THE
FOUR-
★ ★ ★ ★
STAR
KITCHEN

THE FOUR-★★★★ STAR KITCHEN

Classic Recipes from New York's Great Restaurants

Arthur Hettich
with Ann Seranne

𝕿𝖎𝖒𝖊𝖘 BOOKS

Copyright © 1986 by Arthur Hettich

Photographs copyright © 1986 by Lou Manna

All rights reserved under International and Pan-American Copyright Conventions. Published in the United States by Times Books, a division of Random House, Inc., New York, and simultaneously in Canada by Random House of Canada Limited, Toronto.

Library of Congress Cataloging-in-Publication Data

Hettich, Arthur, 1927–
The four star kitchen.

Includes index.
   1. Cookery, International.   2. Restaurants, lunch rooms, etc.—New York (N.Y.)   I. Seranne, Ann, 1914–   .   II. Title.
TX725.A1H44   1986   641.5′09747′1   86-1418
ISBN 0-8129-1227-6

Designed by Marjorie Anderson

Manufactured in the United States of America

9   8   7   6   5   4   3   2

First Edition

To Matthew

ACKNOWLEDGMENTS

Thank you to the following people:

To Ann Seranne, the sage of cookbook writers—author of thirty cookbooks in her own right—my sincere appreciation for her invaluable contributions to this book. For her wise counsel and her personal home-kitchen testing of each and every recipe to make sure that it works for you, the reader, "thank you" seems too little to say.

To Frances Rothenberg, whose time-consuming research provided the background for each restaurant writeup.

To Linda Oliveri, whose assistance was invaluable.

To Elizabeth Randolph, my wife, for her advice and editing.

And to Kathleen Moloney and Ruth Fecych, my editors at Times Books, for all their help.

☆ ☆ ☆ ☆

CONTENTS

☆ ☆ ☆ ☆

Contents

x

Contents

x i

INTRODUCTION

☆ ☆ ☆ ☆

*T*his is a cookbook for several categories of food lovers. First but not necessarily foremost, it is for New Yorkers and visitors to New York who want to learn about good restaurants where they can find the kinds of food they know they like from a particular social or cultural group, or perhaps try great dishes that are new to them.

Second, it is bedtime reading for armchair cooks who enjoy drifting off to sleep dreaming of exotic, elegantly prepared and served foods.

Third, it is for sophisticated home chefs who like nothing more than to watch family and friends enjoy the dishes in a carefully planned and executed meal. If, as Craig Claiborne maintains, ". . . fine cooking on an international or national scale is one of the greatest pleasures known to man," then preparing and serving a delicious meal to an appreciative audience is nothing short of heaven for these cooking addicts.

This book is also for inquisitive novice cooks who are intrigued by the fascinating "new" items appearing in retail food stores and would like to be adventurous and try them. Here are answers about how to use many of these ingredients.

I decided to write this book for several reasons. First, New York City and its environs is a virtual treasure trove of restaurants of all kinds, and I like nothing better than going to restaurants, both to enjoy favorite foods and to try new dishes. I enjoy all styles and types of cooking, some more than others, and am constantly curious about just what goes into a recipe in order to create a particular taste or combination of flavors. The research for this book allowed me the luxury of indulging in one of my favorite pastimes, eating out, without guilt. It also enabled me to visit many wonderful New York restaurants that were new to me and that I might otherwise have felt I would never have the time to visit.

Another reason for my interest in preparing this book is that, although I do like to cook myself, I enjoy reading about food and food preparation even more. I was very lucky to be able to enlist the expert services of Ann Seranne, an experienced chef and food writer, to test all of the recipes in the book in her own kitchen and fill in the kinds of details for our readers that restaurant chefs sometimes know so well they forget to include. She translated vague instructions such as "cook until ready" and "to taste" into concrete terms that even the least worldly cook can follow.

I would like to thank my associate, Fran Rothenberg, who was an invaluable help. She went to some restaurants four or five times in order to taste various offerings, helped decide which dishes to include from which restaurants, and, finally, arranged to obtain the desired recipes.

I would particularly like to thank all of the restaurant owners and chefs who treated us with such grace on our visits and who spent so much time explaining their special preparation tricks and "secrets." Without them, there would have been no book.

We hope you enjoy the recipes in this book and the introductions they give you to the fine restaurants whose chefs created them.

Welcome to the wonderful world of restaurants in the amazing city of New York.

Arthur Hettich

SOME ADVICE FOR THE HOME CHEF

☆ ☆ ☆ ☆

*I*n restaurants and hotel kitchens, the master chef is the overseer who makes sure everything tastes just right and is presented the way he or she wishes it to be. There are many others responsible for the actual preparation of the food, from the chief assistant, or sous chef, through the various specialty chefs, down to the patissiers.

The home chef, on the other hand, is usually on his or her own with, at best, the willing if unskilled help of a friend or family member. The secret of successful home cooking, then, is to undertake only what can be easily accomplished.

There are many easy dishes in this book that can be prepared in half an hour or less. There are other recipes in which almost all preparation and cooking can be done in advance, and the dish finally reheated or finished in just a few minutes. The secret, or "trick," of many of the recipes is the superior quality of the ingredients. Formerly, many of these ingredients were available only to restaurants, but nowadays they can be bought in specialty shops and even via mail order.

Experienced home chefs know that careful advance shopping, assembly of ingredients and necessary tools, and step-by-step preparation can make even the most complex recipe fall into place so that the actual cooking can be performed efficiently and easily.

They also know that "season to taste" is an important rule, adding spices, herbs, and condiments bit by bit until the flavor is just right. They follow the advice of Paul Prudhomme, the famous Louisiana Cajun chef, who seasons a dish at the very beginning of cooking, again in the middle of the cooking time, and makes a final correction in the flavoring just before a dish is served.

No completely foolproof recipe has ever been written. How hot is hot, how high is high, how pungent is pungent? Two people may cook the same dish from the same recipe and come up with two different results. That's why it is important to read all of the chef's notes and comments in each recipe. Good cooking may be a creative art but like all other art forms, the basic rules must be learned and followed before a home chef can let imagination take over.

THE
FOUR-
★ ★ ★ ★
STAR
KITCHEN

Abyssinia

35 Grand Street
New York, N.Y. 10013   226-5959

Since Middle Eastern, Japanese, and Mexican foods are no longer considered exotic in this city of restaurants, it's always refreshing to discover a new cuisine. Abyssinia, in SoHo, offers Ethiopian food in an authentic setting. Once you enter the restaurant (be advised of the usual weekend lines), you'll be seated on a birchooma, *a concave, backless stool, around a* messobe *or "straw table." Native art adorns the walls and tapes of popular Ethiopian music play in the background.*

The basis of Ethiopian food is injera, *a spongy fermented bread that serves also as plate and utensil (no cutlery is ever used). Once you've selected from the slow-simmered meat, vegetable, or fish mixtures offered at Araya Slassie's restaurant, the food will be brought to you on a base of* injera. *If you come in a group you can share a variety of dishes. The most popular dishes are kifto, Ethiopian steak tartare, and doro wot, chicken marinated in a red-hot sauce. The particularly spicy combinations are always served with cooling sour cream or cottage cheese. Tear off bits of the bread and scoop up mouthfuls of the savory stews.*

Tej, a fermented honey wine similar to mead, is served before, during, and after a meal. Beer and wines are also available.

For dessert, choose fresh fruit or one of the exotic American desserts. Most guests choose freshly cut papaya simply served with a wedge of lime, or a sublime pear almond tart baked in an all-butter crust.

☆ ☆   **KIFTO**   ☆ ☆

(Ethiopian steak tartare)

SERVES 4

1 pound sweet butter
2 tablespoons garlic powder
1 tablespoon ground ginger or shredded fresh gingerroot
1 pound lean beef
Mitmata (hot chili powder)*
Salt to taste

1. Make seasoned butter: Combine butter and garlic powder with ginger in a small saucepan and bring slowly to a boil, stirring constantly. Let cool, then pour off the clear liquid (flavored clarified butter), discarding the milk solids that settle to the bottom of the pan. You should have about 2 cups.
2. Put the meat through the medium blade of a meat grinder twice, or use a food processor to chop the meat fine. Empty into a bowl. Gradually stir in the seasoned butter, mitmata, and salt. Serve with injera, pita, or other soft bread.

* Mitmata is a hot chili powder available in Chinese markets. Use 1 tablespoon per pound of meat for a mild flavor.

☆ ☆   **INJERA**   ☆ ☆

(Ethiopian soft bread)

1 envelope active dry yeast
3 cups all-purpose flour
About 1½ cups water

1. Combine yeast and flour with enough water to make a thin crêpelike batter that coats the spoon well. Let stand at room temperature overnight. The batter will separate. Refrigerate until time to make the bread.
2. Stir batter. Heat a Teflon-coated 8-inch pan or griddle and when it is hot pour about ⅔ cup batter to make a thin layer onto it. Cook about 3 minutes or until bubbles appear on the surface and underside is browned. Remove from heat and cool slightly. As the breads cool, stack them on a plate.

Note:

Injera is best prepared ½ to 1 hour ahead of time. It can be prepared up to 2 days ahead and stored in the refrigerator.

Alfredo on the Park

240 Central Park South
New York, N.Y. 10019   246-7050

One of the greatest discoveries in New York is a good restaurant where you can dine before the theater or a concert. The ideal place is close enough to your evening's entertainment so you don't have to spend your dinner hour worrying about finding a cab.

When you're going to Carnegie Hall or any of the festivities at Lincoln Center, Alfredo's fills the bill admirably. This is one of the few restaurants in the city that just seem to go on and on. Regulars love it and newcomers can't wait to become regulars. The atmosphere is plush, the food Italian with a dash of continental style. The wine list is extensive, with Italian, American, and French wines as well as imported beers. Prices are moderately high.

☆ ☆ ZUPPA DI PISELLI E VONGOLE ☆ ☆
(Fresh pea and clam soup)
SERVES 4

A delicious, colorful, very pretty first course.

> *2 dozen tiny littleneck clams*
> *2 tablespoons olive oil*
> *¼ onion, julienned*
> *2 cloves garlic, smashed*
> *1 ripe tomato, peeled and cubed*
> *1 cup cooked fresh peas or steamed snow peas*
> *3 cups water*
> *1 sprig parsley*
> *Reserved clam juice*
> *Pepper to taste*
> *1 cup croutons*

1. Scrub clams and soak in cold water for at least 30 minutes to remove any sand. Rinse well and put into a heavy casserole or pot. Cover tightly and cook over low heat for 8 to 10 minutes, or until clam shells are opened. Remove clams from shells, discard the black necks or valves, and put clams in a deep dish. Cut them in half if too large. Strain their juices over them through a sieve lined with cheesecloth to catch any sand that might have been in the clams. Set aside.
2. In a saucepan heat the oil and in it cook onion and garlic without letting them brown too much—cook until just golden. Discard garlic.
3. Add tomato, peas, water, parsley, clams, and reserved clam juice, bring to a boil and simmer for 6 to 7 minutes.
4. Add pepper to taste and a little salt, if necessary.
5. Serve in bouillon cups topped with croutons.

☆ ☆
COSTOLETTE D'AGNELLO GIANNI, SALSA FUNGHI
☆ ☆
(Lamb chops with mushroom sauce)
SERVES 4

4 tablespoons Béchamel Sauce (see below)
Salsa Funghi (see below)
8 rib lamb chops, single bone cut
8 teaspoons freshly grated Parmesan cheese
½ cup flour
2 tablespoons lightly salted butter
Parsley for garnish

1. Prepare béchamel and mushroom sauces.
2. Trim excess fat from chops, split meat in half and pound open, butterfly fashion. Do not remove the bone.
3. On one side of each chop put ½ tablespoon béchamel sauce and sprinkle with 1 teaspoon grated cheese. Fold other side of meat over filling and press edges closed.
4. Coat chops lightly with flour, shaking off any excess, and brown them lightly in hot foaming butter for about 2 minutes on each side or until lightly browned.
5. To serve: Cover half of each plate with a little mushroom sauce. Place 2 chops on bare part of plate with bones crossed and pointing to the opposite side of the plate. Garnish with parsley.

BÉCHAMEL SAUCE

¾ cup

1 cup milk
1 onion slice
2 tablespoons butter
2 tablespoons flour
Pinch salt, pepper, and nutmeg, or to taste

1. Heat milk with the slice of onion until very hot, but do not let boil.
2. In a small saucepan melt butter and stir in flour. Remove from heat and pour in the hot milk, whisking rapidly. Return to heat and continue whisking until sauce is smooth and slightly thickened. Cook over low heat for 20 minutes, stirring occasionally.
3. Discard onion slice.

SALSA FUNGHI

(Mushroom sauce)

1 cup

¼ small onion, julienned
1 cup sliced fresh mushrooms
2 tablespoons butter
½ cup chicken broth or consommé
1 cup heavy cream (not ultrapasteurized; see page 303)
Salt and pepper to taste

1. In saucepan sauté onion and mushrooms in butter, shaking pan frequently, until onion is lightly golden.
2. Add chicken broth or consommé, bring to a boil, and simmer for 2 minutes.
3. Cool for a few minutes, then empty into container of an electric blender and blend until smooth. Return to saucepan and bring to a simmer. Stir in cream and salt and pepper to taste. Cook over moderate heat until sauce is reduced to about 1 cup. Keep warm over hot water.

☆ ☆ # TIRAMISÙ ☆ ☆

SERVES 6

One of the most popular desserts on Alfredo's menu.

1 pound mascarpone cheese*
5 eggs
¾ cup confectioner's sugar
5 ladyfingers, halved, to make 10 pieces
2 to 3 cups freshly brewed espresso
Dutch cocoa

1. Put cheese, eggs, and sugar into container of a food processor and process until smooth and well blended.
2. Cover the bottom of a 7- by 10- by 2-inch cake pan with a layer of the cheese mixture about ½ inch thick. Cover the cheese mixture with ladyfinger halves.
3. Gradually pour espresso over the ladyfingers until they are saturated, then spread remaining cheese mixture on top.
4. Refrigerate for several hours or overnight.
5. Before serving sprinkle surface of the dessert with cocoa powder.

* This is a fresh double cream cheese available at most good cheese stores.

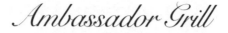

Ambassador Grill

1 United Nations Plaza (East 44th Street off 1st Avenue)
New York, N.Y. 10017   702-5014

Ambassador Grill is an apt name for a restaurant owned by the United Nations Developmental Corporation. The breathtaking Mylar-backed glass panels created by Kevin Roche and John Dinkeloo form a multifaceted backdrop for an equally multi-faceted international crowd.

Although the restaurant, with its Swiss-trained American chef, is known for its emphasis on American grilled foods, many business people begin their day with a breakfast meeting at the Grill. They may return later in the day for blackened redfish or filet mignon; grilled swordfish; shallot- and chile-marinated butterflied chicken; or salmon with dill sauce. Other popular dishes that escape the coals include scallop and crab meat appetizer with vin blanc sauce, and sautéed calf's liver with mustard sauce. For those watching their weight, the Grill offers a daily "Menu Manhattan," a three-course lunch at under 550 calories with a low fat content. Less conscientious souls will find desserts such as bread and butter pudding and crème brûlée.

The bar, which is set at an angle from the dining area, is sometimes filled with a lively international crowd; those people partake of a separate cafe-type menu. Although pricey, the Grill's Sunday brunch buffet, with unlimited champagne, is always a sellout, so reserve early. Wine connoisseurs will be impressed with the Grill's long wine list, frequently updated to keep up with an ever-changing stock.

☆ ☆ # Piña Colada Scallops with Chutney Sauce ☆ ☆

SERVES 6

This recipe has definite Caribbean overtones. It makes an intriguing entrée when served with a vegetable and rice.

> *2 to 2½ pounds sea scallops*
> *½ cup all-purpose flour*
> *1 cup cornstarch*
> *1 teaspoon baking powder*
> *2 tablespoons sugar*
> *1 teaspoon vinegar*
> *1 tablespoon pineapple juice*
> *2 eggs*
> *2 tablespoons rum*
> *2 tablespoons coco Lopez*
> *1¼ cups water*
> *2 tablespoons vegetable oil*
> *Additional flour to coat the scallops*
> *Oil for deep-frying*
> *Chutney Sauce (see below)*

1. Wash scallops, drain on absorbent paper, and set aside.
2. Combine dry ingredients. Combine wet ingredients, including the 2 tablespoons oil, then combine the two mixtures and whip with a balloon whip until batter is smooth.
3. Coat scallops with flour, shaking off any excess, dip in batter, and fry in deep oil heated to 360 degrees until golden brown and firm, about 3 to 5 minutes. Drain and serve hot with the chutney sauce on the side.

CHUTNEY SAUCE

> *2 ripe mangoes, peeled and seed removed*
> *3 ripe apricots, peeled and pitted*
> *2 tablespoons corn syrup*
> *2 tablespoons grated horseradish*
> *2 tablespoons soy sauce*
> *2 tablespoons shredded pineapple*

1. Blend all ingredients in an electric blender or food processor until smooth. Pour into small saucepan and heat to simmering. Do not boil.

☆ ☆ GRILLED MAUI PRAWNS WITH ☆ ☆
SCALLOP AND CRAYFISH
STUFFING

SERVES 6

Another delicious main dish served with rice or boiled potatoes are
these grilled prawns. Prawns are a variety of shrimp, but are 6 to 8
inches long. If they are not available extra-large shrimp may be
substituted.

24 prawns
2 tablespoons olive oil
2 tablespoons butter
6 scallops (or about 3 ounces) sea scallops, finely chopped
2 ounces chopped crayfish meat or shredded lump crab meat
3 large cloves garlic, finely chopped
1 carrot, scraped and chopped
¼ pound fresh spinach
1 ounce brandy
1 cup fresh bread crumbs
½ cup heavy cream
Salt and pepper to taste
2 tablespoons melted butter
Garlic and Sweet Basil Sauce (see below)

1. Split prawns lengthwise down back, cutting almost all the
   way through. Discard shells and rinse out the intestinal vein.
   Flatten prawns to butterfly them. Arrange on a baking sheet,
   cover with a damp towel, and refrigerate.
2. For the stuffing: In a 10-inch sauté pan heat olive oil and
   butter. Add scallops, crayfish or crab meat, garlic, carrot, and
   spinach and cook for 2 or 3 minutes. Add brandy and cook for
   2 minutes longer. Then add remaining ingredients except
   sauce.
3. Remove from heat and empty into container of a food processor. Process until smooth. If stuffing is too moist, add a few
   more bread crumbs; if too dry, add a little more heavy cream.
   Season with salt and pepper.
4. Cool stuffing to room temperature, then spoon a little of the
   mixture onto each prawn. Arrange in a broiler pan, brush
   with a little melted butter, and broil about 5 inches from medium heat for about 10 minutes.
5. Pour the sauce over the hot prawns and serve.

GARLIC AND SWEET BASIL SAUCE

6 ounces lightly salted butter
2 cloves garlic, finely chopped
2 tablespoons chopped fresh parsley
1 tablespoon chopped fresh sweet basil
1 tablespoon lemon juice
Salt and pepper to taste

1. In a small saucepan heat butter and in it sauté the garlic until lightly golden. Add remaining ingredients and keep warm until ready to serve.

Andrée's Mediterranean Cuisine

354 East 74th Street
New York, N.Y. 10021   249-6619

Going to Andrée's is almost like going to a friend's home for dinner. You walk into the ground floor of a house, carrying a bottle of wine—none is available at the restaurant. Leave your coat in the entryway and move right into the parlor. Your host is Andrée's husband; her two daughters are usually found waiting on tables. But make no mistake, this is not a run-of-the-mill family-style restaurant. Food here is of a class found only at places where the ingredients are the best, and the chef knows what to do with them. Andrée has mixed the cuisine of her Egyptian background with that of its Mediterranean neighbors. People come for the couscous, stay for the lamb, and feast on the fabulous fish dishes. We take champagne or sparkling Spanish white wine—they suit the mood of the place. Remember to bring cash or a checkbook, for no credit cards are accepted here.

☆ ☆ ## KOBEBA ☆ ☆
(Stuffed bulgur)
ABOUT 3 DOZEN

The first recipe is for stuffed kebabs, known as kobeba. The technique may be difficult for the home chef to master and will require some practice, but once made, they freeze well and may be taken directly from the freezer to the deep fryer. In Egypt they are served with baba ghanoush, an eggplant dip; in Lebanon with yogurt; in Syria with lemon juice; and in Israel with hummus or chick-pea dip.

2 cups finely ground bulgur (cracked wheat)
1 pound lean lamb or beef, cubed
1 onion, quartered
Salt and pepper to taste

Filling:
1 large onion, chopped
2 tablespoons vegetable oil
1½ pounds ground lamb or beef
¼ cup pine nuts
1 teaspoon allspice
Salt and pepper to taste
2 tablespoons pomegranate juice,
or ¼ cup lemon juice mixed with 2 teaspoons sugar
Vegetable oil for deep-frying

1. Cover bulgur with water and let it soak for 30 minutes. Drain and rinse, then squeeze dry in cheesecloth or a towel. Empty into a large bowl.
2. Add cubed meat, onion, and salt and pepper and put through a meat grinder at least 3 times, or until mixture is smooth. Then knead further by hand if necessary. Set aside.
3. Prepare filling: Sauté chopped onion in vegetable oil until golden. Add ground meat and cook until meat begins to brown, stirring occasionally. Drain off excess fat and add pine nuts, allspice, salt and pepper to taste, pomegranate juice or lemon juice, and sugar. Cook, stirring, a few minutes longer. Let cool.
4. Take large walnut-sized lumps of the ground bulgur mixture and shape them into hollow 3-inch tubes, moistening fingers with ice water as you work. Smooth out any cracks in the tubes with wet fingers. Then, using a tiny spoon such as a demitasse spoon, fill each tube with about 1 tablespoon of the filling. Seal the ends firmly.
5. To cook: Deep-fry in vegetable oil heated to 365 degrees for about 5 minutes, or until golden brown, turning occasionally with a spatula as they cook. Serve hot as an appetizer.

☆ ☆ # BOUILLABAISSE ☆ ☆
(*Fragrant fish stew*)
SERVES 4

A traditional Marseillaise bouillabaisse can be made only from species of fish that abound in the Mediterranean Sea. We can, however, come close enough not to offend the purist who might quibble over our use of the word bouillabaisse. An innovative addition to the classic in this recipe is a goodly amount of Pernod or ouzo. The stew is served with toasted French bread dipped into rouille, a hot garlicky purée.

> *2 or 3 leeks, white part only, coarsely chopped*
> *1 large onion, peeled and chopped*
> *4 or more cloves garlic, peeled and finely minced*
> *¼ cup olive oil*
> *1 1-pound can Italian plum tomatoes, drained and chopped*
> *1 teaspoon thyme*
> *¼ cup chopped parsley*
> *1 teaspoon ground fennel seeds*
> *1 large bay leaf*
> *1 small head fresh fennel with leaves, chopped*
> *1 teaspoon dry basil or 1 tablespoon fresh, chopped*
> *½ teaspoon oregano*
> *¼ teaspoon Tabasco*
> *¼ teaspoon saffron threads*
> *1 cup dry white wine*
> *5 cups water*
> *Salt and pepper to taste*
> *2 pounds firm-fleshed fish such as sea trout or haddock*
> *1 small lobster (preferably female)*
> *2 tablespoons flour*
> *3 tablespoons butter*
> *1 cup Pernod or ouzo*
> *12 littleneck clams, scrubbed*
> *12 mussels, scrubbed and debearded*
> *12 shrimp, shelled and deveined*
> *Rouille (see below)*

1. In a heavy casserole or kettle large enough to hold all ingredients, cook the leeks, onion, and garlic in olive oil until onion is transparent.

2. Add tomatoes, thyme, parsley, fennel seeds, bay leaf, fresh fennel, basil, oregano, Tabasco, saffron, wine, water, and salt and pepper to taste. Bring to a boil and simmer for 10 minutes.
3. Meanwhile cut fish into steaks; split lobster, clean, reserving the coral and liver, and cut claws and tail into serving pieces. Add lobster head and fish head to the stewing vegetable mixture. Cover and simmer for 30 minutes.
4. Blend flour and butter to a smooth paste (beurre manié) and mix with the reserved coral and liver. Set aside.
5. Strain soup through a food mill, pushing through the sieve as much of the solids as possible. Return soup to heat, bring to a low boil, and gradually stir in butter-flour mixture. When soup returns to a boil, stir in Pernod or ouzo.
6. Add lobster and shellfish to the stew, cover, and simmer for 8 to 10 minutes, or until clams and mussels have opened. Place fish steaks on top, cover, and cook for 5 minutes longer.
7. Serve immediately with toasted, buttered French bread slices, and pass the rouille separately.

ROUILLE
(Hot garlic sauce)
ABOUT 1 CUP

Rouille literally means "rust."

8 cloves garlic, peeled
2 or 3 small hot chile peppers, softened in warm water and seeded
1 slice white bread, trimmed of crust
¼ cup olive oil
2 tablespoons tomato paste
1 teaspoon paprika
½ cup fish stock

1. Put all ingredients into container of an electric blender, cover, and blend on medium speed to a smooth purée.

Angelo's of Mulberry Street

146 Mulberry Street
New York, N.Y. 10013   966-1277

Now that new Italian cuisine, like its American and French counterparts, has become popular, it's hard to find restaurants serving authentic Neapolitan food. Luckily, the lusty Southern Italian fare is still being prepared in Little Italy, at Angelo's of Mulberry Street. Co-owned and managed by Naples-born chefs Giovanni Aprea and Luigi Silvestri, Angelo's is an unofficial landmark. Patrons throng here for the kind of food that has been served since 1902: twenty kinds of homemade pasta, fritto misto (a mixed fry), sausages alla casalinga, and more than a dozen veal specialties. One afternoon's "quiet" turnout would be considered a bustling crowd by normal standards. This is a place to have fun and enjoy the food, not to have a quiet dinner for two.

Angelo's attracts regulars and celebrities alike. Aprea and Silvestri are so proud of President Reagan's visit to their restaurant that they named a special dinner for two in his honor. If you have room after the pasta and entrée, enjoy a homemade cannoli or tiramisù, the layered dessert based on Italy's creamy mascarpone cheese laced with espresso and liqueurs. An all-Italian wine list includes reasonably priced half-bottles of red, white, and sparkling wines.

☆ ☆ SPIEDINI DI MOZZARELLA ALLA ☆ ☆ ROMANA

Serves 1 for luncheon with a salad

**2 slices white bread, trimmed of crusts
5 slices whole-milk mozzarella (fresh if possible)
1 cup flour for dredging
2 eggs, beaten**

1 cup vegetable oil
2 tablespoons butter
1 anchovy fillet, rinsed
2 ounces (¼ cup) white wine
1 cup chicken broth
1 tablespoon unsalted tomato sauce
Juice and rind of ¼ lemon
Freshly ground black pepper to taste
1 tablespoon chopped parsley
1 fresh basil leaf

1. Preheat oven to 450 degrees.
2. Cut trimmed bread in half and alternate slices of mozzarella and bread on a skewer or attelet. Dredge in flour, dip into beaten eggs, coating well on all sides, and roll again in flour.
3. Meanwhile have oil in a small skillet very hot (375 to 400 degrees). Fry the spiedini on both sides in the hot oil until golden brown on all sides. Remove from oil and set aside on absorbent paper to drain.
4. In a separate ovenproof and flameproof pan or au gratin dish, melt butter and anchovy over low heat. Add wine and simmer until wine is reduced to about half its original quantity. Add chicken broth, tomato sauce, lemon juice and rind, and remaining ingredients.
5. Slip spiedini from skewer directly into the sauce and cook over moderate heat until sauce thickens. Place pan in the preheated oven for about 5 minutes. Serve very hot.

☆ ☆ ## CAPELLINI D'ANGELO ALLA CARBONARA ☆ ☆
(Angel hair with Italian bacon and cheese)
SERVES 4

4 tablespoons butter
4 thin slices Italian bacon (pancetta), diced
1 small white onion, peeled and finely chopped
½ cup fresh heavy cream (not ultrapasteurized; see page 303)
Salt and pepper to taste
10 ounces capellini pasta (angel hair)
1 egg yolk, lightly beaten
½ cup freshly grated Parmesan cheese

1. Put butter, bacon, and onion in a skillet and cook over medium heat until onion is golden brown. Add cream and salt and pepper, and boil the sauce, stirring constantly, until it thickens.
2. Meanwhile bring a large kettle of lightly salted water to a rapid boil. Add the capellini gradually so the water does not stop boiling, and boil for just 3 minutes. It is so thin it needs little cooking.
3. Drain the capellini and empty into a large mixing bowl. Add the egg yolk and toss quickly so the egg yolk will spread evenly throughout the pasta before it has a chance to cook.
4. Continue tossing while adding the cheese and half the sauce from the skillet. Serve on four warm pasta plates and top each portion with some of the remaining sauce.

☆ ☆ # FEGATO DI VITELLO ALLA VENEZIANA ☆ ☆
(Calf's liver Venetian style)
SERVES 4

This next recipe is such a flavorful way to cook calf's liver that it might even tempt those at home who think they don't like it. Baby beef liver may be used, but it will not make as delicate a dish.

4 tablespoons vegetable oil
1 large sweet onion, peeled and finely chopped
1½ pounds thinly sliced calf's liver
2 bay leaves
2 tablespoons red wine vinegar
5 large fresh sweet basil leaves, sliced
Salt and freshly ground black pepper to taste

1. Heat vegetable oil in a large skillet over high heat. Add onion and fry until onion is lightly browned, stirring constantly.
2. Add liver slices and bay leaves and cook for 1 minute, turning the slices of liver after 30 seconds.
3. Pour off most of the oil, leaving just enough to keep bottom of pan coated lightly. Add the vinegar, basil leaves, and salt and pepper, shaking pan back and forth constantly until vinegar is evaporated.
4. Serve as quickly as possible with a colorful vegetable in season at the time. Broiled fresh tomatoes are hard to beat as an accompaniment to this dish.

Arcadia

21 East 62nd Street
New York, N.Y. 10022   223-2900

Everything about this restaurant is lush and beautiful—the painted walls, the food presentation, even the people who eat here and its co-owner and chef, Anne Rosenzweig, former chef of Vanessa. The place is small. In the narrow front room are a tiny but inviting mahogany bar and a few tables. Mauve banquettes encircle the main dining room below the murals by Paul Davis. The food is what might be called haute cuisine, American style. It is imaginative, luxurious, and created with an eye for color and taste. For example, lobster served as a lobster club sandwich on brioche for lunch and cut into succulent chimney-smoked bites at dinner are two house favorites. So, too, are the appetizing corn cakes with caviar and crème fraîche.

Anne Rosenzweig began her career as a pastry chef, so it is natural to have great expectations for dessert; you won't be disappointed. Her chocolate bread pudding with brandy custard sauce is sublime. Another winner is a fresh pear baked in phyllo pastry with a chocolate sauce. As a lighter alternative you might choose the mango mousse with fresh raspberries.

Arcadia is not inexpensive, nor is it a place for spur-of-the-moment dining—you'd be well advised to make reservations in advance.

☆ ☆ CRAB AND LOBSTER CAKES WITH ☆ ☆ CORIANDER AND MUSTARD SAUCE

Serves 6 for lunch or 8 for an appetizer

2 tablespoons melted sweet butter
½ cup minced onion
½ cup minced carrot
½ cup minced celery
1 teaspoon minced garlic
1 pound lump crab meat
3 tablespoons chopped parsley
3 tablespoons chopped chives
3 egg yolks
2 teaspoons dry mustard
4 tablespoons heavy cream
2 tablespoons Worcestershire sauce
1 1½-pound lobster
Salt and pepper to taste
Flour to coat cakes
4 tablespoons clarified butter (page 301)
Coriander and Mustard Sauce (see below)

1. In a medium skillet heat the 2 tablespoons butter and in it
    sauté the onion, carrot, celery, and garlic for about 2 minutes,
    or until onion is transparent. Empty into a bowl and let cool.
    Add crab meat, parsley, chives, yolks, mustard, cream, and
    Worcestershire sauce, mix lightly, and set aside.
2. Steam the lobster for about 7 minutes. Let cool until cool
    enough to handle. Remove meat from shell, discarding intes-
    tine that runs down the back and the sac that lies in the back
    of the head. Chop the meat, add to crab mixture, and toss
    lightly. Season to taste with salt and pepper.
3. Form shellfish mixture into rather thin cakes, 3 to 4 inches in
    diameter, and set aside until ready to cook.
4. To cook, dredge the cakes in flour and sauté in the clarified
    butter until golden brown on both sides. Serve with Corian-
    der and Mustard Sauce.

CORIANDER AND MUSTARD SAUCE

½ cup minced shallots
Juice of ¼ lemon
2 cups dry white wine
2 sticks (½ pound) sweet butter
½ cup chopped coriander
3 tablespoons prepared mustard such as Pommery or Dijon

1. Put into a small saucepan the shallots, lemon juice, and wine. Bring to a boil and cook over high heat until liquid is reduced to about 2 tablespoons.
2. Reduce heat to low and whisk in the butter, 2 tablespoons at a time, until all butter is incorporated and the sauce is the consistency of mayonnaise. Do not let the butter melt.
3. Whisk in coriander and mustard and keep warm without melting until ready to serve.

☆ ☆   # CHOCOLATE TERRINE WITH ALMOND TUILES   ☆ ☆

SERVES 8 TO 10

4 eggs
2 cups sugar
½ cup strong coffee
½ pound bittersweet chocolate, preferably Belgian
½ pound sweet butter, at room temperature
Whipped cream

1. In a large bowl whisk together the eggs, sugar, and coffee.
2. In a saucepan melt together the bittersweet chocolate and the sweet butter. Gradually whisk into the egg mixture. Pour into a 9- by 5- by 3-inch loaf pan and set pan into a larger baking pan containing about 2 inches of hot water. Cover pan with aluminum foil and bake in a preheated 325-degree oven for 2 hours, or until set.
3. Let cool, then refrigerate until ready to serve.
4. To serve, cut terrine into thin slices. Top each slice with a heaping spoonful of whipped cream, and insert the tip of a tuile into the whipped cream.

TUILES

MAKES ABOUT 8

¼ pound almonds, blanched and sliced
½ cup sugar
¼ cup all-purpose flour
2 eggs

1. Mix all ingredients into a batter.
2. Line a sheet pan with parchment paper and drop the batter onto the parchment to make 4 cookies at each baking. Use 2 to 3 tablespoons of the batter for each cookie, and spread the batter out into 6-inch rounds with a spatula.
3. Bake in a preheated 425-degree oven for about 7 minutes or until golden brown, checking occasionally to make sure they are browning evenly and not too much. They should be a pale beige.
4. Remove from the oven and as soon as they have cooled enough to handle, remove, one at a time, from the sheet, and quickly pleat one edge to shape the cookie into a fan. Insert the tip of the fan in the whipped cream.

The Ballroom

253 West 28th Street
New York, N.Y. 10001   244-3005

The Ballroom is a unique New York institution that combines an exceptionally fine restaurant with a separate but adjacent theater/cabaret. This is the place to go when you feel like sampling dozens of tidbits and snacks, selected from a repertoire of some sixty different appetizers, known as tapas in Spain, where they are traditionally nibbled while sipping dry sherry to provide nourishment until dinner, which is served very late in Spain.

The tapas concept was introduced to America by Peruvian-born chef and executive owner Felipe Rojas-Lombardi, and they seem to have become the hottest new food fad of this decade. Those served at The Ballroom are as good as any found in Spain. An additional plus is that the restaurant's sitdown dinners are just as good as the tapas, if you can tear yourself away from the bar. Main course entrées feature such popular dishes as rack of lamb and grilled duckling. There are also evening specials such as moules marinara, a casserole of seafood, or Cornish game hens with green peppercorns. The dessert cart has some tempting sweet treats such as hazelnut cheesecake and pecan pie, but it is the plentiful and unique display of tapas that attracts customers, who are mostly youngish people from the surrounding Chelsea district. Dress runs the gamut from business to casual.

☆ ☆ # CHILES RELLENOS ☆ ☆
(Stuffed peppers)
Serves 8 as an appetizer

This tapas recipe contains fresh or dry ancho chile peppers. If the ancho peppers are freshly dried, 4 to 8 hours is sufficient time to restore them; otherwise, soak dry chiles overnight.

8 dry ancho chile peppers
1¼ pounds fresh mozzarella cheese,
1 pound shredded, and ¼ pound cut into small cubes
1 cup fresh white bread crumbs
¼ cup chopped fresh thyme leaves
¼ cup chopped Italian parsley
¼ cup ground almonds
⅓ cup drained capers
Salt to taste
½ pound thinly sliced Serrano ham or prosciutto
1 small onion, peeled and sliced
2 tablespoons chicken stock
2 tablespoons white wine
2 tablespoons olive oil

1. In advance soak chiles in warm water overnight to restore them. Next day drain. Slit each pepper open lengthwise with scissors, beginning at stem end and cutting to the tip. Remove seeds with a spoon and discard. Set peppers aside.
2. In a small bowl combine the mozzarella, both cubed and shredded, the bread crumbs, herbs, almonds, and capers. Chop half the ham and add it and salt to taste.
3. Line each pepper with a thin slice of ham and stuff with the mozzarella mixture. Place another slice of ham on top and repeat until all peppers are filled.
4. Line a baking dish or ceramic casserole with the sliced onion. Arrange peppers over the onion and sprinkle with the stock, wine, and oil. Cover with a sheet of parchment paper and seal with a sheet of foil.
5. Bake in a preheated 400-degree oven for 25 to 30 minutes. Serve hot.

☆ ☆ YUCCA WITH ROMESCO SAUCE ☆ ☆

Serves 6 to 8 as an appetizer

Yucca or manioc is also known as cassava, a large starchy root used
in the making of tapioca. It is available in Spanish, Mexican, and
California markets.

3 pounds yucca
3 quarts water
2 bay leaves
1 whole bulb garlic, sliced in half horizontally
2 teaspoons salt
1½ cups vegetable oil
Coarse sea salt
Romesco Sauce (see below)

1. With a paring knife, remove the rough, barklike skin from the
   yucca. In a large saucepan bring the water to a boil with the
   bay leaves, garlic, and 2 teaspoons salt. Add the yucca, return
   the water to a boil, reduce heat, and simmer for approximately 1 hour or until yucca can be easily pierced with a fork.
   Drain yucca on kitchen towels and let cool. Then cut into
   pieces or sticks 3 inches long and 1½ inches thick.
2. In a small, deep saucepan, 5 to 6 inches in circumference,
   heat the oil until very hot (almost smoking) and in it deep-fry
   the yucca in several batches until golden. Drain on paper
   towels.
3. Sprinkle with coarse sea salt and serve hot with Romesco
   sauce.

ROMESCO SAUCE

ABOUT 3 CUPS

¾ cup olive oil plus 1 tablespoon
4 dried hot red peppers
3 roasted, peeled, and seeded sweet red peppers (1 pound)
(see Note)
or a 6-ounce jar roasted sweet red pimientos, drained
2 tablespoons toasted almonds
1 large clove garlic, peeled
2 tablespoons red wine vinegar
1 teaspoon coarse sea salt, or to taste
½ Granny Smith apple, peeled, cored, and chopped

1. In a small skillet heat the 1 tablespoon olive oil and in it toast the hot red peppers until black, shaking the pan frequently. Set aside to cool. Prepare sweet red peppers.
2. In container of an electric blender combine all ingredients, cover, and blend to a smooth purée, stopping occasionally to stir down if necessary.

Note:

To roast the peppers rub the skin of the peppers with a little oil and bake them on the rack in a 400-degree oven for 30 minutes, turning them once or twice to roast them evenly. Remove them from the oven and enclose them in a paper sack until cool enough to handle. Then cut each in half and discard seeds and sinews with a spoon and gently pull away stem and skin with your fingers.

☆ ☆   # LECHON ASADO   ☆ ☆
(Roast suckling pig with adobo)

The suckling piglets serve 2 to 4;
the larger 6- to 8-pound pigs serve 8 to 12

2 or 3 suckling pigs, about 2½ to 3 pounds each,
or 1 6- to 9-pound pig, ready to cook
Adobo Marinade (see below)

1. Prepare the pig or pigs for roasting: Remove any hair from piglets by singeing over a gas burner, and wipe clean with a damp cloth. Split pigs in half along backbone and press open. Rub inside and out with adobo marinade. Leave in the marinade for 24 to 48 hours, then leave at room temperature or close to a fan for 6 to 8 hours to dry out the skin so it will be crisp and crunchy when baked.
2. Place pig or pigs skin side up on a rack in a large roasting pan and roast in a preheated 475-degree oven for 45 minutes for the small piglets; the larger pig will take about 1½ hours or even a little more. Remove from oven and let sit in a warm spot to rest for 10 minutes before serving.

ADOBO MARINADE

3 tablespoons finely chopped garlic
1 tablespoon dry oregano, crumbled
2 teaspoons ground cumin
2 teaspoons ground coriander
¼ teaspoon ground cloves
1 tablespoon ground white pepper, preferably freshly ground
¼ cup Achote Oil (see below)
½ cup lemon juice
½ cup bitter orange juice
or regular orange juice plus 1 teaspoon Campari

1. Mix marinade ingredients and let stand at room temperature for at least 1 hour before using.

ACHOTE OIL

1 cup vegetable or olive oil or equal parts of each
½ cup annatto seeds (see Note)
1 dried hot pepper, crumbled
1 bay leaf

1. Combine all ingredients in a saucepan, bring to a low boil, and cook over low heat for 5 minutes.
2. Set aside to cool and when cool, strain through a fine sieve or cheesecloth. The oil is now ready to use and it may be kept in the refrigerator for as long as one year. The seeds should be discarded.

Note:

Annatto seeds or achote (also achiote) are seeds used to give a golden color to oil, shortening, and margarine. They may be purchased in specialty grocery stores. You might try asking for them by their Argentinian name, *urucu*.

☆ ☆ # CAZUELA DE MARISCOS ☆ ☆
(Casserole of seafood)
SERVES 6 TO 8

Filipe, owner-chef of The Ballroom, sent us such a wealth of material that we could not resist making room for just one more delicious seafood "stew."

18 to 24 littleneck clams in their shells
18 to 24 medium mussels, about 1¼ pounds
6 to 8 langoustine or large shrimp
12 to 16 sea scallops, from ½ to ¾ pound
¼ cup olive oil
1 cup finely chopped onion
1 teaspoon minced fresh garlic
1 teaspoon peeled, finely chopped fresh ginger
1 hot chile pepper, fresh or dried, seeded and finely chopped
2 tablespoons chopped fresh lemon thyme
or ½ teaspoon dried thyme
1 bay leaf
½ cup finely chopped carrots
½ cup finely chopped celery
3 pounds fresh or canned plum tomatoes
½ teaspoon sugar
½ cup white wine
4 cups fish stock (page 35)
1 teaspoon coarse sea salt
Salt and white pepper to taste (optional)
1 tablespoon grated lemon peel for garnish

1. Prepare fish: See Note below.
2. In a large saucepan heat the olive oil, add the onion, garlic, ginger, and chile pepper and sauté over moderate heat for 5 to 10 minutes, stirring occasionally. When onion turns translucent, stir in the thyme and bay leaf. Then add the chopped carrots and celery. Continue to sauté all ingredients together for another 5 minutes, or until carrots soften slightly.
3. While the vegetables are cooking peel tomatoes if fresh, drain if canned, quarter, and squeeze out the seeds.
4. Add tomatoes and the sugar to the vegetable mixture and cook over moderate heat for about 10 minutes, stirring occasionally, or until liquid thickens.

5. Add the wine and cook for another 3 to 5 minutes, to evapo-rate the wine.

6. Add the fish stock and sea salt and bring soup to a boil. Dis-card bay leaf, cover saucepan, and turn off heat.

7. Select a shallow skillet large enough to hold all the seafood in one or two layers. Gently transfer the clams to the pan, add the mussels and shrimp, then cover all the shellfish with the hot stock in the saucepan. Cover skillet and cook for 5 to 10 minutes, or until clams and mussels are open completely and the shrimp have turned red. Be careful not to overcook the seafood as this will make them tough. Watch carefully, lifting lid off every few minutes.

8. About 1 minute before they are done, drop in the scallops, which will in a minute or so become firm and white. Immedi-ately turn off heat. Correct seasoning.

9. Working quickly, divide the contents of the skillet into heated soup plates, lifting out the shellfish with tongs and adding a couple of large scallops to each serving. Then ladle the hot soup into each plate and sprinkle each serving with grated lemon rind. Serve immediately with crusty bread.

Note on the preparation of the shellfish:

Scrub the clams in cold water to remove any sand. Remove from water and place in a container in one layer. Refrigerate. Clean the mussels by scraping the shells with a sharp knife and removing the "beards." Cover them with water to which has been added a little flour or cornmeal, and refrigerate. The mus-sels will disgorge any sand they have concealed within their shells. Both clams and mussels may be kept in the refrigerator for several hours to several days. Discard any "gapers" before cooking. These are clams or mussels which have opened slightly and do not snap shut when touched with the hand. Defrost the shrimp in cold water and strip away the shells, leaving the shell only on the tail section. Wash out the vein that runs down the back of each shrimp, rinse, drain, cover, and refrigerate until needed. Check the scallops, removing any specks of foreign material or seaweed with a damp towel, and refrigerate.

Berry's

180 Spring Street
New York, N.Y. 10012   226-4394

You might guess that Berry's is named for the luscious fruit of the season. Actually, there really is a Berry, and her restaurant is very much a reflection of her philosophy toward serving people fine food and drink in a comfortable setting.

This SoHo spot, decorated with wainscotting and wallpaper, lit ever so gently to maintain a relaxed aura, has been a mecca for regulars since it opened ten years ago. Berry and her husband, Kenny, who owns the nearby Broome Street bar, took over an Italian restaurant and turned it into this favorite lunch, brunch, and dinner rendezvous. For the past four years, chef Helen Stewart has been at the helm, creating specialties such as sautéed calf's liver with shallots; pan-sautéed veal chop stuffed with St. André cheese; chicken with crab and cream sauce; straw and hay scampi; and bananas Foster, a banana and ice cream bonanza with raisin and rum sauce. The menu changes every two weeks to take advantage of the best of the season, which often includes fresh produce and herbs from Berry's own country home.

Brunch at Berry's is a SoHo tradition. Who could resist the special waffles, extra-thick French toast, and omelets filled with unusual mixtures? Dinner is also an event, whether you're a single diner (Berry and Helen take special care of lone customers) or a group of gallery-hoppers. The draft beer selection may tempt you —stout, Dinkelacker light and dark, Dortmunder Dab, Watney's Red Barrel, or Beck's—especially when poured into one of the frosty beer mugs embedded in crushed ice at the bar. Do try the apricot-flavored breakfast eggnog, or a Bloody Mary made with aquavit.

☆ ☆   # TOSSED TORTELLINI   ☆ ☆

Serves 6 as an appetizer

You might think you'd ordered a tossed salad for a first course instead of pasta when you see this green and white dish of tortellini being tossed with its "marinade."

1 large garden-ripe tomato, peeled and diced
1½ teaspoons each chopped fresh basil and oregano
(or ½ teaspoon each dried basil and oregano)
6 ounces smoked mozzarella cheese, shredded
½ cup pitted and quartered calamata olives
1 medium clove garlic, peeled and pulverized
2 tablespoons olive oil
1 pound green and white tortellini (half of each)

1. In a large bowl combine the tomato, herbs, cheese, olives, garlic, and olive oil. Set aside to marinate for about 30 minutes.
2. Meanwhile in a large pot bring 1 gallon of lightly salted water to a boil. Add the tortellini; when the water returns to a boil and the tortellini have floated to the top of the water, they are done. *Do not overcook.* They should be al dente, or tooth tender.
3. Drain the pasta and mix it with the marinade. Serve immediately on warm plates.

VEAL CHOPS WITH FRESH
☆ ☆   HERBS AND ST. ANDRÉ   ☆ ☆

SERVES 4

Fresh herbs make all the difference in the world to this dish. If you don't have a spot of good earth where you can plant an herb garden, try large clay pots in a sunny window or on a glassed-in porch. See page 300 for a source of excellent herb plants.

4 loin veal chops with pocket for stuffing
6 ounces St. André or any French triple crème cheese
Flour for dredging
Salt and pepper to taste
2 tablespoons peanut oil
1 tablespoon sweet butter
2 shallots, minced
1 tablespoon chopped fresh herbs to taste
(rosemary, thyme, marjoram, tarragon, or oregano)
⅔ cup dry red wine
1 teaspoon meat glaze or ¼ cup meat gravy

1. Fill the pocket in the chops with the cheese, using about 1½ ounces, or ¼ of the cheese, per chop.
2. Dust chops lightly with flour and sprinkle with salt and pepper. Easy with the salt if you are using meat glaze.
3. In a large ovenproof skillet or pan brown the chops in the peanut oil over high heat, turning to brown both sides. Then place skillet or pan in a preheated 425-degree oven for 12 to 15 minutes.
4. Remove pan from oven and place chops on a platter to keep warm.
5. Discard any excess oil and liquid from the pan and return to medium heat. Add the butter, shallots, herbs, and red wine and cook until wine is reduced by one-quarter. Add the meat glaze or gravy and bring to a full rolling boil, stirring constantly. Correct seasoning and serve each chop on a warm plate with a spoonful of the herb sauce poured over.

Bon Temps Rouler

59 Reade Street
New York, N.Y. 10007   513-1334

Not too long ago, if you had a hankering for something to eat in the City Hall/TriBeCa area, you had to choose between a coffee shop and Chinatown. Bon Temps Rouler, a lively Cajun/Creole restaurant, has joined the ranks of smart places opening up downtown.

Owner/chef Susan Trilling and her four partners offer hearty, plentiful portions to an eclectic crowd. For the adventurous (and apparently there are many because it's the most popular appetizer) there's alligator sausage. Those less daring can enjoy such regional favorites as jambalaya, gumbo, and the blackened redfish that Paul Prudhomme made famous in his New Orleans mecca. A basket of homemade breads such as spicy jalapeño cornbread, miniature banana muffins, and tiny dill rolls comes to every table. Be sure to save room for such desserts as deep-dish apple pie or a bourbonized bread pudding accompanied by a cup of rich coffee with chicory, New Orleans style.

Rhythm and blues tapes are occasionally supplanted by the real thing. Even with the music and the almost always packed tables of lively diners, the noise level remains tolerable.

☆ ☆   **VOODOO STEW**   ☆ ☆
SERVES 4

Every night Susan Trilling creates this popular fish stew.

3 cups fish stock (see below)
3 cups canned thick tomato sauce
2 tablespoons fennel seeds

> *1 teaspoon saffron threads*
> *½ cup freshly chopped parsley*
> *¼ cup Pernod*
> *2 or 3 red chile peppers*
> *2 bay leaves*
> *8 ounces trout, catfish, or redfish chunks*
> *12 shrimp, shelled and deveined*
> *12 oysters, shucked*
> *8 ounces crayfish tails*
> *4 whole crayfish for garnish*

1. Heat fish stock to boiling, then add an equal amount of tomato sauce and bring to a simmer. To this mixture add fennel seeds, saffron, parsley, Pernod, chiles, and bay leaves. Simmer for 20 minutes.
2. Cook the fish and shellfish in the tomato sauce mixture for 3 minutes. Ladle out into large soup plates and garnish each serving with a whole crayfish. Serve with garlic toast.

FISH STOCK

> *3 pounds fish heads and tails (salmon, flounder, or striped bass)*
> *Half water and half Chablis wine, sufficient to just cover the fish*
> *2 onions, quartered*
> *3 stalks celery, halved*
> *Small bunch fresh parsley*
> *2 garlic cloves, smashed*
> *1 bay leaf*
> *2 lemons, sliced*
> *½ teaspoon peppercorns*
> *½ teaspoon thyme*
> *1 tablespoon fennel seeds*
> *Salt to taste*

1. Clean heads and tails of fish, discarding any blood clots and the gills in the heads. Put them in a large stockpot, press down, and cover with liquids. Add remaining ingredients, bring slowly to a boil, and simmer for 30 to 45 minutes. Strain, reserving the liquid.

☆ ☆ # BON TEMPS BREAD PUDDING ☆ ☆
SERVES 6

With its bland, soothing flavors, this is a perfect dessert to polish off a Cajun dinner.

5 cups milk
6 ounces sweet butter
¾ cup seedless raisins
5 large eggs
2 cups granulated sugar
1 teaspoon freshly grated nutmeg
1 teaspoon cinnamon
1 teaspoon vanilla extract or 1 teaspoon paste scraped
from inside 1 inch of vanilla bean
Pinch salt
About 15 cups French or Italian bread
torn into 2-inch chunks (2 to 3 loaves)
Whiskey Sauce (see below)

1. In a saucepan combine milk and butter. Heat until milk is scalded and butter is melted.
2. Meanwhile cover raisins with water in a small saucepan and bring to a boil to plump them. Drain well and set aside.
3. In a bowl whisk together the eggs, sugar, nutmeg, cinnamon, vanilla, and salt. Add milk in a slow steady stream, whisking constantly so eggs do not curdle. Add raisins and bread. Push down the bread to make sure it soaks up most of the custard mixture.
4. Empty bread-milk mixture into a 2-quart buttered dish about 10 inches in diameter. Place this pan in a larger baking pan half-filled with hot water. Cover it all with aluminum foil.
5. Bake in a preheated 350-degree oven for about 1 hour. Remove foil and continue to bake for 15 minutes longer. Serve hot with Whiskey Sauce.

WHISKEY SAUCE

MAKES ABOUT 3 CUPS

1 pound light brown sugar
3½ ounces bourbon
½ pound (2 sticks) sweet butter
1 cup heavy cream
Pinch salt

1. Measure all ingredients into a saucepan and bring to a boil. Cook until sauce is thickened, about 1 hour, whisking frequently. Serve hot over the pudding. Excess sauce may be refrigerated and used for other desserts or ice cream.

Café des Artistes

1 West 67th Street
New York, N.Y. 10023   877-3500

It was just ten years ago that George Lang took over the Cafe des Artistes and restored it to its original glory. And glorious it is, ornate and elegant, the walls filled with huge murals and mirrors, the windows filled with plants—the entire scene harking back to another era. This is not so odd, for 1985 was the seventieth anniversary of the café, which was built, together with the Hotel des Artistes, in 1915. The dishes served consist of the Sunday-type fare to be found on the tables of typical French middle-class families, combined with distinguished American food.

☆ ☆ # POT-AU-FEU ☆ ☆

SERVES 10

The French version of our New England boiled dinner, considered one of the great dishes of the world.

6 pounds short ribs of beef
3 pounds beef brisket
1 veal shank (about 3 pounds)
Coarse salt
1 spice bag containing 6 sprigs parsley, 1 sprig fresh thyme, 2 teaspoons cracked black peppercorns, and 1 bay leaf, wrapped in a double thickness of cheesecloth and tied with twine
1 onion, peeled and halved, each half studded with 2 cloves
10 marrowbones, each about 6 inches long, individually wrapped in cheesecloth with both ends tied
1 3- to 4-pound chicken
10 small carrots, peeled and tied in a bunch
1 knob celery, peeled and quartered
5 leeks, trimmed, sliced in half lengthwise, washed well to remove sand, and tied in a bunch
10 small white turnips, peeled and trimmed
Freshly ground white pepper to taste
Toast

Condiments:
Cornichons
Dijon mustard
Dark stone-ground mustard
Fresh grated horseradish

1. Put ribs, beef brisket, and veal shank in a large, deep soup kettle; add salt and enough cold water to cover the meat (about 6 quarts). Bring to a simmer.
2. Add a few tablespoons cold water to retard boiling and skim foam from surface. Keep skimming as needed.
3. Add spice bag and studded onion halves and simmer, uncovered, for about 2 hours.
4. Add marrowbones and chicken and continue to simmer for 1 hour. Skim foam from surface occasionally to give a clear broth.

5. Add vegetables and simmer approximately 45 minutes more, removing each vegetable when it becomes tender when pricked with a fork.
6. Remove string from cooked vegetables, and keep vegetables warm by putting in a small pot with some of the cooking stock. Do not place over direct heat.
7. Drain cooking stock from meats and keep warm as above with the vegetables.
8. Strain stock through cheesecloth moistened with water into another soup pot. Bring to a simmer. Skim off any fat from surface, and season to taste with coarse salt and white pepper.
9. Discard spice bag, and remove cheesecloth from marrow-bones.
10. Remove chicken and reserve for another use. It's good for salad, creamed, or as sandwich filling.
11. Serve the bouillon in cups as a first course. Pass thinly sliced toast with the marrowbones and individual marrow spoons for scooping out the marrow. This is usually spread on the toast. Serve the brisket and short ribs with the vegetables as a separate course with the condiments on the side.

☆ ☆   # VINEGAR PIE   ☆ ☆

This recipe from Cafe des Artistes is a good example of hard times, when imaginative use of simple materials compensated for expensive raw ingredients. This type of "forgotten" dessert, plus delicious cakes and tortes, is made by neighboring housewives for the restaurant.

Pastry:
1¼ cups all-purpose flour
¼ teaspoon salt
6 tablespoons very cold sweet butter, cut into 6 pieces
2 tablespoons solid vegetable shortening
3 tablespoons ice-cold water

Filling:
4 large eggs
1¼ cups granulated sugar
¼ cup sweet butter, melted and cooled
1½ tablespoons cider vinegar
1 teaspoon vanilla extract
1 cup heavy cream, whipped until stiff
¼ cup chopped pecans or walnuts for garnish

1. Measure flour and salt into mixing bowl. Add butter and vegetable shortening. With a pastry blender or two knives, cut shortening into flour mixture until mixture looks like coarse cornmeal.
2. Sprinkle water over flour mixture and mix rapidly with tines of a fork until ingredients form a ball in center of bowl. Shape dough into a rough ball, wrap in wax paper, and chill for about 1 hour.
3. Preheat oven to 450 degrees.
4. When ready to make pie, roll dough out on floured pastry cloth with floured rolling pin into a thin round, and with it line a 9-inch pie plate. Trim edges and crimp to form a decorative edge. Chill until firm.
5. Set a square of wax paper inside pie shell and fill with raw beans or rice. Bake in the hot oven for 6 to 8 minutes or until pastry looks set. Remove from oven, prick dough with a fork, and return to the oven for about 6 minutes longer, or until edge is golden brown. Remove from oven.
6. Reduce oven temperature to 350 degrees.
7. In a large bowl beat eggs. Gradually beat in sugar, melted butter, vinegar, and vanilla, mixing well. Pour into baked pie shell, place on baking sheet, and bake in a 350-degree oven for 35 to 40 minutes, or until firm and a knife inserted in center of filling comes out clean.
8. Remove pie from oven and place on a wire rack to cool completely. When cool, spread whipped cream over the pie, and sprinkle with chopped nuts. Refrigerate until ready to serve.

Cafe Loup

18 East 13th Street
New York, N.Y. 10003   255-4746

If you have a longing for a neighborhood pub where the regulars all seem to know one another and you can eat your meal at the bar if you wish, welcome to Cafe Loup. This place is what Greenwich Village is all about, or at least what it used to be. During lunch, antique dealers share the space with the publishing crowd, and even an artist or two who haven't left for another section of the city. Part of what makes this place work is Jorge, the bartender. He welcomes you, makes sure your glass is filled, helps you feel like a member of the club, makes the wait for a table more tolerable. The food is good, basically bistro fare—coarse pâté, onion soup, lamb and veal in hearty variations, a chicken dish or two, plus beef for those who still yearn for a good steak. But don't come just for the food, come to enjoy the casual atmosphere, and the nice small-town feeling.

☆ ☆ # CHEF FEIT'S SCALLOP AND CORN CHOWDER ☆ ☆

SERVES 4 TO 6

The chowder served at the Cafe Loup is rich and wonderfully characteristic of a true chowder—that is, seafood and lots of good vegetables.

6 medium potatoes
½ cup butter, divided
2 medium onions, peeled and diced
2 stalks celery, thinly sliced
1 quart clam broth or half clam and half chicken broth
1 pint (2 cups) water
3 strips of bacon, diced (see Note)
10-ounce box frozen corn, defrosted
1 pound bay scallops
½ cup flour
1 pint (2 cups) heavy cream
Salt and white pepper to taste
Chopped parsley

1. Peel and cut potatoes into ½-inch dice. Set aside.
2. In a soup pot, heat half the butter (4 tablespoons) and in it sauté onion and celery until onion is transparent and celery is limp.
3. Add potatoes, clam broth, and water and bring to a simmer.
4. Meanwhile, in a small skillet fry bacon until crisp. Strain off the drippings and reserve. Add bacon to the soup and simmer for 20 minutes.
5. Add corn and simmer for 10 minutes. Add scallops.
6. Make a roux or paste by combining remaining 4 tablespoons butter with the flour and the reserved bacon drippings. Whisk it gradually into the simmering soup to thicken it. Cook over low heat for 15 minutes, stirring occasionally.
7. Add cream and salt and pepper to taste. Garnish each serving with chopped parsley.

Note:
   If you slice bacon while it is very cold the slices will not stick to the knife.

☆ ☆ CALF'S BRAINS WITH JULIENNE ☆ ☆
OF HAM AND CAPERS

SERVES 4 TO 6

If you don't like calf's brains (some people just don't like the consistency), you may substitute sweetbreads.

3 sets of fresh calf's brains
Salt and pepper
½ cup flour
⅓ cup vegetable oil
¼ cup dry white wine or vermouth
½ cup veal stock or strong beef consommé
2 tablespoons capers
2 tablespoons sweet butter
6 tablespoons cooked ham or prosciutto, julienned
4 teaspoons chopped parsley for garnish

1. Rinse the brains in cold water.
2. Place the brains upright in a pot and cover with cold water by
   about 1 inch. Add a little salt, bring water to a boil, and simmer the brains over low heat for 20 minutes. Drain and immediately rinse in cold water until brains are cool to the touch.
   Cover with cold water and set aside for 1 hour.
3. When ready to cook, remove brains from their water bath, pat
   dry, and slice each hemisphere lengthwise in two or three
   pieces. Sprinkle with salt and pepper and coat each side of
   each medallion lightly with flour.
4. In a large sauté pan, heat vegetable oil until very hot and in it
   sauté the brains until golden brown on each side, from 3 to 5
   minutes. Remove from pan to paper towels to drain. Discard
   the oil.
5. To pan add the wine, veal stock, and capers and boil until
   liquid is reduced to half its original quantity. Reduce heat to
   low and add the butter in small amounts to thicken the sauce
   slightly.
6. Arrange 3 or 4 medallions of brains on a warm serving platter,
   sprinkle each serving with about 1 tablespoon ham, and
   spoon over a little of the caper-wine sauce. Garnish with the
   parsley.

Cajun Restaurant

129 Eighth Avenue (between 15th and 16th Streets)
New York, N.Y. 10011 691-6174/5

Chef Mickey Campbell is from the South and has seriously researched the Cajun/Creole fare he prepares at Herb Maslin's Cajun Restaurant. The French Quarter atmosphere—red walls with ornamental wrought iron—is a fitting backdrop for the live Dixieland music and the very reasonably priced food. Many patrons come to Cajun on Sunday for a Dixieland jazz brunch.

When in season, crayfish are served in pies or etouffée-style (in a dark, spicy sauce). Soft-shell crabs are also available in season. Although some diners enjoy oysters on the half shell, others opt to share a baked oyster selection: six briny specimens with a trio of toppings. Blackened bluefish, a Northern version of the now famous Louisiana redfish dish, is popular, as are jambalaya and shrimp Tchoupitoulas. The latter may sound Greek, but is really a Southern concoction of shrimp sautéed with mushrooms, artichoke hearts, garlic, and white wine.

Beignets, those airy New Orleans fritters, are made to order. Dunk a few in a cup of rich French roast chicory coffee, or indulge in bourbon pecan pie or bread pudding with zabaglione.

There is a limited wine selection. Better yet, choose a frosty glass of Dixie beer; the New Orleans brew is more appropriate with this spicy food.

☆ ☆   **SHRIMP, CRAB, SAUSAGE, AND**   ☆ ☆
OKRA GUMBO

SERVES 8

No Cajun restaurant would be caught without its very special gumbo served in large bowls over rice. Chef Campbell suggests preparing all the vegetables before making the roux.

¾ cup vegetable oil
¾ cup flour
2 pounds smoked sausage such as Polish kielbasa,
andouille or the like
2 cups chopped onion
¼ cup chopped green pepper
½ cup sliced scallions
⅓ cup sliced celery
2 tablespoons minced parsley
1 tablespoon minced garlic
1 can (28 ounces) Italian plum tomatoes
2 quarts Shrimp Stock (see below)
1½ cups red wine
2 tablespoons Worcestershire sauce
3 bay leaves
1 teaspoon thyme
½ teaspoon basil
½ teaspoon oregano
2 teaspoons salt or to taste
½ teaspoon cayenne
½ teaspoon ground black pepper
½ teaspoon ground white pepper
¼ teaspoon mace
¼ teaspoon allspice
2 pounds okra (fresh or frozen), sliced ½ inch thick
2 pounds shrimp, peeled and deveined
1 pound crab, cleaned and halved

1. In a heavy 7- to 8-quart kettle, heat the oil. Add the flour, a third at a time, stirring constantly. Cook over low heat for 20 to 30 minutes, or until the mixture is a rich brown. Constant stirring is essential or the roux will stick and burn.

2. Add the sausage and cook, stirring, for 5 minutes. Add all the fresh vegetables except the okra plus the parsley and garlic and simmer, stirring occasionally, for 20 to 30 minutes, or until vegetables are soft.
3. Add the tomatoes and their juice, the stock, wine, and Worcestershire sauce. Stir in all the seasonings and simmer for 1 hour. If using fresh okra, add it now; if using frozen okra, add it after 30 minutes.
4. Add the shrimp and crab and simmer for 10 to 12 minutes longer. Serve in large bowls over cooked rice.

SHRIMP STOCK

Shells from 2 pounds shrimp, well washed
1 carrot, sliced
2 ribs celery, sliced
1 onion, quartered
1 orange, quartered
1 lemon, quartered
2 quarts water
2 bay leaves
1 teaspoon thyme
1 teaspoon whole black peppercorns

1. Combine all ingredients in a large pot and bring slowly to a boil. Reduce heat and simmer for one hour, adding more water if too much boils away.
2. Strain and use for gumbos and sauces.

☆ ☆   # SHRIMP TCHOUPITOULAS   ☆ ☆
SERVES 4

Shrimp blend flavorfully with mushrooms, artichoke hearts, pimiento, and of course garlic in this dish, which is more Creole than
Cajun.

> *1 pound medium shrimp, shelled and deveined*
> *½ pound mushrooms, sliced*
> *3 tablespoons butter*
> *2 tablespoons minced garlic*
> *¼ cup dry white wine*
> *4 cooked artichoke hearts, quartered*
> *4 tablespoons chopped pimientos*
> *½ cup thinly sliced scallions*
> *2 tablespoons chopped parsley*
> *1 cup shrimp stock (see Note)*
> *¼ cup lemon juice*
> *2 tablespoons Blond Roux (see below)*
> *Salt, cayenne, and Worcestershire sauce to taste*
> *Cooked rice*

1. Sauté shrimp and mushrooms in the butter, stirring constantly, for about 5 minutes or until shrimp lose their translucence.
2. Add garlic, being careful not to let it burn. Add wine and
   cook over high heat until most of the wine has evaporated.
3. Add artichoke hearts, pimientos, scallions, and parsley. Cook
   for 1 minute longer, then stir in stock and lemon juice.
4. Add the roux, a little at a time, to make the sauce the desired
   thickness. Add seasonings. Serve with rice.

BLOND ROUX

1. This is made with equal parts by weight of flour and butter
   cooked together but not allowed to color like the dark roux in
   the preceding recipe for gumbo. In a saucepan melt 2
   tablespoons butter, stir in 4 tablespoons flour, and cook,
   stirring, until mixture is smooth. Makes 2 tablespoons.

Note:
   If you want to make this recipe and don't have any shrimp stock
   on hand, you can substitute bottled clam juice.

The Coach House

110 Waverly Place
New York, N.Y. 10011   777-0303

For many years the Coach House has been considered one of Manhattan's finest restaurants. Its reputation for good food is legion. Nothing but the highest quality ingredients are used, and they are simply prepared and beautifully served in a handsome setting. Fresh flowers adorn the tables, priceless paintings decorate the walls, and the lighting is rosy and flattering.

Two of the dishes most popular with the clientele are roast rack of baby lamb with sauce bordelaise and fresh artichoke hearts, and chicken pie, with its rich, flaky crust filled with chunks of tender chicken and flavorful vegetables. The black bean soup is one of the best and most popular first courses, and the striped bass is nothing short of sensational. Expensive, but you'll love it.

☆ ☆ ## STRIPED BASS ADRIATIC ☆ ☆
SERVES 6

This spectacular fish dish for a party of six is served at The Coach House on special order. A whole striped bass, surrounded by herbs, vegetables, shrimp, clams, and mussels, is baked in white wine and served in all its glory with crusty bread and a tangy feta cheese salad. It's an easy dish to serve at home, next time you catch that fresh striper.

A 4-pound very fresh striped bass
12 large shrimp
12 littleneck clams
12 mussels
¾ cup chopped flat-leaf Italian parsley
½ teaspoon oregano
½ teaspoon dry basil or 1 tablespoon chopped fresh
2 bay leaves
1 teaspoon chopped fresh dill
3 cloves garlic, finely chopped
4 scallions or green onions, finely chopped
2 pounds fresh tomatoes, chopped
2 carrots, thinly sliced lengthwise
1 heart of celery, finely chopped
Juice of 2 lemons
Salt to taste
2 teaspoons crushed black pepper
1 cup dry white wine
¾ cup olive oil
1 lemon, thinly sliced

1. Have the fish market remove the gills from the bass and clean and scale it, leaving the head on and removing the spine. You can do this yourself if you wish. Wash fish well, removing any leftover scales. Wash shrimp and slit backs with sharp scissors, but do not remove shells. Rinse out the black vein that runs down the back. Scrub clams well and rinse to remove any sand. Scrub mussels and rinse well, making sure there are no "clinkers" among them—that is, empty shells filled with sand.
2. Combine all herbs and vegetables and set aside.
3. Preheat oven to 375 degrees.
4. Dry the striped bass and slit it lengthwise on both sides. Rub well with lemon juice and season with salt and pepper.
5. Place the bass in the center of a large baking pan or casserole, and spread the herbs and vegetables around it.
6. Pour the wine and olive oil over the fish and vegetables, and arrange thin lemon slices all down its length.
7. Place pan over high heat on top of stove and cook for about 15 minutes. Arrange the shrimp, clams, and mussels around the fish, and bake in the hot oven for 30 to 40 minutes, or until clams and mussels open and the fish flakes with a fork.
8. Serve in its baking dish.

☆ ☆   # COACH HOUSE BLACK BEAN SOUP   ☆ ☆

MAKES ABOUT 10 CUPS

"Every restaurant needs a special dish of its own by which the restaurant is known," said Leon Lianides, owner of the Coach House. At the Coach House that specialty is an outstandingly different and delicious black bean soup, which the restaurant serves with hot corn sticks.

3 cups black beans (also called turtle beans)
3 quarts water
5 strips bacon cut into small pieces
2 stalks chopped celery
2 coarsely chopped onions
2 tablespoons flour
Rind and bone from a smoked ham or two smoked ham shanks, split
3 pounds beef bones
2 sprigs parsley
1 bay leaf
2 cloves garlic, cut in half
2 coarsely chopped carrots
2 coarsely chopped parsnips
½ teaspoon freshly ground black pepper
1 cup Madeira wine
2 hard-boiled eggs, chopped fine

1. Wash the beans, cover them with cold water, and refrigerate overnight.
2. Drain the beans and wash them again. Place them in a casserole, add the 3 quarts of water, cover, and simmer for about 90 minutes.
3. Place the bacon in a heavy kettle and sauté for a few minutes. Add the celery and onion and cook until tender. Do not brown.
4. Blend in the flour and cook the mixture stirring for one minute. Add the ham and beef bones, parsley, bay leaves, garlic, carrots, parsnip, black pepper, and beans with the cooking liquid.
5. Cover and simmer for 3 to 4 hours. Add more water if necessary.
6. Remove bones and ham rind, and put the soup through a sieve, pressing through thoroughly. Return the soup to the fire to reheat.
7. Add the Madeira wine and chopped eggs. Mix well and serve hot.
8. Adjust salt and pepper to taste.

☆ ☆ COACH HOUSE RACK OF LAMB ☆ ☆

SERVES 4

This is a favorite dish of the restaurant's faithful clientele. It is usually served with bordelaise sauce and fresh artichoke hearts on the side.

2 6-chop racks of lamb, about 2 pounds each
1½ cups Coach House Bordelaise Sauce (see below)
1 clove garlic
1 teaspoon lemon juice
1 teaspoon French olive oil
Salt and freshly ground pepper to taste
2 tablespoons minced parsley

1. Have the butcher scrape ends of bones of all fat and meat, and trim meat of any excess fat.
2. Make bordelaise sauce and set aside.
3. Crush the garlic clove and rub it over the bone side of the meat. Then rub the meat with lemon juice and olive oil and sprinkle with salt and pepper and minced parsley.
4. Preheat the oven to very hot, 500 degrees.
5. Put racks in a shallow roasting pan, meat side up, and roast for 10 minutes. Turn the racks and roast for 10 minutes longer, or until lamb is well browned on outside, but still pink within.
6. Serve half a rack per person with sauce on the side.

COACH HOUSE BORDELAISE SAUCE

ABOUT 1½ CUPS

2 tablespoons finely chopped shallots
2 tablespoons butter
¾ cup red wine
1½ cups Brown Sauce (see below) or 1 10½-ounce jar brown gravy
¼ cup sherry or port wine
2 teaspoons lemon juice
Salt and pepper to taste

1. Sauté shallots in butter in a medium saucepan until translucent but not brown. Add red wine and boil down until quantity is reduced by half.
2. Stir in brown sauce or gravy, sherry or port, and the lemon juice. Add salt and pepper to taste. Heat sauce and simmer for 5 minutes.

BROWN SAUCE

MAKES 1 QUART

½ cup (2 sticks) butter
8 tablespoons flour
4 cups brown stock (see below)
1 carrot, sliced
1 onion, chopped
1 leek, quartered
1 clove garlic, minced
2 tablespoons tomato purée
1 cup dry white wine
½ teaspoon thyme
1 large bay leaf
Salt and pepper to taste
½ cup sherry or Madeira

1. In a heavy skillet melt the butter, stir in the flour, and cook until mixture becomes a good dark brown, the color of dark brown sugar.
2. Add the stock and cook, stirring, until sauce is thickened. Add carrot, onion, leek, garlic, tomato purée, white wine, thyme, and bay leaf. Simmer for 30 minutes, skimming off the fat that rises to the surface. Remove bay leaf.
3. Blend 2 cups at a time in container of an electric blender until sauce is smooth. Return blended sauce to saucepan, add a little salt and pepper to taste, and stir in the sherry or Madeira.
4. Cool, and if not using immediately, pour into clean jar with tight-fitting lid and refrigerate. Sauce will keep for several days to a week.

BROWN STOCK

MAKES 3 QUARTS

2 pounds beef shin, cubed
3 pounds beef or veal knuckle, cubed
¼ pound lean raw ham, diced
2 tablespoons cooking oil
3 carrots, sliced
2 onions, sliced
2 stalks celery, sliced
3 cloves garlic
2 cups water plus 4½ quarts water
A bouquet garni consisting of parsley, ½ teaspoon thyme,
2 large bay leaves, and 1 teaspoon crushed peppercorns
2 teaspoons salt

1. Preheat oven to 475 degrees.
2. In a flat baking pan spread the beef shin, beef knuckle, and ham and sprinkle with the oil. Bake in the preheated oven for 1 hour, or until well browned.
3. Add carrots, onions, celery and garlic, and bake for 30 minutes longer.
4. Transfer meat and vegetables to a large soup kettle. Rinse baking pan with the 2 cups water and add to the kettle. Add remaining water and the bouquet garni tied in a cheesecloth bag. Add salt.
5. Bring water to a boil, skim well, reduce heat, and simmer for 3 hours. Cool, remove fat from surface, and strain through a sieve lined with cheesecloth. Pour into containers, cool, and use as needed. Freeze what is not needed in the recipe for future use.

☆ ☆   # COACH HOUSE BAVARIAN CREAM   ☆ ☆

SERVES 12

A lovely egg-enriched cream, served plain or with fresh fruit or berries, makes a suitable and refreshing conclusion to a Coach House dinner.

1 quart milk
1 cup sugar
10 egg yolks
4 tablespoons cornstarch
2 envelopes plain gelatin
½ cup water
1 tablespoon pure vanilla extract
1 pint heavy cream, whipped

1. In a saucepan combine 3 cups of the milk and the sugar. Bring to a boil, stirring until sugar is completely dissolved.
3. Meanwhile combine egg yolks and cornstarch with remaining 1 cup milk, stirring until smooth.
3. When milk comes to a boil, stir in cornstarch mixture and cook for 3 minutes, stirring constantly.
4. Strain the thickened custard into a chilled bowl and cool completely.
5. Soften gelatin in ½ cup water, then dissolve over low heat.
6. Add 1 cup of the cooled custard to the dissolved gelatin and stir to combine thoroughly. Add this to the larger quantity of cooled custard, stirring quickly so the gelatin will be evenly distributed. Stir in vanilla.
7. Fold in whipped cream gently but thoroughly. Pour into a chilled 8-cup mold and refrigerate for 3 to 4 hours before turning out onto chilled serving plate.

Crêpe Suzette

363 West 46th Street
New York, N.Y. 10036   581-9717

Along West 46th Street between 8th and 9th Avenues, or Restaurant Row as the street sign states, is an almost overwhelming choice of restaurants. Located on the ground or street levels of a series of row houses, these places are almost all perfect for pre-theater dining. Among them is Crêpe Suzette, an old-fashioned French bistro that offers the type of fare once found in many New York French restaurants, but now rare. There's beef, veal, always some fish, and of course chicken on the menu. The nightly fixed price meal offers two choices of entrées and several choices of appetizers. The atmosphere is simple, comfortable, and relaxing, and the food fits that description as well. If you are in doubt as to what to order, the owner, Madelaine Ribes, will be glad to help.

☆ ☆ VEAL SCALOPPINE NORMANDE ☆ ☆
SERVES 1

The first recipe from this charming restaurant is a veal scallop dish with mushrooms in an apple brandy cream sauce. Serve with several colorful julienned vegetables, steamed until just tender.

1 tablespoon flour
Pinch salt
Freshly ground pepper to taste
3 slices veal scallops, pounded until very thin and trimmed
1½ tablespoons clarified butter (page 301)
2 fresh mushrooms, washed, trimmed, and sliced
2 tablespoons (1 ounce) calvados (apple brandy)
2 tablespoons heavy cream

1. Combine flour, salt, and pepper. Spread on wax paper and dip veal slices in the mixture to coat both sides lightly.
2. In a skillet heat the butter and in it sauté the veal briefly on each side, about 2 to 3 minutes. When lightly browned, add mushrooms and calvados. Light the calvados and let the flame die out. Then add the cream and shake the pan over the heat until the cream has picked up all the brown glaze from sides and bottom of pan.
3. Transfer veal slices to a warm serving plate and pour the sauce over. Garnish with vegetables and a spray of watercress.

☆ ☆   # CRÊPES MADELAINE   ☆ ☆

And here is Madelaine Ribes's very own recipe for dessert crêpes that should not be missed on your first visit. Some people go there just for this delicately delicious dessert.

CRÊPES
3 DOZEN 6-INCH CRÊPES

2½ cups flour
5 tablespoons sugar
Dash salt
2 eggs
3 eggs, separated
1 teaspoon vanilla
2 tablespoons imported Belgian mandarin orange liqueur
1 cup milk
2 cups light cream
4 tablespoons melted butter

1. In advance, combine flour, sugar, and salt. Beat in 2 whole eggs, one at a time, and 3 egg yolks. Stir in vanilla, mandarin orange liqueur, milk, and cream.
2. Beat egg whites until they hold a light peak and fold into egg yolk mixture. Let rest for at least 2 hours.
3. To bake: Heat a 6-inch crêpe pan over medium heat until it sizzles a drop of water. Brush pan lightly with melted butter. For each crêpe pour in just enough batter to coat bottom of

pan with a thin layer. As the batter is poured in, immediately rotate and tilt pan to swirl batter quickly and evenly in a thin layer over the bottom. If you have poured in too much batter, tilt pan over the container of batter so that any excess will run out. If the crêpe has holes, patch with a drop or two of batter.

4. Brown crêpe on one side. This should take only a minute. When evenly browned and set, turn it carefully, using a spatula. It's very delicate. Let the other side dry for about one-half minute. It will not be as evenly browned as the first side so this will be the inside of the finished crêpe.

5. Invert pan over a strip of paper toweling, emptying out the crêpe to cool, and repeat until all batter has been used, brushing pan with melted butter after every two or three crêpes. When crêpes are thoroughly cooled, they may be stacked one on top of the other on a plate. Cover with foil or plastic wrap to keep them moist, and set aside until needed. Those not needed may be sealed in a plastic bag and frozen.

CRÊPES MADELAINE SAUCE
SERVES 6

2 tablespoons clarified butter (page 301)
4 teaspoons fine granulated fruit sugar
Grated rind and juice of 1 lemon
Grated rind and juice of 1 orange
¼ cup Cognac
2 tablespoons mandarin orange liqueur

1. In a large shallow skillet combine butter, half the sugar, grated lemon and orange rinds, and juices and mix well.

2. Place 12 crêpes, one at a time, in the sauce, fold in half, then in half again, and arrange side by side in the sauce remaining in the skillet.

3. Sprinkle crêpes with the remaining sugar, pour in the Cognac and orange liqueur, ignite the liqueurs, and let the flame burn out.

4. Serve two crêpes per person with a spoonful of the pan juice poured over them.

Diane's

7 East 54th Street
New York, N.Y. 10022   644-5700

If you are away from home and miss the dishes "mom used to make," you'll love Diane's, which features traditional cuisine. Many recipes for the dishes at Diane's have been passed down from Diane Roupe's grandmother, mother, and friends in her native Iowa. At a time when Americans are eating more meals in restaurants than ever before, Diane's makes it possible for New Yorkers weary of nouvelle cuisine, cuisine minceur, and sushi to dine in elegant surroundings and enjoy the wonderful, simple flavors of a home-cooked meal.

☆ ☆ ## SCALLOPED CHICKEN ☆ ☆
SERVES 8

This first recipe from Diane's is a comfortable scalloped chicken with a sauce of mushrooms and olives.

1 4- to 5-pound chicken
½ cup plus 2 tablespoons butter
½ cup flour
2½ cups chicken broth, divided
1½ cups milk
½ teaspoon salt
⅛ teaspoon freshly ground pepper
3 eggs, separated
1 cup sliced mushrooms
2 cups fresh bread crumbs
Mushroom Olive Sauce (see below)

1. A day in advance, poach the chicken until done to taste. Do *not* overcook. Remove from stove, let stand in broth until cool to the touch. Remove meat from the bones, cut into large chunks, and refrigerate in a loosely covered container.
2. In a 2-quart saucepan melt the ½ cup butter. Remove from heat and stir in flour. When mixture is smooth, add 2 cups of the chicken broth and all the milk and return to moderate heat. Cook, stirring, until sauce thickens. Remove again from heat and stir in salt, pepper, egg yolks, and the remaining ½ cup chicken broth. Let mixture cool.
3. Meanwhile arrange chicken meat in an oiled 13- by 9-inch baking dish.
4. Sauté the mushrooms in the remaining 2 tablespoons butter until most of the excess moisture has evaporated. Drain and sprinkle the mushrooms evenly over the chicken.
5. Stir the bread crumbs into the sauce. Beat egg whites until stiff enough to hold a soft peak and fold into the sauce. Pour sauce evenly over chicken mixture.
6. Bake in a moderate 325-degree oven for 60 minutes.
7. Cut the scalloped chicken into 8 serving portions and, using a spatula, remove from baking dish to a warm serving plate. Top each portion with Mushroom Olive Sauce.

MUSHROOM OLIVE SAUCE

SERVES 8

2 tablespoons butter
1 cup sliced mushrooms
¼ cup sliced stuffed olives
¼ cup pitted ripe olives

1. In a skillet or small saucepan melt the butter and in it sauté the mushrooms until they are lightly golden. Add olives and heat.

☆ ☆ # FROSTED BROWNIES ☆ ☆

MAKES 8 LARGE RECTANGULAR PORTIONS

One of the most popular desserts served at Diane's is her frosted brownies. The rich cookie is crunchy with English walnuts, and it is topped with a luscious mocha frosting.

1 cup butter
4 squares unsweetened chocolate
2 cups sugar
4 eggs, well beaten
1 teaspoon pure vanilla extract
1½ cups sifted flour
½ teaspoon salt
1 cup broken English walnuts
Chocolate Mocha Frosting (see below)

1. In the top of a double boiler melt butter and chocolate over hot water. Add sugar and mix well.
2. Transfer chocolate mixture to an electric mixer and, while beating slowly, add eggs, vanilla, then the flour and salt, mixing thoroughly after each addition.
3. Fold in walnuts with a large metal spoon.
4. Spread mixture in a well-oiled 13- by 9-inch baking dish and bake in a preheated 400-degree oven for 20 minutes. Cool.
5. Spread with frosting and let frosting set before cutting into rectangular serving pieces.

CHOCOLATE MOCHA FROSTING

1 pound confectioner's sugar
½ cup melted butter
⅓ cup cocoa
3 tablespoons cool brewed coffee
2 teaspoons pure vanilla extract

1. Measure all ingredients into bowl of an electric mixer and beat until completely smooth. If too thick, add a little more coffee.

Dieci X

1568 First Avenue (between 81st and 82nd streets)
New York, N.Y. 10028   628-6565

Years ago First Avenue was the backwater of Manhattan. Every few blocks you might find a neighborhood restaurant in between the corner drugstore and the local meat market, but for the most part it wasn't an area that attracted diners from other neighborhoods. Now First Avenue bustles, and restaurants are spiffy enough to attract Upper East Siders who live more than a few blocks away.

Dieci X is one of these. Its long bar, wood-enhanced interior, and white linen tablecloths beckon to both neighbors and visitors. The cuisine is what might be called "restaurant Italian"—chicken, veal, and fish dishes, complete with a choice of many different kinds of pastas—all satisfying, all commendable.

☆ ☆ ## FETTUCCINE AL RADICCHIO ☆ ☆

Serves 2 as an appetizer

Chef Michael Orsini might suggest this for an appetizer. Garlic, cream, plum tomatoes, and chopped radicchio make this pasta hard to beat.

1 large clove garlic, peeled and minced
2 tablespoons sweet butter
1 head radicchio (Italian red lettuce), trimmed and chopped
¼ cup dry white wine
1 cup whole, peeled plum tomatoes
1 tablespoon heavy cream
Salt and pepper to taste
½ pound freshly made fettuccine
½ cup grated fresh Parmesan cheese

1. Sauté chopped garlic in the butter in a 10-inch skillet for about 1 minute. Do not let it brown. Add chopped radicchio, wine, and tomatoes, and cook for 3 minutes. Stir in cream, salt, and pepper, and simmer for 4 minutes longer.
2. Meanwhile, in a large saucepan bring 4 quarts lightly salted water to a rapid boil. Gradually drop in the fettuccine and boil for about 4 minutes, or until just tooth tender. Do not overcook.
3. Drain noodles, transfer to a warm bowl, and toss with the Parmesan cheese. Slowly pour the radicchio sauce on top of the fettuccine and serve in heated soup bowls.

☆ ☆   # SHRIMP IMPERIAL   ☆ ☆
SERVES 2

An excellent entrée to follow the pasta course. Salad and a good cup of espresso would complete a memorable meal.

10 fresh jumbo shrimp
1 Spanish onion, peeled and sliced
2 tablespoons sweet butter
1 clove garlic, peeled and minced
1 whole red pepper, seeded and sliced
1 medium zucchini, sliced
3 fresh mushrooms, sliced
5 or 6 large fresh basil leaves or 1 tablespoon drained pesto
Salt and pepper to taste
3 tablespoons dry white wine
2 sprigs parsley

1. Peel and devein the shrimp and set aside.
2. In a large skillet over medium heat simmer the onion in butter until soft but not brown. Add minced garlic and let it become golden. Then add the red pepper, zucchini, mushrooms, sweet basil or pesto, salt, and pepper. Pour in the wine and cook until it has completely evaporated.
3. Add the shrimp and cook for about 5 minutes, or until they have lost their translucence, stirring and tossing the shrimp constantly. Serve garnished with a sprig of parsley.

El Internacional Tapas Bar and Restaurant

219 West Broadway
New York, N.Y. 10013   226-8131

If you are a secret nibbler whose idea of a perfect meal is a grand buffet where you can munch on bits and pieces all evening long, El Internacional is the place for you. You won't find a buffet but you will find tapas, a variety of appetizing dishes like those served in the great bars in Spain. You can order one dish or several at a time. For those who prefer not to pick and taste, there is a choice of main courses that also reflect the owner's origins—Barcelona, Spain. The clientele combines residents of the downtown neighborhood and uptown "visitors" who soon become regulars. If you want to see and be seen, sit in the downstairs area off the bar. If you prefer anonymity, go upstairs to either the Marina or the Crystal Room, each capturing a different feeling and period. El Internacional is a mix of Spanish food, red velvet, and a group of food-conscious people who are ready to try something new and interesting. The place is large—four rooms—and noisy. When it comes to dressing, anything goes. Reservations are necessary.

☆ ☆ # Tortilla Española ☆ ☆
(Spanish potato omelet)
SERVES 8 TO 12

Some people like tortillas hot, others like them cool. In Spain the custom is to serve them at room temperature.

20 eggs
Salt to taste
8 large potatoes
2 large Spanish onions
½ cup olive oil
¾ cup vegetable oil

1. Break the eggs in a large bowl and season wth salt. Set aside.
2. Peel and slice the potatoes and onions.
3. Combine the two oils. Pour half of the oil mixture into a large nonstick frying pan and begin to heat. When the oil is hot, put in the potatoes and onions and sauté them gently until tender and golden brown.
4. Remove the pan from the heat and add the vegetables to the eggs. Mix together thoroughly and correct seasoning with salt.
5. Heat the remaining oil mixture in a large nonstick omelet pan. When hot pour the egg-vegetable mixture into the pan. Lower the heat, cover the pan, and let eggs cook gently until they become firm. Use a dish or the cover of the pan to turn the tortilla over, and brown it on the other side.
6. Cut like a pie to serve.

☆ ☆   # Mar y Montaña   ☆ ☆
(Sea and mountain)
SERVES 6

The mixture of meat and seafood is no rarity in Catalonia, especially in the northern part near the Costa Brava. Mar y montaña is a festive dish, usually prepared inland because lobsters are one of the few aquatic animals that survive for quite a long time out of water if kept cool and packed in seaweed. It is said that this dish was invented to save chickens, more expensive and much harder to come by than lobster. Chef Montse Guillen added that the secret to the dish's success is the sauce—the picada.

2 large tomatoes, about 1½ pounds total weight,
or 1¾ cups drained, chopped, canned tomatoes
1 frying chicken, about 2¾ pounds, cut into serving portions
(discard backbone)
Salt and freshly ground pepper to taste
2 live lobsters, 1½ pounds each
⅓ cup olive oil
1 cup chopped onion
1½ tablespoons finely minced garlic
2 tablespoons finely chopped parsley
1 cup dry white wine
⅔ cup Picada (see below)

1. If fresh tomatoes are used, peel and put them in a shallow casserole. Bake in a preheated 375-degree oven for about 20 minutes, or until soft but not mushy. Set aside.
2. Sprinkle chicken pieces with salt and pepper and set aside.
3. Split each lobster in half crosswise at the point where the tail and body meet. Then split tail and body lengthwise and discard the intestinal vein and the sac that lies in back of the head. Cut the tail piece crosswise into 3 or 4 pieces. Crack the lobster claws. Arrange all the lobster pieces in a dish and sprinkle lightly with salt and pepper.
4. Heat the oil in a large heavy casserole and add the lobster pieces. Cook, stirring, over high heat for 2 to 3 minutes. Using a slotted spoon, transfer lobster pieces to a dish, leaving the oil in the casserole.

5. To oil remaining in casserole add chicken pieces, skin side down. Sauté until golden, then turn and brown the other side, about 5 minutes a side. Remove chicken pieces and add them to the lobster, leaving the oil in the casserole.
6. Add onion and garlic to the oil and cook, stirring often, until onion is golden brown, about 15 minutes.
7. Add the parsley.
8. Chop the baked tomatoes and add them, or add the canned tomatoes. Cook, stirring occasionally, about 5 minutes. Add the wine and simmer for 5 minutes.
9. Return the lobster and chicken to the casserole and cook for 5 minutes. Add the picada, cover the casserole, and cook another 5 minutes. If desired, remove the lobster claws and break them open. Remove the meat and return it to the casserole, discarding the claw shells.

PICADA
(A Spanish nut and chocolate condiment)
ABOUT ⅔ CUP

3 cloves garlic
12 blanched hazelnuts, skinned
12 blanched almonds, skinned
1½ tablespoons pine nuts
1½ tablespoons grated bitter chocolate
½ teaspoon saffron stems or threads
½ cup fresh or canned chicken broth or clam juice

1. Sprinkle the unpeeled garlic, hazelnuts, almonds, and pine nuts in a shallow dish such as a pie plate and bake in a 350-degree oven for 20 minutes, or until nuts are browned, stirring occasionally. Remove and cool.
2. Crush the nuts to a paste in a mortar and pestle or blender. Slip the garlic out of its skin and add to the nuts. Continue mashing or blending for about 5 minutes.
3. Add the chocolate and saffron, and continue mashing or blending about 1 minute. Add 2 tablespoons of broth, and continue mashing or blending and stirring until mixture is smooth.
4. Add the remaining broth and stir to blend.

Ennio & Michael

504 La Guardia Place
New York, N.Y. 10012   677-8577

When you first hear of this place, you may not be sure whether it's a restaurant or chic hairdressing salon. But restaurant it is. It first opened its doors in a storefront on Bleecker Street, but it was such an immediate success that it quickly moved to a larger site. Ennio & Michael's is not noted for its decor, which is casual at best, whether it be at the tables up front closest to the bar or in the main dining room farther back. On the other hand, most of the waiters know what they're doing—they've been at it a long time. There are no surprises here, just something to please anyone who wants a straightforward Italian meal: Stuffed mushrooms, deep-fried zucchini, manicotti, tortellini, veal scaloppine, or a nice thick chop are some of the basics that fans of Italian food somehow never seem to tire of.

☆ ☆ # Spiedini alla Romana ☆ ☆
(Mozzarella cheese appetizer)
SERVES 4

Maître d' Michael Savarese suggested spiedini as a first course. He added the tip that in the home kitchen it may be prepared a few hours before cooking time and kept refrigerated, a big boon to the home chef.

40 rectangles of slightly stale bread, each approximately
2 by 1 by ⅓ inch
32 slices of mozzarella cheese (about 1 pound),
cut the same size as the bread
About 1 cup flour
2 eggs, lightly beaten
⅓ stick lightly salted butter
6 anchovy fillets
1 tablespoon capers
1 cup dry white wine
1 cup chicken broth
Vegetable oil for frying

1. Well in advance of serving time prepare the spiedini: On each of four 8- or 9-inch skewers alternate 10 squares of bread and 8 squares of cheese, beginning and ending with bread. Roll in flour, beaten egg, and again in flour, making sure the layers stay together. Place on wax paper or foil and refrigerate.
2. Make the sauce: In a shallow pan, melt butter, add anchovies, and mash with a fork until anchovies are blended into the butter. Add capers and wine. Simmer for about 3 minutes. Add broth and continue to simmer for about 5 minutes longer, until sauce is well blended. Set aside.
3. In a large skillet heat oil to a depth of about 1 inch to 350 degrees. Fry the spiedini in the hot oil until nicely brown all over, turning as necessary to brown all sides evenly.
4. Meanwhile reheat sauce to simmering.
5. Remove spiedini from the hot oil and drain on paper towels to absorb any excess oil. Prick all sides with a fork and dip in the sauce.
6. Serve on warm plates with a little of the sauce poured over each serving.

☆ ☆ SPAGHETTI ALLA PUTTANESCA ☆ ☆
SERVES 4

For a main course, Michael suggests what he calls a "white version" of the popular spaghetti alla puttanesca. He includes no tomatoes and uses 3 or 4 leaves of fresh oregano. This herb is available some seasons of the year in Italian markets and gives the dish a flavor never achieved with the dried facsimile.

¼ cup olive oil
4 large cloves garlic, peeled, smashed, then minced
32 black pitted olives, sliced
3 anchovy fillets, chopped
2 cups chicken broth
Salt to taste
Lots of freshly ground black pepper
3 or 4 leaves fresh oregano*
1 pound spaghetti

1. In a large skillet heat oil, add garlic, and let it brown very lightly—only to a pale gold.
2. Add remaining ingredients except spaghetti and simmer for 5 to 6 minutes, or until sauce thickens slightly.
3. In a large kettle bring 5 quarts water to a boil. Add salt to taste, and cook spaghetti al dente, following directions on the package.
4. Drain spaghetti, return to kettle set over direct heat, and add half the sauce. Simmer for 1 to 2 minutes.
5. Serve on heated plates, topping each serving with a spoonful of the remaining sauce.

* A pot of oregano thrives in a sunny kitchen window.

Felidia

243 East 58th Street
New York, N.Y. 10022 758-1479

What's amazing about East 58th Street is that even though it seems to be almost overwhelmed by Italian restaurants, each manages to have its own distinct personality. At Felidia the personality changes twice a day. During lunch this is a warm, friendly place, where you can eat and drink in a sunlit room or an intimate balcony area. At night there is no decrease in the warmth and friendliness, but there is a definite increase in the hustle and bustle. It's the owners, Felix and Lidia Bastianich, who make it work. The pastas are all homemade, as are the cakes and breads, but this is one place to deviate from the pastas—at least on your second visit, try the polenta. Felidia's menu changes often to make the best possible use of whatever is freshest and in season, so listen carefully as the specials are enumerated.

☆　☆　　　## CHICKEN IN SGUAZET　　☆　☆
WITH POLENTA
(Chicken in spiced wine sauce)
SERVES 4

One of the most popular dishes at Felidia, this is an easy chicken sauté flavored with rosemary and cloves. It is served with polenta.

1 large onion, diced
2 slices lean bacon, diced
3 bay leaves
1 teaspoon fresh or dried rosemary
4 whole cloves

¼ cup olive oil
1 chicken, cut into 8 pieces
2 teaspoons tomato paste
1 cup dry white wine
2 cups chicken stock
Salt and freshly ground
black pepper to taste
Polenta (see below)

1. Sauté the onion, bacon, bay leaves, rosemary, and cloves in the olive oil for about 3 minutes or until onion is wilted and transparent. Add chicken pieces and sauté until pieces are lightly brown on all sides.
2. Add tomato paste and mix it into the drippings in the pan. Add wine and cook, scraping the pan to remove brown bits from bottom and sides. Add chicken stock, and salt and pepper to taste. Cover and simmer for 20 minutes to cook the chicken and reduce the sauce.
3. Remove pieces of chicken and strain the sauce.
4. To serve: Spoon hot polenta into center of warm serving plates and flank each serving with 2 pieces of chicken. Spoon some sauce over polenta and chicken.

POLENTA

SERVES 4 TO 6

6 cups cold water
1 tablespoon unsalted butter
½ teaspoon salt
1 bay leaf
1½ cups cornmeal

1. In a heavy saucepan, combine water, butter, salt, and bay leaf. Bring water to a boil. Pour in cornmeal in a thin stream, stirring constantly, and continue to cook over medium heat until mixture is smooth and very thick and pulls away from the sides of the pan, or for about 15 to 20 minutes.
2. Cover and keep warm over simmering water.

☆ ☆ # PASUTICE WITH SEAFOOD ISTIANA ☆ ☆
SERVES 6

Pasutice means little diamonds of noodle dough, and at Felidia it is homemade, as are all the pastas, and served with a garlicky seafood sauce. It's hard to beat the combination of pasta, seafood, tomatoes, and garlic. If fresh seafood is available in your area, this is a simple recipe for the home chef.

½ pound small shrimp, shelled and deveined
½ pound sea scallops, quartered
10 littleneck clams, opened and chopped (reserve liquor)
4 cloves garlic, peeled and crushed
4 tablespoons olive oil
1 cup crushed peeled tomatoes
Freshly ground black pepper to taste
1 tablespoon chopped Italian parsley
Pasutice (see below)

1. Prepare seafood and set aside.
2. In a heavy skillet brown garlic very lightly in hot olive oil. Do not let it burn.
3. Add shrimp and scallops and cook for 2 minutes. Add chopped clams, then stir in the clam liquor, tomatoes, and pepper. Cook over high heat, stirring and tossing ingredients, for 3 minutes. Add parsley.
4. Mix half the sauce into the pasta and spoon the rest on top.

PASUTICE

3½ cups unbleached flour
2 whole eggs
¼ teaspoon salt
1 teaspoon salad oil
½ cup warm water
3 teaspoons salt

1. Pile 3 cups of the flour on work surface and make a well in the center. Beat eggs lightly with ¼ teaspoon salt and pour into the well. Mix with fingers, gradually working in flour and oil and as much of the water as needed to make a workable mass that is not too sticky. If too dry, add a little more water.

2. Knead the dough for about 10 minutes, cover, and let it rest for 30 minutes to lose its elasticity.
3. Cut dough in half and roll out one half at a time on a floured surface with floured rolling pin until it is no more than ⅛ inch thick. Cut rolled dough into diagonal strips 1 inch wide, then cut across the strips, also on the diagonal, at 1-inch intervals, making diamond shapes.
4. To cook: Bring 6 quarts of water to a boil and add 3 teaspoons of salt.
5. When water returns to a boil add the pasta slowly, stirring constantly.
6. Boil vigorously for 3 minutes, then drain.
7. Immediately add half the sauce to the pasta and toss together, otherwise pasta will stick.
8. Top with some of the remaining sauce and serve.

☆ ☆   # TAGLIO RUSTICO   ☆ ☆
(Roast veal)
SERVES 6

5 pounds shoulder of veal, cut into 2-inch chunks, bone and all
2 stalks celery, coarsely cut
2 medium carrots, scraped and sliced
1 large onion, sliced
4 bay leaves
½ teaspoon fresh or dry rosemary
1 cup dry white wine
½ cup olive oil
¼ cup balsamic or herb vinegar
2 cups beef stock
Salt and freshly ground pepper to taste

1. A day in advance, in a shallow glass or enamel roasting pan combine meat, celery, carrots, onion, herbs, white wine, olive oil, and vinegar and toss well. Refrigerate overnight.
2. Next day add beef stock, homemade or canned, and salt and pepper to taste.
3. Roast in a preheated 450-degree oven for 1 hour; reduce oven temperature to 425 degrees and continue to roast for 1½ hours longer, or until meat falls off the fork. During the roasting time, turn the meat and baste it frequently.

4. Transfer all meat to a warm serving dish. Place roasting pan over direct heat and reduce remaining liquid over medium heat, stirring and scraping in all brown bits from sides and bottom of pan. If necessary, stir in 1 teaspoon cornstarch mixed with 1 tablespoon cold water, to thicken the pan sauce slightly. Strain the gravy over the meat and serve with cooked rice.

☆ ☆ # STRIPED BASS SALAD ☆ ☆
SERVES 4

Another popular dish on Felidia's menu is this salad made with fresh poached bass.

> *2 pounds fillet of striped bass*
> *2 bay leaves*
> *1 small onion, chopped*
> *1 medium carrot, sliced*
> *2 tablespoons white vinegar*
> *1 teaspoon salt*
> *2 medium cucumbers, peeled and sliced*
> *1 Bermuda onion, peeled and thinly sliced*
> *1 tablespoon chopped Italian parsley*
> *4 tablespoons olive oil*
> *3 tablespoons wine vinegar*
> *Salt and pepper to taste*
> *Lettuce leaves*
> *Parsley for garnish*

1. Wash fish and remove any skin on it. Tie it in cheesecloth to keep it flat and put into a shallow pan with enough water to cover.
2. Bring water to a boil and add bay leaves, chopped onion, sliced carrot, white vinegar, and the salt. Simmer over low heat for 20 minutes. Let fish cool completely in the pan liquid.
3. Remove fish and break it into large flakes. In a bowl mix the fish with all remaining ingredients except lettuce and parsley. Toss lightly until all the ingredients are well moistened with the oil and vinegar. Chill.
4. Serve salad on lettuce leaves on individual plates and garnish with a sprig of parsley.

Fonda la Paloma

256 East 49th Street
New York, N.Y. 10017   421-5495

Long before Mexican food became the latest "in" cuisine, there was Fonda la Paloma with its strolling guitarists, Latin decor, and boisterous atmosphere. In the early evening, the downstairs area with its long bar is the place to pick up your margaritas or pitcher of sangria—if you like your sangria tart be sure to ask them to go easy on the sugar. For dinner and some lucid conversation, the smart thing to do is to move the party upstairs. The food here is, was, and probably always will be a mix of what some experts refer to as Tex-Mex plus some not-too-spicy Mexican specialties. Come to Fonda la Paloma for a combination of the cuisine and the light-hearted, friendly atmosphere.

☆ ☆ GUACAMOLE FONDA STYLE ☆ ☆
SERVES 2

The restaurant's guacamole is spicy hot and chunky, with the haunting flavor of cilantro.

*1 medium-sized ripe avocado
½ medium Spanish onion, peeled and chopped
1 medium tomato, peeled and chopped
2 teaspoons chopped fresh cilantro
1 teaspoon chopped fresh jalapeños
Salt and pepper to taste*

1. Peel and halve the avocado. Remove and discard the pit and cut the flesh into small cubes.
2. Transfer avocado cubes to a bowl and add remaining ingredients. Mix carefully so you do not mash the avocado. Serve with tortilla chips.

☆ ☆ # CAMARONES A LA FONDA ☆ ☆
(Shrimp sautéed in wine with spices)
SERVES 2

This may be served either as an appetizer or a main dish. As an appetizer it serves two. For a main course for two, you should double the ingredients and serve it with cooked rice. This dish is a Fonda la Paloma exclusive.

12 medium-sized fresh shrimp
2 tablespoons sweet butter
¼ cup dry white wine
½ cup Creole Sauce (see below)
4 tablespoons mole powder*

1. Shell shrimp, leaving tails intact. Devein and rinse in cold water. Then split each shrimp in half lengthwise.
2. In a medium saucepan melt butter, add shrimp, and cook them until they turn pink, stirring frequently, about 3 minutes. Add wine, continuing to stir until wine is evaporated.
3. Add Creole Sauce, stir, and simmer for 1 minute. Sprinkle with mole powder and stir until mole is completely blended into the sauce.

* Mole powder may be purchased from Casa Moneo, 210 West 14th Street, New York, NY 10011 and from other Mexican-Spanish specialty shops throughout the country.

CREOLE SAUCE

About 1 cup

This is a very versatile sauce. It may be made well in advance and reheated. Quantities may be doubled or quadrupled, and what is not used may be frozen for future use.

3 tablespoons olive oil
1 medium-sized Spanish onion, peeled and chopped
1 small clove garlic, peeled and minced
2 large tomatoes, peeled, seeded, and chopped
1 green pepper, seeded and chopped
1 stalk celery, chopped
Salt and pepper to taste
¼ cup chopped cilantro or parsley

1. Heat oil in a small skillet. Add onion and garlic and sauté until golden.
2. Add tomatoes. Mash with a fork, stirring constantly. Simmer for 2 minutes.
3. Add green pepper and celery. Sprinkle with salt and pepper to taste, and simmer for 20 minutes. Stir in cilantro or parsley.

The Four Seasons

99 East 52nd Street
New York, N.Y. 10022   754-9494

The cuisine at The Four Seasons includes traditional seasonal dishes of every nationality. The menu not only changes with the seasons, but new dishes, discovered by owners Paul Kovi and Tom Margittai in their world travels, are regularly incorporated into the restaurant's repertoire. There are two elegantly simple rooms. The bar, or Grill Room, with its enormously high ceiling, has floor-to-ceiling windows covered with shimmering aluminum chain draperies and two abstract Richard Lippold sculptures. Lunch and dinner are served in the Grill Room from a shorter (but no less fascinating) menu than that in the more formal Pool Room, aptly named for its bubbling twenty-foot-square white Italian marble pool. The room is further graced by a Picasso on a curtained stage.

This magnificent restaurant has received innumerable awards. In addition to the two main dining rooms, there are private dining rooms. Reservations are imperative. Although it is expensive, The Four Seasons is not overpriced for the quality of its food and service.

☆ ☆ LOBSTER AND CAVIAR IN SAVOY ☆ ☆ CABBAGE LEAVES

SERVES 4

This first recipe from The Four Seasons requires quite a bit of advance preparation, but once that is done, your work is finished until time to cook.

1 1½-pound live lobster
Freshly ground pepper
5 cabbage leaves, preferably savoy, blanched and prepared
as directed (see below)
¼ cup fish stock (page 35)
4 teaspoons caviar, preferably fresh (beluga, red salmon,
or golden American)
Fish Sauce (see below)

1. Bring a large pot of salted water to a boil. Add the live lobster. When water returns to the boil, lower heat to a simmer, cover, and cook for 18 minutes. Drain lobster and let cool.
2. When cool, remove meat from tail and claws. Cut claws in half. Cut the tail meat crosswise into eight pieces, setting aside any roe. Sprinkle lobster meat with freshly ground pepper.
3. Arrange four cabbage leaves on a work surface, curved side down, and divide the lobster pieces evenly among them in the center of each leaf. Gather each cabbage leaf around the lobster meat to make packages like little string-tied purses (the leaves will hold together by themselves, although they can be loosely tied with a chive). Place them, one at a time, on a kitchen towel. Wrap towel around and squeeze to eliminate excess liquid. Place the packages, gathered side down, on a plate. Cover the packages with the fifth cabbage leaf to keep them moist, and sprinkle with the fish stock. Refrigerate until ready to cook, or cook immediately.
4. To cook: Arrange the packages, still covered by the extra cabbage leaf, in a steamer over simmering water. Cover and heat through for 3 to 5 minutes.
5. Discard cabbage leaf cover. Remove packages and gently pat dry. Place a package on each of four individual plates, still upside down, and spoon some fish sauce around them. Top each package with a teaspoon of caviar. Mix any roe which may have been in the lobster with the caviar.

FISH SAUCE

2 cups strong fish stock (page 35) or clam juice
1 cup heavy cream (not ultrapasteurized; see page 303)
¼ pound (1 stick) lightly salted butter, cut into 1-inch pieces
Juice of ½ lemon

1. Put stock in a wide saucepan and bring to a boil. Remove any scum that rises to the surface and cook rapidly until reduced to about half its original quantity.
2. Add cream and boil over high heat again until liquid is reduced to about half, about 5 minutes.
3. Whisk in butter. Stir in lemon juice. Serve hot.

How to Prepare the Cabbage:

The cabbage must be blanched thoroughly so it will be soft enough to roll easily without breaking. Bring a large pot of salted water to a boil. Have ready a large container of ice water. With a paring knife, cut the core out of the cabbage and discard. Also discard any obviously tough outer leaves. Put the head of cabbage into the boiling water. It will rise to the top, so turn it from time to time so that all the leaves cook evenly. The exact cooking time varies from cabbage to cabbage and with the variety. Savoy cabbage will be done in about 2 minutes; regular white cabbage will take 5 minutes or longer. The outer leaves will cook faster than the inner leaves, so these can be peeled off as they are tender. Plunge them immediately into ice water, adding more ice if the water gets too warm. The cold water bath is important to preserve the bright color of the leaves. Once the leaves are cooled, remove and pat dry. When leaves are all blanched, put them, one by one, on the work surface and, with a sharp paring knife, trim down the center vein until it is no thicker than the rest of the leaf, being careful not to puncture the leaf.

☆ ☆ FOUR SEASONS STEAK TARTARE ☆ ☆

SERVES 4

Four Seasons triumph is its steak tartare, a popular luncheon dish. It is different from any other served in the city.

> *2 pounds fresh lean top round*
> *Juice of ½ lemon*
> *1 small white onion, peeled and finely chopped*
> *2½ tablespoons finely chopped fresh parsley, divided*
> *1½ teaspoons English or Dijon mustard*
> *1 teaspoon salt*
> *1 teaspoon coarsely ground pepper*
> *2 fresh raw egg yolks*
> *3 tablespoons Cognac*
> *Crisp raw vegetables*
> *Crusty bread*

1. Use the leanest meat possible. Trim off any fat and wipe the beef with a clean wet cloth. Cut meat into workable chunks and run twice through a meat grinder with the medium blade.
2. Spread the meat on a chopping board and, with the tines of two forks, blend in lemon juice, onion, and 2 tablespoons of the chopped parsley. Fold the meat in from edge to center, and spread out again. Follow the same technique adding the mustard, salt, pepper, and egg yolks. Fold again, spread, add Cognac. Fold once more, then work ingredients thoroughly into the meat.
3. Form the meat into 4 oval-shaped patties. Carefully smooth all surfaces with a dinner knife. Sprinkle the remaining parsley on top, and garnish plate with crisp raw vegetables. Serve with crusty bread.

MAPLE SYRUP BOURBON SOUFFLÉ GLACE

☆ ☆   ☆ ☆

An elegant dessert after any luncheon or dinner entrée.

> *5 tablespoons sugar*
> *2 large eggs*
> *2 large egg yolks*
> *2 tablespoons bourbon*
> *3 tablespoons maple syrup*
> *2½ cups heavy cream*
> *Toasted chopped macadamia nuts*
> *Maple Bourbon Sauce (see below)*

1. Oil a 6-cup soufflé dish and fit it with an oiled collar extending about 2 inches above the top of the dish. Set aside.
2. Put sugar, eggs, egg yolks, and bourbon in the top of a double boiler and place over simmering water. The water in the bottom pan should not be allowed to touch the bottom of the upper pan. Cook over the simmering water until mixture is smooth and quite warm, about 5 minutes.
3. Empty egg mixture into the bowl of an electric mixer and beat on high speed until it is very thick, fluffy, and thoroughly cooled. Beat in maple syrup.
4. In a separate bowl beat the cream until soft peaks form. Fold the whipped cream into the egg mixture and spoon into the prepared soufflé dish. Smooth the top with a rubber spatula and put in the freezer for a few hours until firm. If you have prepared the dessert a few days or weeks in advance cover the top with foil to prevent freezer burn.
5. When ready to serve, remove dish from freezer and discard collar. Firmly but gently press macadamia nuts around exposed sides of the mousse.
6. Serve with Maple Bourbon Sauce (see below).

MAPLE BOURBON SAUCE

ABOUT 2 CUPS

2 cups milk
4 large egg yolks
½ cup sugar
3 tablespoons bourbon
2 tablespoons maple syrup

1. Heat milk in a saucepan until boiling. Remove from heat.
2. In a small bowl beat egg yolks and sugar. Slowly whisk in the hot milk to raise the temperature of the egg yolks. Return to the saucepan and cook over low heat, stirring constantly until mixture thickens just enough to coat the spoon. Be careful not to let the mixture boil or eggs will curdle.
3. Strain sauce through a fine sieve into a clean bowl and stir in bourbon and maple syrup. Cool to room temperature.

Frank's

431 West 14th Street
New York, N.Y. 10014   243-1349

This no-frills restaurant is located in the heart of the meat district. As an accommodation to early morning employees of meat wholesalers, it opens as a diner at 2:00 A.M. and functions that way through the noon hours until 3:00 P.M. It opens again in the evening, transformed as if by the touch of a magic wand into a full-service restaurant. The tile-floored room with its oak bar holds just nineteen tables, and it is illuminated by genuine Tiffany lamps. Frank's was founded by the Molinari family in 1912, and they still retain ownership. One of the sons, George Jr., is chef, while son Christopher serves graciously as the maître d'. Chris says that they aim to serve patrons the same good food and give them the same warm hospitality that they would have received at his father's home in Staten Island. The food is excellent indeed, and the tagliarini puttanesca is reputed to be the best in town. Try it for yourself and see. Prices are moderate for the quality.

☆ ☆   # SWEETBREADS EUGENIE   ☆ ☆
SERVES 4

This may be served either as a luncheon dish or dinner appetizer.

4 sweetbreads
Salt
Flour
Freshly ground pepper
4 teaspoons butter
2 ounces Cognac
3 or 4 fresh mushrooms, sliced
3 ounces dry white wine (preferably Soave)
1 cup heavy cream (see page 303)
1 cup brown sauce or good brown gravy
4 slices Virginia ham

1. Arrange sweetbreads in large skillet, and just cover with lightly salted water. Bring slowly to a boil and simmer for 10 minutes. Drain, rinse in cold water, and carefully remove the thin skin covering them and any connecting tissue.
2. Slice sweetbreads ½ inch thick, coat lightly with flour, and sprinkle with freshly ground pepper.
3. Heat butter in a large skillet until it just begins to give off a nutty aroma, and in it sauté sweetbread slices for about 5 minutes on each side, or until lightly browned. Flame with Cognac.
4. Add mushrooms and wine, and simmer about 4 minutes. Add cream and brown sauce and simmer for 2 minutes, spooning sauce over sweetbreads constantly.
5. Serve each portion on a slice of Virginia ham with some of the sauce spooned over.

☆ ☆ # SEA TROUT ADRIA ☆ ☆

SERVES 2

George Jr. believes that every dish derives its flavor from the ingredients used in its making. The quality of each ingredient is most important. Don't settle for anything but the freshest and best.

> *2 fillets of sea trout, about 10 ounces each*
> *3 ounces (6 tablespoons) butter*
> *2 tablespoons well-drained capers, washed*
> *1 cup dry white wine*
> *1 clove garlic, minced*
> *4 large mushrooms, sliced*
> *2 tablespoons chopped fresh parsley*
> *Freshly ground white pepper*
> *Salt to taste*

1. Wash fish well, then drain and dry on paper towels.
2. Melt butter in a large skillet, place fillets in the melted butter, and sprinkle with capers, half the white wine, garlic, and mushrooms. Bring wine to a boil, and simmer for 4 minutes, or until wine has almost evaporated.
3. Add remaining wine and continue to cook for about 10 minutes, or until fish is done to taste, basting frequently with the pan sauce.
4. Remove fish to a warm serving platter, add parsley to sauce remaining in pan, and boil hard to reduce sauce until slightly thickened. Add freshly ground pepper and salt to taste, and spoon over the fish.

☆ ☆ # FRANK'S PUTTANESCA SAUCE FOR PASTA ☆ ☆

Serves 4 as an entrée; 6 as an appetizer

George recommends serving this sauce with either cooked linguine or tagliarini. The sauce is sufficient for a pound of pasta.

1 large clove garlic, chopped
4 tablespoons butter
4 anchovy fillets, chopped
1 tablespoon capers
½ cup chopped, pitted black olives
3 cups Sauce Marinara (see below)

1. Sauté garlic in hot foaming butter until it is lightly golden, then add anchovies, capers, and olives, and simmer for 2 minutes.
2. Add marinara sauce, and simmer for 4 minutes longer.
3. Drain pasta, mix with the sauce, and serve while very hot.

SAUCE MARINARA

MAKES 2 CUPS

4 cups imported Italian plum tomatoes
6 tablespoons salad oil (part olive)
1 tablespoon finely chopped garlic
¼ cup dry white wine
1 teaspoon dried oregano
1 tablespoon chopped fresh parsley
Salt and freshly ground pepper to taste

1. Crush tomatoes with hands or in a food processor. Set aside.
2. In a saucepan heat the oil and in it cook the garlic until golden. Do not let it brown. Add dry white wine and cook until wine has evaporated.
3. Add tomatoes, oregano, parsley, salt, and pepper. Simmer for 20 minutes.

Note:
If available, add 8 fresh sweet basil leaves, chopped, with the oregano.

Fuji Restaurant

238 West 56th Street
New York, N.Y. 10019   245-8594

Many people note that Lou Castioni must be the only Italian manager of a Japanese restaurant, if not in all the United States, then at least in New York City. It's not so surprising when you learn that Mr. Castioni married into the family that runs Fuji Restaurant. Centrally located, it's a favorite lunch hangout for local TV, record, and publishing people; at dinner, locals and the pretheater crowd take over. As knowledgeable as and perhaps even more proud than a native, Mr. Castioni happily explains Fuji's specialties. Unlike most Japanese restaurants caught in the fury of sushi, Fuji doesn't have a sushi bar, although varieties of raw fish are prepared in the kitchen. The focus here is on other well-known Japanese dishes, notably tempura; sukiyaki, the broth-based mixture simmered at your table and available with beef, chicken, pork, or seafood; negimaki, tender marinated beef wrapped around scallions and grilled; fried oysters; and tatsuta agi, the dish of marinated, then fried chicken that Mr. Castioni feels is prepared better at Fuji than anywhere else in the city. In the spring, Fuji tops fresh steamed asparagus with a special crab meat dressing.

Though the Japanese do not generally crave sweets, Fuji serves exotic ginger and red bean ice creams, in addition to more traditional fresh fruit. Sake, Takara plum wine, and an Italian house wine are available from the service bar, as is a regal assortment of Japanese beers plus Budweiser—for Fuji's Japanese customers.

☆ ☆ # TATSUTA AGI ☆ ☆
SERVES 4

Moist bits of tender chicken are marinated in a special sauce and deep-fried for a Fuji appetizer known as tatsuta agi.

½ cup Japanese soy sauce
½ cup Japanese rice wine (sake)
1 teaspoon shredded fresh ginger
1 boned chicken breast
1 boned chicken leg and thigh
Vegetable oil for frying
2 cups cornstarch
Salad greens
Lemon wedges

1. Combine soy sauce, sake, and ginger.
2. Cut chicken meat into cubes, about 7 to 8 pieces per breast or leg. Put chicken cubes into the marinade, and mix well to make sure all pieces are well coated. Refrigerate for at least 1 hour. The longer it sits the saltier it becomes.
3. Heat enough oil to cover a layer of chicken in a wok or electric skillet to 375 degrees. Dip chicken pieces, one at a time, in cornstarch, shake off excess, and drop gently into the hot oil. Cook until the outside is crisp and brown, about 3 minutes. Drain on draining rack or on a layer of paper towels. Serve on a bed of shredded head lettuce or romaine with wedges of lemon to be squeezed over the chicken.

☆ ☆   # NEGIMAKI   ☆ ☆
(Broiled beef rolls)
SERVES 2

This next recipe from Lou Castioni is suggested as an entrée after the chicken tidbits, to be served with cooked rice. Tender slices of beef are rolled around green onions and marinated before they are briefly broiled.

> *1 cup (8 ounces) Japanese soy sauce*
> *½ cup sugar*
> *12 scallions or green onions*
> *6 thin slices boneless rib steak or round*
> *Curly endive*
> *1 cup cooked rice*

1. Combine soy sauce and sugar in a small saucepan. Stir over low heat until sugar is completely dissolved.
2. Wash and trim scallions to the same length as the meat slices. Broil or blanch until fork tender.
3. Arrange beef slices side by side. Rub 1 teaspoon of the soy sauce mixture into each slice. Arrange 2 scallions on the edge of each slice nearest to you and roll beef into a cylinder. Secure the roll with wooden picks.
4. Arrange rolls in broiler pan and broil about 4 inches from heat for about 3 minutes on each side, or until done to taste, preferably medium rare.
5. Remove wooden picks from meat, cut each roll into 3 sections, and arrange the cut rolls, cut sides up, on a bed of curly endive or other attractive green. Pour balance of the sauce over and serve with cooked rice.

Gage & Tollner

372 Fulton Street
Brooklyn, N.Y. 11201   (718) 875-5181

Some places are meant for eating, others have become famous for their view, or maybe because you want to tell your friends you've been to the newest hot spot in town. Then there are those restaurants that are venerable institutions. Every town, luckily, has at least one and in New York City—for those who are wont to forget, Brooklyn is definitely part of the city—Gage & Tollner is a famous landmark. Go for the grand atmosphere and the traditional American food. Seafood and steaks simply done are what to look for on the menu. During the day the place is jammed with the business crowd. At night the pace is more leisurely. Don't be put off by the deserted neighborhood in the evening hours. Cabbies know how to get back and forth to Brooklyn from Manhattan, and you can always call a car service to get you back to your apartment or hotel. It's well worth the trip.

☆ ☆ # CRAB MEAT VIRGINIA ☆ ☆
SERVES 1

This first recipe gives a clue to the simplicity of the restaurant's food.

6 ounces fresh lump crab meat
3 tablespoons butter
1½ tablespoons lemon juice
Parsley sprig and lemon wedge for garnish

1. Pick over crab meat and discard any bits of shell or cartilage. Spread crab meat evenly in a single-serving ramekin or a small shallow baking dish.
2. Dot crab meat with butter and sprinkle with lemon juice.
3. Bake in a preheated 400-degree oven for 8 minutes, or until delicately brown.
4. Garnish with a sprig of parsley and a wedge of lemon and serve at once.

☆ ☆ ## CLAMS OR OYSTERS CASINO ☆ ☆

Serves 2 as an appetizer

12 clams or oysters on the half shell
Rock salt
¼ cup chopped parsley
½ cup chopped pimiento
¼ cup chopped green pepper
¼ cup crumbled crisp bacon
Lemon wedges for garnish

1. Arrange the clams or oysters on a baking sheet on a bed of rock salt to keep them steady.
2. Combine parsley, pimiento, green pepper, and bacon and sprinkle a good tablespoon of the mixture on each clam or oyster.
3. Place under a hot broiler, about 4 inches from the source of heat, and broil for 5 minutes.
4. Carefully place 6 clams or oysters on each serving plate and garnish with lemon wedges.

Gargiulo's

2911 West 15th Street
Coney Island, N.Y. 11224   (718) 266-0906

Since 1907, Gargiulo's has been as much a part of Coney Island as the amusement area flanking the waterfront. But although Coney Island has changed through the years, this classic Italian restaurant has remained pretty much the same. The large (seating for 1,000), busy restaurant attests to the ongoing popularity of Gargiulo's among people from all over the New York area.

At least one of the three Russo brothers (they bought the restaurant 20 years ago) is always on hand. In addition to the usual Italian fare offered (including homemade pasta with a choice of twelve sauces, and six varieties of risotto), the Russo brothers are especially proud of their chef's veal valdostana, a veal chop stuffed with mozzarella and prosciutto, egg-battered and fried; red snapper livornese, fish steamed in a lusty tomato sauce with onions, capers and olives; and insalata caprese, a salad of fresh mozzarella, ripe tomatoes, and fresh basil leaves. Cheesecake and cannoli are two of the desserts prepared at the restaurant. Although the house wine is Paul Masson, Italian and French wines are also available, in addition to the standard cocktails prepared at the service bar.

☆ ☆   # TAGLIATELLE ALLA DIVA   ☆ ☆
(Noodles with meat, vegetables, and cream)
SERVES 6

This is a delicious egg noodle appetizer (it may also be served as an entrée if preferred) aromatic with porcini mushrooms.

1 medium onion, peeled and chopped
6 tablespoons (3 ounces) butter
½ pound fillet of beef, cut into tiny cubes
¼ pound prosciutto, shredded
½ ounce dried porcini mushrooms, soaked in warm water
and squeezed dry
½ pound fresh mushrooms, cleaned and sliced
4 ounces (1 cup) fresh or cooked frozen peas
2 ounces (4 tablespoons) brandy
1 cup heavy cream
Salt and pepper to taste
1 pound flat egg noodles, preferably Italian brand
4 ounces (1 cup) grated Parmesan cheese

1. In a skillet sauté the onion in the butter over low heat until golden. Add the beef and prosciutto and cook for 8 to 10 minutes.
2. Add the porcini and fresh mushrooms, the peas, and the brandy, cover skillet, and cook gently for a few minutes. Add the cream, salt, and pepper.
3. Cook the egg noodles in an abundant amount of lightly salted water until barely tender (al dente). Drain and toss with half the sauce and the Parmesan cheese. Serve the remaining sauce separately.

☆ ☆ # BEEF AMALFITANA ☆ ☆
(Rolled stuffed filet mignon
with tomato sauce)
SERVES 6

In the fall when sweet basil is abundant and the tomatoes hang red and sun-ripened on the vine, use 1 large or 2 medium fresh tomatoes in place of the canned ones.

12 filets mignons, ½-inch thick
4 ounces (1 stick) sweet butter, divided
1 large clove garlic, peeled and chopped
2 tablespoons chopped parsley
5 ounces thinly sliced prosciutto
½ cup cooking oil
½ cup dry white wine
Salt and pepper to taste
1 cup peeled and diced fresh or canned tomatoes
2 tablespoons chopped sweet basil or 1 teaspoon pesto
4 ounces mozzarella cheese (fresh if possible), diced

1. Pound the filet slices between two pieces of wax paper with a meat cleaver until flat.
2. Combine half the butter (4 tablespoons) with the chopped garlic and parsley and work ingredients together until they form a paste.
3. Spread a little of the paste over each beef slice and top with a slice of prosciutto.
4. Roll meat like little jelly rolls and secure each roll with a wooden pick.
5. Heat the remaining butter and oil and in it brown the beef rolls on all sides. Add the wine and salt and pepper to taste. Then add the diced tomato and sweet basil and cook for a few minutes over low heat. Sprinkle with the mozzarella, cover, and cook until cheese is melted. Serve immediately.

Giambelli 50th

46 East 50th Street
New York, N.Y. 10022   688-2760/1

With sixty years of restaurant experience (beginning with his Pesce
d'Oro in Voghera, Italy) Frank Giambelli still talks of food and its
preparation with the zeal of a neophyte. He regards food as "the
best medicine" known to man and he's still drawing avid "pa-
tients" for lunch and dinner.

With the help and friendship of general manager Virgilio Gatti,
Mr. Giambelli serves some of the lightest homemade pasta, tender-
est veal, and sultriest desserts this side of the Atlantic. But regular
customers know there's more to the kitchen's repertoire than
what's on the menu. Mr. Giambelli and Gatti cater to a diner's
individual appetite, disposition, and taste. This specialized individual attention makes Giambelli's two private rooms hot dining
spots for a select group of steady corporate customers. The rooms
are booked weeks, if not months, in advance. The extensive à la
carte dinner menu offers such specialties as capelli d'angelo al
salmone (angel hair pasta with Scottish smoked salmon) and von-
gole sorrentina (clam stew Sorrento style). Desserts may be selected from the wagon (the classic tiramisù is uniquely prepared
here— airy little cream puffs with an ethereal mascarpone cheese
sauce) or ordered specially.

Giambelli's wine list is a veritable tome, with more than 1,000
wines. With all this variety there's still an Italian wine available
by the glass or carafe.

☆ ☆ GAMBERI OR SCAMPI RAIMONDO ☆ ☆

SERVES 4

Mr. Giambelli sent us this appetizer recipe made of either baby Danish lobster tails or large shrimp.

½ cup salad oil
16 baby Danish lobster tails or 1 pound shrimp (16 per pound),
shelled and deveined
¼ cup flour to coat lobster or shrimp
¼ pound (1 stick) sweet butter
½ cup dry white wine
Juice of 1 lemon
Pepper to taste and salt if really needed
8 thin slices prosciutto or boiled ham, halved
16 thin slices mozzarella cheese (fresh if possible)
½ cup grated Parmesan cheese
Sauce Raimondo (see below)

1. Pour oil into a 10-inch skillet over low heat. Dredge or coat each lobster tail or shrimp with flour and place in the skillet. Cook for about 2 minutes on each side or until golden brown.
2. Drain oil from pan and add butter. When butter is melted, add the wine, lemon juice, pepper, and salt only if necessary. Cook and stir for another 2 minutes. Set aside.
3. Wrap each shrimp in a half slice of ham and arrange in a baking dish side by side, in two rows. Pour the sauce from the skillet over the shrimp, cover with slices of mozzarella, and sprinkle with the grated Parmesan.
4. Bake in a preheated 400-degree oven until cheese is melted and tinged with brown, about 5 minutes. Serve at once with sauce Raimondo.

SAUCE RAIMONDO

1 CUP

1 shallot, chopped
1 clove garlic, minced
2 tablespoons sweet butter
2 anchovies, rinsed and chopped
5 capers
1 tablespoon chopped parsley
½ cup dry white wine
Few drops lemon juice
½ cup brown sauce or gravy
Salt and pepper to taste

1. Sauté shallot and garlic in butter until golden and transparent. Add anchovies, capers, and parsley. Simmer for 5 minutes.
2. Add wine, lemon juice, and brown sauce. Mix well and season to taste.

☆ ☆ CAPELLI D'ANGELO GRANSEOLA ☆ ☆

SERVES 4

Unless you have a pasta machine in which you can turn out angel hair pasta at home, you may have to buy it at an Italian pasta shop. The finest commercial pasta may be substituted.

2 tablespoons olive oil
2 teaspoons chopped shallots
½ teaspoon minced garlic
1 pound fresh lump crab meat
8 ounces peeled Italian plum tomatoes,
drained and coarsely chopped
15 leaves fresh sweet basil, chopped, or 1 tablespoon
drained pesto or basil preserved in oil
Salt and pepper to taste
2 teaspoons chopped parsley
1 pound capelli d'angelo (angel hair pasta)
½ pound whipped sweet butter

1. Pour olive oil into a 10-inch skillet over low heat and in it sauté the shallots and garlic until golden and translucent but not brown. Add crab meat and mix thoroughly, being careful not to break the large lumps.
2. Add chopped tomatoes and basil or pesto and toss again over low heat for 5 minutes. Season with salt and pepper and sprinkle with parsley.
3. Meanwhile add the angel hair pasta to 5 quarts boiling, salted water. Stir immediately so that the pasta will not stick. Boil 1 to 2 minutes and drain.
4. In a large skillet or serving dish toss the pasta with the whipped butter and half the sauce. Serve, topping each portion with some of the remaining sauce.

Girafe

208 East 58th Street
New York, N.Y. 10022   752-3054

If you didn't look at the menu, you'd never believe this was an Italian restaurant. Even before you open the door you're surrounded by jungle animals. Rumor has it that the original owner went on a safari and that inspired the decor of the restaurant. This big brassy restaurant is a favorite of visitors to the city and those who are entertaining guests. The food is what most people want when they go to an Italian restaurant—veal, fish, hot antipasti, zuppa inglese, and lots of pasta. For a more soothing atmosphere, ask for a table upstairs.

☆ ☆ ## VEAL GABRIELLA ☆ ☆

SERVES 4

1 pound or 8 thin slices veal from the leg
Flour to coat
8 tablespoons (1 stick) butter, divided
1 teaspoon minced shallots
¼ pound mushrooms, cleaned and sliced
12 small cooked artichoke hearts, fresh,
drained canned, or defrosted
½ cup dry white wine
2 tablespoons lemon juice
Salt and freshly ground pepper to taste
¼ cup canned concentrated beef bouillon
2 tablespoons chopped parsley

1. Pound the veal lightly between two pieces of wax paper until very thin. Coat both sides lightly with flour.
2. Heat 3 tablespoons of the butter in a large skillet, add the veal, and brown on both sides. Add shallots, mushrooms, artichoke hearts, and white wine and cook for about 1 minute longer over moderately high heat.

3. Transfer meat to a warm serving platter and add lemon juice, salt and freshly ground pepper, and beef bouillon to pan drippings and vegetables. Cook, stirring briskly to scrape loose all the brown particles from bottom and sides of pan.
4. Reduce heat and whisk in the remaining 5 tablespoons butter, about 1 tablespoon at a time. Add parsley and pour vegetables and sauce over meat.

☆ ☆   # NAPOLEONS   ☆ ☆

These delectable layers of puff pastry are a favorite dessert in French and Italian restaurants. Now that one can buy frozen puff pastry in most supermarkets, these rich pastries are within the scope of every good cook. It is important to follow the thawing directions on the package.

1 pound frozen puff pastry, defrosted
according to package directions
2 cups (1 pint) heavy cream
4 tablespoons sugar
Few drops vanilla
2 tablespoons Galliano
2 tablespoons anisette
1 8-ounce block semisweet chocolate for shaving

1. Roll out pastry into a rectangle and cut into thirds. Roll out each third on floured pastry cloth to 1/16 inch thick, and trim to 4 or 5 inches in width. Reserve the trimmings.
2. Brush baking sheets with cold water and transfer the pastry to the sheets. Prick all over with tines of a fork and bake with the trimmings for about 20 minutes, or until puffed and evenly brown. Cool on racks.
3. When ready to assemble, whip the cream until very thick, gradually adding the sugar. Continue whipping while adding the vanilla and liqueurs. Put the 3 layers together with flavored cream between, saving enough to coat top and sides.
4. Garnish with chocolate curls. Crumble the trimmings and sprinkle on top of the pastry and press against the sides.

Note:
This dessert should be made no more than 4 hours in advance. When completed put in the freezer for 20 minutes, then transfer to the refrigerator.

Il Monello

1460 Second Avenue (between 76th and 77th streets)
New York, N.Y. 10021   535-9310

The Upper East Side of Manhattan has a plethora of restaurants. Some have their moments in the sun, with limos lined up night after night, and then, for some unknown reason—oblivion. Not so for Il Monello, one of the best Italian restaurants in the city specializing in Northern cuisine. It has been around a long time and has never lacked customers. It is so spacious that with luck you can decide to dine here at the last minute and usually get a reservation. There seems to be a myriad of rooms, all plushly decorated, starting with a front area that houses an active square bar. The back room is the quietest, but also the least appealing. The menu has a long list of pasta dishes, always a happy choice, such as angel hair with seafood. Half a portion is sufficient for an appetizer. After that there is a wide array of entrées of fish or seafood, chicken, or veal. Creamy Italian desserts are also tempting. Expensive. Reservations usually advisable, especially for dinner.

☆ ☆ # CAPELLI PRIMAVERA ☆ ☆
Serves 4 as a main course; 6 as an appetizer

This is Il Monello's version of the popular pasta topped with a variety of vegetables in a delectable tomato sauce.

1 large carrot, cooked
1 large zucchini
¼ pound fresh mushrooms
½ cup diced, cooked string beans
½ cup diced, cooked broccoli
¼ cup olive oil
1 large onion, finely chopped
8 ounce can (1 cup) tomato sauce
¼ pound (1 stick) butter
1½ cups chicken broth
Salt and freshly ground pepper to taste
1 pound angel hair pasta
Freshly grated Parmesan cheese

1. Slice carrot, zucchini, and mushrooms into julienne strips and set aside with the string beans and broccoli.
2. In a large saucepan heat the olive oil and in it simmer the onion until soft but not brown. Add zucchini and mushrooms and cook for 5 minutes, stirring occasionally. Add remaining vegetables and simmer for 2 to 3 minutes.
3. Add tomato sauce, butter, and broth. Add salt and pepper to taste. Heat to boiling.
4. Meanwhile cook pasta in lightly salted boiling water for the least amount of time specified on package. Pasta should be al dente and not overcooked.
5. Drain pasta in a colander and empty into the saucepan with the vegetables. Toss all together over very low heat.
6. Serve steaming hot with the cheese served on the side.

☆ ☆ # VITELLO ALLA MOLESE ☆ ☆
SERVES 4

This time colorful vegetables are teamed with thinly sliced veal and Italian sausages.

8 thin slices veal scaloppine, trimmed and well pounded
Flour
¼ cup cooking oil
2 cloves garlic, peeled and chopped
2 tablespoons sweet butter
4 medium mushrooms, washed and sliced
1 sweet red or green pepper, seeded and cut into julienne strips
6 pickled Tuscan peppers, seeded and cut into julienne strips
2 sweet Italian sausages, sliced
⅔ cup dry white wine
Salt and pepper to taste

1. Coat veal with flour on both sides and shake off any excess.
2. Heat oil in a large frying pan and in it cook the veal until it is golden on both sides. Transfer to a platter and keep warm.
3. Add garlic to oil remaining in pan and cook until it is pale gold in color. Carefully drain off excess oil from pan and add butter, mushrooms, sweet peppers, pickled peppers, sausage, wine, and salt and pepper to taste. Simmer for 3 minutes.
4. Serve the veal with vegetables and sauce.

☆　☆　　　　　# ZUCCOTTO　　　　　☆　☆

SERVES 8

For dessert, Adi Giovannetti highly recommends his scrumptious zuccotto: slices of sponge cake saturated with crème de cacao, surrounding chocolate cream and whipped cream. It's sure to evoke bravos. Definitely *not* for dieters. Start this production one or two days before it will be needed.

1 Sponge Cake, 9 inches in diameter and about
2 inches thick (see below)
1 cup crème de cacao
Whipped Cream Filling (see below)
Chocolate Cream Filling (see below)
¾ cup heavy cream, whipped
¼ cup grated semisweet chocolate

1. Cut sponge cake from side to side in slices ¼ inch thick and 2 inches wide. Line the inside of an 8-inch bowl with the slices, and sprinkle the slices with three-quarters of the crème de cacao. You will have some cake slices left. Set them aside.

2. Pour the whipped cream filling into the lined bowl and, with a spatula, push it toward the sides of the bowl, completely covering the cake slices and leaving a hollow in the center.
3. Pour the chocolate cream filling into the hole in the center, smooth the top, and cover with reserved sponge cake slices. Sprinkle cake slices with the remaining crème de cacao.
4. Cover with plastic wrap and freeze for at least 3 hours.
5. When ready to serve, remove bowl from freezer and set it up to its rim in hot water for 60 seconds. Place a serving plate over bowl and invert the bowl. The zuccotto should slide out easily without cracking.
6. Coat the frozen molded cream and cake with whipped cream and sprinkle with grated chocolate.

SPONGE CAKE

This is a very delicate French sponge, known as a genoise.

7 eggs, at room temperature*
6 tablespoons superfine granulated sugar
5 tablespoons sifted flour

1. In a bowl placed over a pan of warm water beat eggs and sugar until thick and pale in color. This may also be done in an electric mixer, beating at high speed for 5 minutes. When the beaters are lifted, the batter should form a ribbon that takes some time to level out.
2. Meanwhile oil and flour a 9-inch cake pan 2 inches deep, and preheat oven to 350 degrees.
3. Add flour to egg mixture, a little at a time, and fold it in with a large stainless steel spoon or your hand. Continue to fold until smooth.
4. Pour batter into prepared pan and bake in the preheated oven for 30 to 40 minutes, or until cake pulls away from sides of pan and a cake tester inserted in the center comes out clean.
5. Run a spatula around edge of cake to loosen it from sides, and carefully turn out onto a rack to cool.

* If you forget to take eggs out of the refrigerator, drop them into a bowl of water just hot to the hand for 10 minutes.

WHIPPED CREAM FILLING

2 cups heavy cream, stiffly whipped
2 tablespoons minced candied orange peel
2 tablespoons minced candied cherries
2 tablespoons minced candied citron
2 tablespoons crushed chocolate bits
2 tablespoons blanched minced almonds
2 tablespoons minced hazelnuts

1. Fold all ingredients together thoroughly.

CHOCOLATE CREAM FILLING

2 cups heavy cream, whipped
5 ounces semisweet chocolate bits, melted

1. Blend whipped cream and melted chocolate together until mixture is uniform in color. Keep cold until ready to use.

Note:

When possible buy pasteurized fresh cream, not ultrapasteurized. Buy it at least 2 days in advance and keep it in the coldest part of your refrigerator until ready to whip. If you will whip it in your blender until very thick, the cream will not weep upon standing. Just be careful not to whip it to butter. Use low speed, and when cream is thick, stop, stir, and blend again briefly. Repeat this as many times as necessary until the cream is as stiff as you wish it to be.

Il Nido

251 East 53rd Street
New York, N.Y. 10022   753-8450/1

Il Nido is one of the best Italian restaurants in New York, specializing in Northern Italian cuisine. Two attractive rooms hold a total
of only 30 tables. Formerly a French restaurant, Il Nido still retains the original Tyrolean European decor. The owner, Adi Giovannetti, also owns Il Monello and Il Nido Cafe. The menu at Il
Nido is extensive and includes an ample selection of pastas, fish,
cooked vegetables and salads, to appeal to non-meat eaters, and,
of course elegant desserts, both lean and rich. Mr. Giovannetti
often recommends his tomatoes and buffalo-milk mozzarella, with
sweet basil and virgin olive oil, freshly roasted red and yellow
peppers topped with capers, or his salad of thinly sliced mushrooms and celery with shredded Parmesan in oil and wine vinegar.
For the main course you might decide on a Fritto Misto of mixed
vegetables, spinach-filled dumplings (ravioli malfatti), or the particularly good manicotti.

☆ ☆   # MALFATTI   ☆ ☆
(Little spinach and cheese dumplings in tomato sauce)
SERVES 4

An appetizer that appeals to vegetarians, whose numbers are increasing rapidly.

10 ounces fresh spinach or frozen chopped, defrosted
½ cup ricotta cheese
2 tablespoons Parmesan cheese
Salt, pepper, and nutmeg to taste
Tomato Sauce (see below)

1. If spinach is fresh, wash it well in cool water, remove the thick stems, and put leaves into a large saucepan with just the water clinging to them. Cover and steam for 5 minutes, or until spinach is wilted. Chop and drain, pressing out as much of the liquid as possible.
2. Empty spinach into a mixing bowl and add ricotta and Parmesan cheeses and seasonings.
3. With floured hands, form the spinach mixture into balls about the size of small walnuts. Drop the balls gently into a saucepan or skillet of simmering water, and simmer for about 2 minutes, or until they rise to the top of the water and turn over.
4. Remove the balls with a slotted spoon and drop them into a gratin dish. Cover with tomato sauce and serve.

TOMATO SAUCE

2 tablespoons minced parsley
1 clove garlic, peeled and minced
2 tablespoons finely chopped onion
2 cups canned tomato sauce
Freshly ground pepper to taste
Pinch cayenne or to taste
2 tablespoons sweet butter

1. Simmer the parsley, garlic, and onion in the tomato sauce for 10 minutes. Season with pepper and cayenne, and swirl in the sweet butter. Keep hot.

☆ ☆   # CHICKEN BOLOGNESE   ☆ ☆
SERVES 2

This is a deliciously easy dish to make once the chicken is prepared. You can do it yourself quite easily with a sharp knife, or ask
your butcher if he will do it for you. Use chicken legs with thighs
attached or breasts, or half of each, whichever suits your taste.
Serve with artichoke hearts or broiled tomato halves and
pan-roasted potatoes.

2 chicken legs with thighs or 1 chicken breast, halved
Flour to coat chicken, about 2 tablespoons
2 tablespoons olive oil
1 tablespoon butter
2 tablespoons chopped shallots or green onions
2 tablespoons white wine or dry sherry
1 tablespoon brown sauce or gravy
1 tablespoon chicken broth
2 slices prosciutto
2 slices Italian fontina or Port-Salut cheese
2 tablespoons grated Parmesan cheese

1. Bone chicken legs, leaving lower leg and thigh attached, or
   bone breast and cut into two portions. Pound chicken parts
   between pieces of waxed paper until flattened, and coat
   lightly with flour.
2. In a heavy skillet heat olive oil and in it sauté the chicken
   pieces for about 3 minutes on each side, or until golden. Pour
   off any excess oil.
3. Add butter and shallots or green onions and cook until shallots are lightly browned.
4. Sprinkle with white wine or sherry, brown sauce, and
   chicken broth. Simmer until sauce is thickened, stirring
   frequently.
5. Transfer the chicken to a gratin dish and pour the pan sauce
   on top. Arrange slices of prosciutto over the chicken, top with
   the slices of cheese, and sprinkle with Parmesan.
6. Broil about 5 inches from source of heat for 5 to 6 minutes, or
   until golden brown.

☆ ☆   # MELANZANE PARMIGIANA   ☆ ☆
(Eggplant with cheese and tomatoes)
SERVES 2

For this colorful vegetable dish of eggplant and tomato it's worth finding an Italian market that carries imported Italian fontina cheese.

2 tablespoons olive oil plus a few drops
½ cup chopped onion
1 cup peeled, seeded, and coarsely chopped tomatoes
Salt and freshly ground pepper to taste
1 1-pound eggplant, peeled and sliced ½ inch thick
½ cup unseasoned Italian bread crumbs
4 ounces fontina cheese, sliced
4 tablespoons freshly grated Parmigiano-Reggiano cheese

1. In a saucepan heat the 2 tablespoons olive oil, and in it sauté the onion until translucent, about 6 minutes.
2. Add tomatoes, season to taste with salt and pepper, reduce heat, and simmer, partially covered, for 45 minutes, stirring occasionally.
3. Meanwhile rub each side of the eggplant slices with a little olive oil. Arrange the slices on a baking sheet and broil 5 inches from source of heat for about 3 minutes on each side, or until lightly browned.
4. Dip each slice of eggplant into bread crumbs and arrange in a single layer in a baking dish. Top with tomato sauce and slices of fontina cheese, and sprinkle with the Parmigiano-Reggiano.
5. Bake in a preheated 325-degree oven for 20 minutes, or until cheese is melted and bubbling.

Jane Street Seafood Cafe

31 Eighth Avenue (at the corner of 8th Street)
New York, N.Y. 10014   243-9237

There are two reasons to come to this restaurant—the seafood and the desserts. The atmosphere is simple and unadorned—wooden walls and tables with some nautical decoration thrown in almost as an afterthought. But there's also a feeling of comfort that quickly makes you forget what may be lacking in adornments. The house favorite is sole Portuguese—a fillet sautéed with tomatoes, mushrooms, garlic, butter, herbs, and wine. The desserts are made by two neighborhood women, but don't let that fool you. If the place has one drawback, it's the fact that you can't reserve and often must wait for a table.

☆ ☆ ## CLAMS OREGANATO ☆ ☆
SERVES 4

This first recipe is an appetizer. For anyone who has difficulty opening bivalves such as clams and oysters, there's another way. Preheat oven to 400 degrees. Arrange clams on a baking sheet and bake in the hot oven for 8 to 10 minutes, or until shells pop open. Remove clams from oven and continue with the recipe. Reduce oven to 350 degrees.

2 dozen fresh littleneck clams, well scrubbed
4 ounces (1 stick) sweet butter, at room temperature
6 cloves garlic, peeled and minced
2 tablespoons minced fresh parsley
¼ teaspoon thyme
¼ teaspoon oregano
2 tablespoons freshly grated Parmesan cheese
1 slice white bread, trimmed and blended to crumbs
Lemon wedges

1. Open clams and leave on the half shells in their own juice. Arrange on a baking sheet and set aside.
2. Combine butter, garlic, parsley, thyme, and oregano, mixing and mashing thoroughly.
3. Combine cheese and bread crumbs.
4. Put a dab of the herb butter on each clam and sprinkle lightly with the cheese–bread crumb mixture.
5. Bake in a preheated 350-degree oven for 8 to 10 minutes. Serve immediately with wedges of lemon.

☆ ☆ FILLET OF SOLE PORTUGUESE ☆ ☆

SERVES 2

After an appetizer of clams, a colorful and most flavorful dish of sole with tomatoes and mushrooms makes a suitable main course. It is served with brown rice.

1 small ripe tomato, peeled
4 medium mushrooms
3 tablespoons butter
1 teaspoon soy sauce
2 cloves garlic, minced
1 tablespoon lemon juice
Pinch each oregano, sweet basil, and thyme
Salt and freshly ground pepper to taste
2 4-ounce fillets of sole
¼ cup flour to coat the fish
2 tablespoons cream sherry
1 cup cooked brown rice
2 lemon wedges and parsley sprigs for garnish

1. Cut tomato into bite-sized pieces and quarter the mushrooms. Set aside.
2. In skillet large enough to hold the fish fillets, heat butter slowly. Add soy sauce, garlic, lemon juice, herbs, and vegetables, and cook until the vegetables begin to soften. Season with salt and pepper to taste.
3. Coat fillets on both sides with flour and place in pan, pushing vegetables to one side. Sauté for 2 minutes on each side.
4. Pour sherry into pan and ignite. Let flame burn out.
5. Spoon ½ cup brown rice on a warm serving plate, place a fish fillet halfway across the rice and arrange vegetables over both. Garnish with lemon wedge and parsley. Serve.

John Clancy's

181 West 10th Street
New York, N.Y. 10011 242-7350

Cookbook mavens know the name John Clancy because of his dessert books, so they may be slightly surprised to find that the specialty of his restaurant is seafood. Located on a heavily trafficked corner in the center of Greenwich Village, Clancy's attracts a professional crowd from all corners of the city. The two-story restaurant is pretty—lots of pinks and grays. The downstairs area, which many regulars prefer, may be noisy, so the upstairs room is the place to head for quiet dining. Mesquite grilling is as popular here as elsewhere, and the number one dish is skewered swordfish grilled in this manner. For dessert, the lemon pie wins hands down. Some people make a habit of ordering dessert as they walk in, to be sure their favorite has not been sold out. An overloaded English trifle is also available, as is the ubiquitous chocolate roulade.

☆ ☆ ## LOBSTER À L'AMERICAINE ☆ ☆
SERVES 4

This classic lobster dish from John Clancy's is easy to make at home.

4 1½-pound live lobsters
¼ cup olive oil
⅓ cup Cognac or brandy
½ cup dry white wine
Sauce à l'Americaine (see below)
Salt and pepper
2 tablespoons chopped parsley

1. Kill the lobsters instantly by plunging the tip of a sharp knife just behind the eyes of each lobster.
2. Prepare the lobsters: Cut the claws from the body and set aside. Split the lobster in half lengthwise and discard the sac that lies in the head and the black intestinal vein that runs down through the body. Set aside the tomalley and coral, if any. Now cut the tail section crosswise into three sections. Sever each large claw at the joint and crack the shells with the flat side of the cleaver. Each lobster will be in nine pieces.
3. Heat the olive oil in a very large shallow skillet. Add the lobster pieces and cook them until the shells turn red. Add Cognac or brandy and ignite it. When the flame dies out add the dry white wine and boil until it is reduced by half.
4. Pour the sauce à l'Americaine over the lobster pieces, bring to a boil, and simmer, covered, for 12 minutes.
5. Remove lobster pieces to a large warm serving platter. Beat the tomalley and coral together until smooth, stir into the sauce with the parsley, and cook for 2 to 3 minutes longer. Correct seasoning of sauce with salt and pepper, and spoon over the lobster. Serve with cooked rice or pasta.

SAUCE À L'AMERICAINE
ABOUT 1 QUART

The sauce may be made well in advance and refrigerated or frozen until needed. It should be at room temperature before you begin to make the dish.

¼ cup olive oil
¼ cup finely chopped carrots
½ cup finely chopped onion
1 teaspoon finely chopped garlic
3 cups canned Italian plum tomatoes, including juice
1 tablespoon tomato paste
1½ cups chicken broth, fresh or canned
1 bay leaf
1 teaspoon dried thyme
1 teaspoon dried tarragon
1½ teaspoons salt or to taste
Lots of freshly ground black pepper to taste

1. Heat the olive oil in a 2-quart saucepan. Add the carrots, onion, and garlic. Cook the vegetables until they are lightly colored, stirring frequently. Add the tomatoes, tomato paste, chicken broth, bay leaf, thyme, tarragon, salt, and pepper. Partially cover the pan and simmer the sauce for 40 minutes. Remove bay leaf. Purée the sauce through a food mill into a bowl or in the container of an electric blender. Set aside until needed.

☆　☆　　　# LEMON MERINGUE PIE 　　　☆　☆

1 9-INCH PIE

No book on the best recipes from New York restaurants would be complete without instructions for John Clancy's lemon meringue pie. Every day dozens of these giant pies are enjoyed by his customers. So popular is the dessert that many people call in advance to reserve it.

Pastry:
1½ cups all-purpose flour
6 tablespoons unsalted butter, chilled and cut into small pieces
2 tablespoons vegetable shortening
2 teaspoons sugar
½ teaspoon salt
3 to 5 tablespoons ice water

1. Put the flour, butter, shortening, sugar, and salt in a medium-sized bowl. With tips of your fingers, rub the ingredients together until they form small granules. Sprinkle 3 tablespoons of the ice water over the pastry mixture and gather it into a ball. If the dough crumbles, add additional ice water, 1 tablespoon at a time; use only as much as it takes to shape the pastry into a ball. Press the dough into a thick cake, wrap it in wax paper, and refrigerate for 30 minutes.

2. Roll out the pastry into a 12-inch circle. Starting at one edge, roll the pastry onto the rolling pin. Lift the rolling pin, hold it over a 9-inch pie pan so that about 1½ inches of the pastry drops over the nearest edge of the pan, then unroll the rest of the pastry, letting it fall into the pan. Gently fit the pastry into the pan and trim off the excess. Refrigerate for 1 hour to let the dough rest before baking.

3. Fit a piece of heavy duty foil into top of the pastry, pressing gently. Place the pan on a rack in the middle of a preheated 375-degree oven and bake the pastry shell for 10 minutes. Remove the foil and prick the bottom of the pastry shell several times with the tines of a fork. Continue to bake the pastry shell for an additional 10 to 12 minutes, or until it is golden brown.
4. Remove the pie shell from the oven and let it cool to room temperature on a wire rack.

Filling:
½ cup granulated sugar
¼ cup cornstarch
Pinch salt
3 large egg yolks
1¾ cups milk
2 tablespoons butter
1 tablespoon finely grated lemon rind
⅓ cup lemon juice or to taste
6 tablespoons granulated sugar
1 tablespoon cornstarch
3 large egg whites
1 tablespoon confectioner's sugar

1. In a heavy saucepan (not aluminum) combine ½ cup sugar, ¼ cup cornstarch, and salt. Beat in the egg yolks and continue beating until the mixture forms a smooth yellow paste. Gradually whisk in the milk.
2. Whisking constantly, bring the mixture just to a boil over medium heat. Remove from the heat and immediately beat in the butter, lemon rind, and lemon juice. Pour the mixture into the cooled pastry shell.
3. When the filling has cooled to room temperature, make the meringue. Sift 6 tablespoons sugar with 1 tablespoon cornstarch. Beat the egg whites until they form soft peaks. Gradually add the sugar and continue to beat until the whites form stiff peaks.
4. Mound the meringue on top of the pie, or, if you wish, make decorations by piping the meringue through a pastry bag fitted with a number 5 star tube. Sift the confectioner's sugar over the top of the pie, place the pie on a rack in the middle of a preheated 400-degree oven, and bake for 10 minutes, or until meringue is nicely browned.

La Caravelle

33 West 55th Street
New York, N.Y. 10019   586-4252

For all their seeming disrespect for tradition, New Yorkers are sentimentalists who like to return to a favorite restaurant for a special dinner or to celebrate an auspicious occasion. Unfortunately, should you stay away from some restaurants for a month or two, they disappear! Fortunately, La Caravelle with its traditional French cuisine seems in no danger of disappearing, and we hope it never will. The fresh flowers, sparkling white linen, and slightly formal atmosphere are still intact. So are the sauces, the fish dishes, and the slightly exotic pigeon offerings. Whatever you desire—veal, steak, Dover sole—you'll find it beautifully prepared, and that is heartwarming.

☆ ☆   # CRÈME DE TOMATES AU FENOUIL À LA GOUTTE DE PERNOD   ☆ ☆

(Cream of tomato soup flavored with fennel and Pernod)

SERVES 6 TO 8

The first recipe given us by executive chef Michael Romano is a delicious tomato soup flavored with anise.

1 medium onion, peeled
1 medium carrot, trimmed and peeled
1 stalk celery
2 cloves garlic, peeled
3 large bulbs fennel, washed and trimmed
2 tablespoons butter
2 tablespoons olive oil
Salt and pepper to taste
12 medium-sized tomatoes (fresh or canned), peeled and chopped
1 quart chicken stock
1 pint (2 cups) heavy cream (see page 303)
½ cup Pernod
½ cup sautéed croutons (see below)

1. Chop onion, carrot, celery, garlic, and fennel into small regular-shaped pieces.
2. In a large 4-quart stockpot heat butter and olive oil. Add vegetables and let them braise for about 10 minutes over low heat, covered, until soft. Do not let them brown.
3. Season with salt and pepper. Add tomatoes, cover, and cook for 5 minutes longer. Add chicken stock, bring to a boil, and simmer, uncovered, for 40 minutes.
4. Remove from stove and purée, 2 cups at a time, in an electric blender. Return to heat, correct seasoning, and add cream and Pernod. Serve with croutons.

SAUTÉED CROUTONS

1. Trim the crusts off 2 slices of bread and cut into ½-inch squares. Heat 2 tablespoons cooking oil or butter in a small skillet, add bread, and sauté, stirring and tossing the bread constantly until golden on all sides. Empty out onto absorbent paper to cool.

☆ ☆ ## PAUPIETTES DE VEAU FARCIS ☆ ☆
À L'AUBERGINE, SAUCE AUX
TROIS POIVRES
(Veal birds stuffed with eggplant,
three-pepper sauce)
SERVES 4

This dish requires quite a bit of work, but is deliciously different, very handsome, and well worth the time. All preparation may be done the day before and the paupiettes refrigerated until cooking time. Serve with wild rice.

3 large eggplants (about 1 pound each)
3 tablespoons cooking oil, divided
1 bay leaf
Pinch each tarragon, thyme, parsley, and chives
Salt and freshly ground pepper
1 pound chopped lean raw veal
1 cup fresh bread crumbs
8 thin slices veal from the leg, pounded flat as for scaloppine
2 sweet yellow peppers
1 sweet red pepper
1 sweet green pepper
4 tablespoons butter, divided
1 clove garlic, peeled and minced
½ cup dry vermouth
1 quart chicken stock
1 pint (2 cups) heavy cream (see page 303)
Chopped parsley

1. Rub the eggplants lightly with 1 tablespoon of the oil and bake in a preheated 350-degree oven for 1 to 1½ hours or until soft to a fork. Remove from oven and let cool. Then slit open lengthwise and, using a metal spoon, scoop out the flesh of two eggplants into a skillet.

2. Cook the eggplant meat over brisk heat to dry it out, at the same time stirring in the bay leaf and the herbs. Season to taste with salt and pepper, and when the eggplant holds together as a tight mass, remove from heat and cool.

3. When the eggplant is cooled a little, discard the bay leaf, add the chopped veal and bread crumbs, mix well, and correct the seasoning.

4. Arrange slices of veal on a work surface and sprinkle each with a little salt and pepper. Divide eggplant-veal mixture into 8 portions and, forming each into a lozenge shape, place one in the middle of each scaloppine. Roll the veal around the stuffing and secure with wooden picks. Set aside.

5. Meanwhile char the skin of the yellow peppers over an open flame or roast them in a 400-degree oven until the skin blackens. Place them in a covered bowl or wrap in a towel to steam for 15 minutes. Then discard skin, stems, and seeds. Set the meat of the yellow peppers aside.

6. Wash the red and green peppers, and discard stems and seeds. Cut the meat into small dice. Heat 2 tablespoons of the butter in a small saucepan and in it braise the green and red pepper with the minced garlic for about 6 minutes, or until soft. This is now called a brunoise. Set aside.

7. In a large ovenproof skillet heat the remaining 2 tablespoons butter and 2 tablespoons oil and in it brown the veal "birds" on all sides. Remove from pan and deglaze the skillet with the dry vermouth. Let the wine reduce by about half, return the "birds," and add the chicken stock. It should come up to the level of the meat in the skillet. Bring liquid to a boil, reduce heat, cover, and bake in a 350-degree oven for 30 minutes, or cook on top of stove over very low heat if preferred.

8. Remove the paupiettes to a warm platter and keep warm. Boil the liquid remaining in the pan over high heat until reduced to one-third its original quantity. Add cream and boil for 5 minutes longer.

9. Pour sauce into container of an electric blender, adding the flesh of the third eggplant and the two yellow peppers. Cover and blend until smooth. Strain through a fine sieve to remove any coarse bits that may remain in the sauce. Stir in the pepper brunoise.

10. Remove wooden picks from the paupiettes and arrange two on each warm serving plate. Cover with sauce and sprinkle with a little chopped parsley.

La Colombe d'Or

134 East 26th Street
New York, N.Y. 10010 689-0666

This cozy, friendly restaurant serves terrific food, which is evident from the crowd that arrives every evening. Lunches are quieter, the clientele consisting primarily of local neighbors and publishing people from the area. One of the best reasons to head for this restaurant is its bouillabaisse maison. Proprietor George Studley first thought about opening an American restaurant while he was living in Nice, but decided he would do better offering provençal specialties in the United States. He was right. In ten years he has made it an art. Located on the ground floor of a row house, this is a casual place that feels warm and welcoming, although a sport jacket or suit won't be out of place at night.

☆ ☆ POULET FARCI AU BASILIQUE ☆ ☆
(Chicken stuffed with sweet basil and garlic)
SERVES 6

This first recipe is a specialty of the house. Chef Rich Steffan rolls breast of chicken around a filling of sweet basil and garlic. In winter months, when fresh sweet basil is not readily available to the home chef, you may use well-drained sweet basil preserved in oil if you have a supply. To preserve basil in oil, see page 302.

4 whole chicken breasts, skinned and boned
Salt and freshly ground pepper
4 teaspoons lemon juice
Sweet Basil and Garlic Filling (see below), divided
½ cup flour to coat chicken
1 egg
2 tablespoons water
1 cup fresh bread crumbs
¼ teaspoon oregano
1 tablespoon freshly grated Parmesan cheese
¼ cup salad oil
1½ cups chicken broth
½ cup heavy cream (see page 303)
1 tablespoon cornstarch
6 lemon wedges
6 sprigs parsley

1. Flatten unsplit chicken breasts between two pieces of wax paper with a mallet or flat side of a heavy cleaver. Sprinkle with salt and pepper and a little lemon juice (about 1 teaspoon per breast).
2. Spread a thin layer of the filling on each breast, reserving about 4 tablespoons for the sauce. Roll each breast on a slant from tip end, tucking in sides as you roll, and place on wax paper, seam side down. Place in freezer for 15 to 30 minutes for easier handling.
3. When breasts are firm but not frozen, roll in flour, coating each lightly. Beat together egg and 1 tablespoon of the water. Roll chicken breasts in the egg and water or brush on to coat each thoroughly.
4. Combine bread crumbs with oregano and Parmesan and coat chicken breasts thoroughly. Place on wax paper and refrigerate until ready to use, but no longer than 1 hour. Breading will become soft after that.
5. When ready to cook, heat the oil in a large skillet over medium heat. Place chicken rolls in the hot oil seam side down and cook for about 5 minutes, or until evenly brown. Carefully turn with a spatula and brown the other side.
6. Transfer rolls to a sheet pan and bake in a preheated 375-degree oven for about 20 minutes, or until chicken meat springs back to the touch. Keep warm while making the sauce.

7. For the sauce, pour chicken broth into a 1½ quart saucepan and bring to a rolling boil. Whisk in the heavy cream and cook over high heat to reduce the quantity of sauce, for about 5 minutes. Whisk in salt and pepper to taste and the reserved filling.
8. Combine cornstarch with remaining tablespoon water and stir into sauce. Cook, stirring, until sauce is slightly thickened, about 2 or 3 minutes.
9. To serve: Slice chicken rolls ¼ inch thick. Ladle a few spoonfuls of sauce on each warm serving plate and arrange a few chicken slices on top. Garnish with a lemon wedge and a sprig of parsley.

SWEET BASIL AND GARLIC FILLING

4 bunches sweet basil
1 bunch parsley
½ cup pine nuts
4 large cloves garlic, peeled
Juice of 1 lemon, or 2 tablespoons

1. Discard thick stems from thoroughly clean sweet basil and parsley and put the leaves into a food processor with the steel blade. Process for 1 minute.
2. Add pine nuts and garlic and process to a paste consistency.
3. Add lemon juice and process again thoroughly to a spreadable paste.

☆ ☆ # BOUILLABAISSE MAISON ☆ ☆
SERVES 6

One of this restaurant's most popular dishes is its provençal bouillabaisse with aioli. If you plan to serve it in your own home, begin a day or two in advance. Make the stocks and clean and prepare the fish. Keep everything cold until time to reheat the soup and assemble the individual serving dishes, which should be cast-iron pans 8 inches in diameter and 1½ inches deep. (You can also use flameproof glass or pottery dishes, approximately 8 x 1½ inches.) You will also need a large stockpot.

For Each Serving:
1 lobster piece, tail or claw
2 shrimp, shelled and deveined
3 sea scallops
3 mussels, cleaned and debearded
3 littleneck clams, well washed
3 2-ounce pieces of meaty fish such as bluefish,
monkfish, or sea trout
Bouillabaisse Stock (see below)
Dash of Pernod
1 tablespoon chopped parsley
1 tablespoon Aioli (see below)

1. In each individual pan arrange the pieces of meaty fish in a single layer in center. Along each side arrange the scallops, mussels, and clams. On top of the fish arrange the shrimp and lobster.
2. Cover fish and seafood with hot bouillabaisse stock. Place a lid or inverted pan on top and cook over medium heat for 6 to 8 minutes, or until clams are fully opened.
3. Remove covers and to each portion add a dash of Pernod and chopped parsley. Serve with the aioli.

BOUILLABAISSE STOCK

¾ gallon Vegetable Stock (see below)
1 bunch leeks, split, well washed, and coarsely cut
2 carrots, trimmed and sliced
1 bulb fennel, washed and coarsely cut
1 whole bulb garlic, separated into cloves and peeled
1 teaspoon thyme
1 teaspoon tarragon
1 teaspoon cayenne pepper
Good pinch saffron threads
1 8-ounce can tomato purée
2 ounces Pernod
2 lobster heads
12 shrimp shells
Sea salt if necessary

1. Combine all ingredients in the stockpot, bring to a boil, and simmer for 1½ hours. Correct seasoning with sea salt if necessary. Strain and degrease.

VEGETABLE STOCK

¾ gallon or 3 quarts

2 onions, coarsely cut
1 bunch leek tops, well washed
½ bunch celery with leaves, coarsely cut
6 bay leaves
1 teaspoon thyme
1 teaspoon black pepper
1 teaspoon sea salt
1 gallon (4 quarts) cold water

1. Put all ingredients into a soup kettle or stockpot and bring to a boil. In order to have a crystal clear broth, skim off foam as it rises to surface. Simmer for about 35 minutes.
2. Strain and cool.

AIOLI

1½ cups mayonnaise, preferably homemade
4 cloves garlic, finely chopped
½ teaspoon cayenne pepper
Pinch saffron threads
1 teaspoon lemon juice
Salt if necessary

1. Combine mayonnaise, garlic, and cayenne pepper. Warm the saffron in lemon juice and when hot add to the mayonnaise. Mix thoroughly. Correct seasoning with salt if necessary.

☆　☆　　# GÂTEAU VICTOIRE　　☆　☆
(Chocolate Cake)
SERVES 8 TO 10

Sinfully rich, but worth every mouthful.

1 pound semisweet chocolate
6 eggs
1 teaspoon vanilla
1 tablespoon dark Jamaican rum
1 cup heavy cream
Additional whipped cream for garnish
Chocolate shavings

1. Cut chocolate into small pieces and place in an ovenproof or stainless steel bowl. Put in a very low 200-degree oven to melt slowly. It will take approximately 40 minutes.
2. In another stainless steel bowl combine eggs, vanilla, and rum. Beat with a whisk until frothy, then place on top of a saucepan of simmering water (the bottom of the bowl should not touch the water) and continue beating until eggs double in volume and hold a soft peak when beater is withdrawn. Remove from the simmering water occasionally to prevent eggs from cooking.
3. When eggs have thickened, remove from heat and whisk in melted chocolate slowly until mixture is smooth and uniform in color.
4. Beat cream until stiff and whisk slowly into the chocolate mixture until thoroughly incorporated.
5. Turn the mixture into an oiled 10- by 4- by 3-inch aluminum loaf pan with bottom lined with wax or parchment paper. Place loaf pan into a shallow pan containing about 2 inches warm water and bake in a 325-degree oven for about 55 minutes, or until cake is slightly cracked on top.
6. Remove cake pan from water bath and cool for 2 hours. Invert and unmold onto serving plate and garnish with whipped cream and chocolate shavings.

La Fenice

242 East 58th Street
New York, N.Y. 10022   759-4660

This Northern Italian restaurant just around the corner from Bloomingdale's is busier at dinnertime than at noon. Pino Castriota and Tony Buonsante have owned La Fenice since 1979. The intimate dining room, decorated in warm tones of red and pink, specializes in classical Italian veal, pasta, and fish dishes.

Scampi rialto, baked scampi rolled in ham with cheese, served with an anchovy sauce, and vitello tonnato, cold veal lavished with a light tuna sauce, are two of the more popular appetizers here. Diners favor such entrées as snapper in seafood sauce, veal scaloppine with dried mushrooms, carrots, and celery in a sherry- and cream-enriched sauce, and fegato alla veneziana, tender calf's liver sautéed with onion and white wine.

Desserts are the province of Mr. Buonsante. His dessert cart specials might include a warming walnut and nocello liqueur mousse, Italian-style cheesecake, zuppa inglese, and cannoli. La Fenice's wine list includes wines from Italy, France, Germany, and California. The house wines, served by the glass or carafe, are always Italian.

☆ ☆   # SCAMPI RIALTO   ☆ ☆

Serves 6 as an appetizer; 4 as an entrée

Scampi is the name given by the Italians to a type of orange-colored, shrimplike shellfish found in the Adriatic. Extra large shrimp may be substituted. Most people confuse the name with any size shrimp that are baked or broiled with the shell still on the tails.

24 large scampi, shelled and deveined
2 tablespoons flour
8 tablespoons butter, divided
8 slices cooked ham
6 slices Muenster cheese, quartered in strips
Caper and Anchovy Sauce (see below)

1. Dust the scampi with flour. In a large skillet melt half the butter over fairly high heat. Add the scampi and cook, tossing and turning the shrimp for 5 minutes, or until they are lightly golden on all sides.
2. Cut ham into strips about 1½ inches wide and roll a strip around each shrimp. Arrange the shrimp in a broiler pan or individual baking dishes, side by side. Place a strip of Muenster cheese over the shrimp.
3. Place about 4 inches below broiler heat and broil for 3 to 4 minutes, or until cheese is melted. Pour a little caper and anchovy sauce over each serving.

CAPER AND ANCHOVY SAUCE

¾ CUP

2 tablespoons drained chopped capers
6 anchovy fillets, washed free of salt and chopped
½ cup butter
1 teaspoon minced shallots
½ cup dry white wine
Chopped parsley

1. Combine the chopped capers and anchovy fillets and set aside.

2. In a small saucepan over medium heat, melt butter and in it
   sauté the shallots until pale gold in color. Add the capers and
   anchovies and continue to sauté for about 3 minutes. Add the
   white wine and simmer for 3 minutes. Add chopped parsley
   and keep warm.

☆ ☆   # VITELLO FENICE   ☆ ☆
(Veal with mushroom sherry sauce)
SERVES 6

A tantalizing combination of flavors created by chef Tony Buonsante especially for La Fenice.

4 ounces dry porcini mushrooms
18 ¼-inch-thick slices veal cut from the upper leg
Flour to coat (about ½ cup)
½ cup or 1 stick butter (4 ounces), divided
2 teaspoons minced shallots
4 tablespoons finely chopped carrot
4 tablespoons finely chopped celery
1 cup dry sherry wine
½ cup veal stock or beef broth
1 cup heavy cream (not ultrapasteurized; see page 303)
Salt and freshly ground pepper to taste

1. Soak the dry mushrooms in warm water just to cover for 10
   minutes. Squeeze dry, drain, and set aside.
2. Place the slices of veal between 2 sheets of wax paper and
   pound them with the flat side of a cleaver or a meat pounder
   to make them as thin as possible without tearing the meat.
   Dust them on each side lightly with flour.
3. Heat 6 tablespoons of the butter in a large skillet over fairly
   high heat and in it quickly brown the veal slices a few at a
   time for about 2 minutes on each side. Transfer the slices to a
   hot serving platter and keep warm.
4. In butter remaining in the pan, sauté the shallots until
   golden. Add the carrot, celery, porcini mushrooms, sherry,
   and stock or broth and cook over high heat until liquid is reduced to one-half its original quantity.
5. Add the cream, salt, and pepper and reduce heat to low. Swirl
   in the remaining 2 tablespoons butter until sauce becomes
   smooth and creamy. Pour the sauce over the veal and serve.

La Gauloise

502 Avenue of the Americas (between 12th and 13th streets)
New York, N.Y. 10011   691-1363

If white tablecloths, wooden wainscotting, and marble bars remind you of a Parisian cafe, you'll feel right at home here. Since cafes are usually noisy, don't expect anything different, but you can find a quiet spot if you ask for one of the banquette tables along the wall and away from the kitchen. As for the food, it's everything you'd expect. Traditional veal, fish, and meat dishes in the French style: coquille St. Jacques, bouillabaisse (Fridays only), cassoulet, and so on. At lunch you can indulge in a simple omelet or a hearty calf's liver sauté. And, of course, any time of the day, try the house pâté. It is excellent.

☆ ☆   # PITHIVIERS DE LA MER   ☆ ☆
(Seafood turnover)
Serves 12 as an appetizer

Mr. Moity, proprietor of La Gauloise, selected as an appetizer for this collection a turnover of puff paste filled with a fish mousse and seafood. Divine! Puff paste may be purchased by the pound at most local supermarkets. The turnover may be triangular or circular, or the dough may be rolled out into two 8-inch squares and sandwiched together with the filling in between.

½ pound fresh pike meat, very cold
1 ice cube
1 egg
½ teaspoon freshly ground white pepper
1½ to 2 cups heavy cream
¼ pound crayfish or shrimp, shelled and diced
¼ pound bay scallops, diced
¼ pound mussels, shelled
¼ pound mushrooms, washed, trimmed, and sliced
1 tablespoon chopped fresh herbs such as parsley, chives,
dill, or tarragon
½ pound puff pastry
1 egg yolk mixed with 1 tablespoon cold water
Beurre Blanc Basilic (see below)

1. First make a fish mousse: Chop pike finely and put it in the container of an electric blender with the ice cube, egg, and pepper. Blend on medium high speed, stopping to stir down frequently, until fish is reduced to a smooth paste. Then begin gradually, with motor on high speed, to add the cream. The raw fish will absorb the cream. Add as much cream as the fish will absorb without becoming too thin. It should be the consistency of a thick creamy pudding. Scrape into a mixing bowl and fold in the prepared seafood, mushrooms, and herbs. Set aside.
2. Cut puff paste in half and roll out each half on a floured cloth with a floured rolling pin into an 8-inch square (one bottom and one cover). We're making the pithivier sandwich-style. Pastry will be very thin.

3. Spread one half with the mousse and seafood mixture, leaving ½ inch rim around edge free of filling. Moisten this edge with egg-water mixture, place cover on top, and press edges firmly together.
4. With wide spatulas or pancake turners, transfer the "sandwich" to a baking sheet, and bake in a preheated 400-degree oven for 40 minutes, or until pastry is well puffed and golden brown.
5. Slice and serve hot with Beurre Blanc Basilic on the side.

BEURRE BLANC BASILIC
(White butter with sweet basil)
ABOUT 1 CUP

4 tablespoons finely chopped shallots
¼ cup dry white wine
½ pound soft sweet butter
Salt and pepper to taste
½ cup chopped fresh sweet basil leaves

1. In a small saucepan combine shallots and wine and bring to a vigorous boil. Let cook over moderate heat, stirring rapidly, until wine is reduced to about 2 tablespoons.
2. Begin to add the butter gradually, about 2 tablespoons at a time, stirring rapidly and constantly, until all butter is incorporated. However, it must never be allowed to melt completely, just get very warm and creamy.
3. When all butter has been added, stir in salt and pepper to taste and the sweet basil.

☆ ☆ ## LAPIN ROTI AU POIVRE VERT ☆ ☆
(Roast hare with green peppercorns)
SERVES 4

For a main course, Mr. Moity selected this saddle of hare. The saddle or *rables* is the upper back portion of the animal, including the loin. If desired, boned chicken breasts may be substituted for the hare.

2 saddles of rabbit, boned
Salt and pepper to taste
¾ cup finely diced ham
½ pound mushrooms, trimmed and sliced
2 tablespoons butter
1 teaspoon chopped fresh tarragon or sweet basil,
or ½ teaspoon dry thyme
¼ pound salt pork or crépinette, sliced paper-thin
Vegetable oil for browning saddles
3 tablespoons finely chopped shallots
1 cup dry white wine
2 tablespoons green peppercorns, well drained
1 cup heavy cream (see page 303)
1 cup brown gravy
4 teaspoons prepared mustard

1. Season the saddles with salt and pepper and flatten them with a meat pounder.
2. For the stuffing: Sauté the ham and mushrooms in the butter until mushrooms give off most of their moisture. Add the herbs and cook, stirring, until mixture becomes quite dry. Let cool for a few minutes. Use the duxelles to stuff the saddles, using half for each saddle. Wrap the meat around the stuffing, wrap each saddle in the *crépinette,* and tie with string.
3. Sauté the prepared saddles in vegetable oil in a hot oven-proof frying pan until lightly browned on all sides. Transfer skillet to a preheated 400-degree oven and roast for 15 minutes.
4. Remove rabbit from oven, remove strings, and transfer the saddles to a warm serving platter. Keep warm while making the sauce: Place skillet in which saddles were cooked over moderate heat and add shallots, white wine, peppercorns, and cream. Cook, stirring, until sauce is reduced and slightly thickened. Stir in brown gravy and simmer, stirring occasionally.
5. Stir in mustard and correct seasoning with salt. Do not let the sauce boil after the mustard is added.
6. Serve the rabbit in thin slices with freshly cooked noodles and some of the pan sauce ladled over.

La Grenouille

3 East 52nd Street
New York, N.Y. 10022   752-1495

Many people living both in and out of New York consider this one of the city's best restaurants. If you've never tasted quenelles nantua, this is the place to enjoy these delicate fresh fish dumplings swimming in a dreamy, creamy fish velouté subtly flavored with lobster butter. It is in Lyon, the capital of French gastronomy, that this dish reaches its peak of perfection, but La Grenouille's come close. There are also many provincial French dishes on the menu at La Grenouille.

☆ ☆ FROGS' LEGS EN CONCASSER À ☆ ☆ LA GRENOUILLE

SERVES 2

This recipe utilizes the bounty of Mediterranean cooking to its greatest advantage, the subtle background flavors of garlic, olive oil, and tomatoes penetrating the fragile flavor of the frogs' legs.

12 pairs medium-sized frogs' legs
1 cup cold milk
Salt and pepper
½ cup all-purpose flour
3 tablespoons vegetable oil
3 tablespoons butter
3 to 4 cloves garlic, finely chopped
Tomatoes Concasser Grenouille (see below)
2 tablespoons minced fresh parsley

132

1. Soak frogs' legs in milk in a glass plate in the refrigerator for at least one hour or until ready to cook. Remove legs from their milk bath, and place on wax paper. Sprinkle lightly with salt and freshly ground pepper.
2. Dredge the seasoned frogs' legs in flour, shaking off the excess.
3. In a large heavy skillet, heat oil. Add the frogs' legs and brown them quickly on all sides. Add the butter and just as it begins to give off a nutty aroma, add the garlic. Be careful not to let the garlic burn or it will taste bitter.
4. Turn the legs immediately onto a heated serving dish or onto individual heated plates, and place a spoonful of tomatoes concasser on the side. Sprinkle with chopped parsley.

Note:

The classic cooking oil for this dish is olive oil, but at La Grenouille, they have found that the flavor of olive oil is too strong for the palates of their American guests. The garniture of tomatoes is a distinctive La Grenouille touch.

TOMATOES CONCASSER GRENOUILLE

Enough to serve 4

What you don't use, pack into moisture-proof bags and freeze for future use.

4 large, ripe tomatoes
3 tablespoons vegetable oil
½ large onion, chopped (½ cup)
Salt and freshly ground pepper to taste
1 clove garlic, finely chopped
½ bay leaf, crumbled
Pinch of sugar

1. Peel tomatoes, slice off the blossom end, and insert a small teaspoon into the tomato sections to remove the seeds. Chop tomatoes coarsely.
2. Heat the oil in a flat-bottomed sauté pan; add onion and sauté for 7 to 8 minutes, or until very soft, but not brown.
3. Add tomatoes, salt and pepper, garlic, bay leaf, and sugar. Reduce heat to low and simmer for 30 minutes, or until tomatoes have thickened to a sauce consistency and most of the liquid has evaporated. Shake the pan occasionally throughout the cooking period.

La Réserve

4 West 49th Street
New York, N.Y. 10022   247-2993

Just when it seemed as if every new restaurant in town was going to have a sleek gray interior, food that looked as if it were meant for photography rather than eating, or a menu that concentrated on every conceivable type of pasta imaginable, La Réserve arrived. Dedicated to the art of classic French cuisine, this place immediately captured the lunchtime expense account crowd, but it is delightfully quiet for dinner.

Not far from the theater district—a nice ten-minute walk—this is a lovely place for an elegant meal before an evening on the town.

☆ ☆ CHARLOTTE DE RIS DE VEAU ☆ ☆
AU BASILIC
(Charlotte of sweetbreads with basil)
SERVES 6

This recipe should revive the popularity of sweetbreads. These delicate glands, once a favorite dish in most middle-class homes, are today monopolized by the good restaurants. If you wish to make the dish at home, make sure you can locate a butcher shop that carries or will order the large lobes. For the charlotte you will need 6 porcelain molds, each 3 inches in diameter.

4 large sweetbreads
4 tablespoons butter
6 shiitakes or chanterelles, canned or
refreshed in cold water, sliced
2 shallots, peeled and minced
2 tomatoes, peeled, seeded, and diced
15 large sweet basil leaves, chopped
¼ cup Cognac
½ cup chicken stock

134

½ cup dry white wine
2 carrots
2 white turnips
¼ pound green beans
Veal Mousse (see below)
Port Wine sauce (see below)

1. Soak the sweetbreads in cold water for several hours, changing water frequently. Then cover with cold water in a saucepan, bring slowly to a boil, and simmer for 15 minutes. Drain and cover again with cold water to cool rapidly. Place sweetbreads between two plates, put a heavy weight on the top plate, and refrigerate until ready to cook.

2. Remove the thin film over the sweetbreads and cut the sweetbreads into small escalopes. Sauté the escalopes in hot butter until lightly brown on both sides. Add the mushrooms and shallots and sauté until the mushrooms release their juices. Add the tomatoes and basil and flame with the Cognac.

3. When the flames die out, add chicken stock and white wine. Cover and cook over low heat for 2 minutes. Remove from heat. Set aside.

4. To prepare the molds: Peel the carrots and turnips. Cut each lengthwise into slices ⅛ inch thick, and cut these into uniform squares or "shingles." The size of the squares is determined by the size of the molds. The squares should be just tall enough to reach from bottom of the mold to its top when placed perpendicularly along its sides. Cut the green beans into similar lengths. Blanch the prepared vegetables in boiling water for about 5 minutes, drain, and dry.

5. Butter the insides of 6 3-inch porcelain molds and line the inside walls with the vegetable "shingles," varying the vegetables and the color all the way around.

6. Spread a thin layer of the veal mousse over the vegetables and on the bottom of the molds. Fill the mousse-lined molds with the sweetbread mixture and cover the top with another thin layer of the veal mousse.

7. Place the filled molds in a pan large enough to contain them and fill it with water reaching halfway up the sides of the molds. Place the pan in a preheated 350-degree oven and bake for 15 minutes, or until mousse is firm.

8. Remove the molds and place them upside down on serving plates. The charlottes should slide right out of the porcelain ramekins. If not, tap the sides and bottoms of the ramekins gently with a knife. Serve with port wine sauce.

VEAL MOUSSE

This mousse is quickly prepared in a food processor.

¾ pound chilled ground lean veal
Salt and pepper to taste
2 eggs
1 cup heavy cream (not ultrapasteurized; see page 303)

1. Put the veal with a bit of salt and pepper into container of the processor, using the metal blade. Turn the machine on and add the eggs. Once they are incorporated into the meat, gradually add the cream and process until the mousse is smooth in texture. Correct seasoning to taste.

PORT WINE SAUCE

1 tablespoon butter
1 tablespoon minced shallots or green onions
1 cup beef bouillon
½ cup homestyle beef gravy
¼ cup port wine

1. To the pan in which the sweetbreads are cooked, add 1 tablespoon butter and in it sauté the shallots or green onions until golden. Add the bouillon and bring to a rapid boil. Add gravy and port and simmer for several minutes. Spoon a little sauce over each charlotte after it is unmolded.

☆ ☆ ☆ ☆

SOLE DE LA MANCHE "STEPHANIE" FARCIE À LA MOUSSE D'ARTICHAUD
(Fillet of Dover sole Stephanie, stuffed with artichoke mousse)

SERVES 4

True Dover sole, as you know, swims only in Mediterranean waters and is seldom available to homemakers in America. Lemon or gray sole or flounder may be substituted, or any small whole fish. Trout would be divine.

4 artichokes
2¼ cups whipping cream (not ultrapasteurized; see page 303)
Salt and pepper to taste
1 tablespoon green peppercorns
4 Dover sole, cleaned
2 shallots, finely minced
½ cup dry vermouth
6 tablespoons butter
½ carrot, cut into julienne strips and blanched
10 snow peas, cut into julienne and blanched
½ small black truffle, cut into julienne (optional)
1 small cooked beet, cut into very fine julienne

1. Make the artichoke mousse: Trim the artichokes, reserving just the bottoms. Cook in salted, slightly acidulated water until fork tender. Remove chokes and purée the bottoms in a food processor with ¼ cup of the cream. Stir in salt and pepper to taste and fold in the green peppercorns. Set aside.
2. Poach the sole in a stainless steel or enamel pan with the minced shallots, vermouth, a bit of salt and pepper, and just enough water to cover the fish. To poach, place fish in the pan, turn heat to a gentle simmer, cover pan, and simmer for 8 to 10 minutes, or until the flesh just begins to pull away from the center bone near the top (the backbone).
3. Remove fish from the poaching liquid and set aside.
4. Make the sauce. To the poaching liquid add the remaining cream and reduce over high heat until the cream has the consistency of syrup and begins to coat the spoon. Stir in the butter, season with salt and pepper, and strain through a fine sieve.
5. Combine julienned vegetables and set aside.
6. Fillet the fish. Separate the top fillet from the center and then run a spatula or thin knife blade above the bottom fillet and under the bones. The bones should lift away easily.
7. Spread ¼ of the artichoke mixture on each of the bottom fillets, and reassemble the fish. Place each fish on a warm serving plate, cover with a bit of the sauce, and top the fish with the vegetable julienne.

La Ripaille

605 Hudson Street
New York, N.Y. 10014   255-4406

This tiny bistro—it seats 45—looks casual. It doesn't have any dress code, but the diners come dressed anyway. For the most part, you'll find young professionals who look as if they haven't noticed the brick walls or casual seating arrangements or the view into the kitchen. They are attracted by the promise of good food—the pâté, the salmon in puff pastry, and the broccoli mousse. The menu is limited and changes often, but some of the favorites remain as long as the fresh ingredients are available. Open only for dinner, and reservations are necessary. Like many French bistros, La Ripaille is closed on Sundays.

☆ ☆ ESCALOPE OF SWEETBREADS IN ☆ ☆ CREAM SAUCE

SERVES 4

The first recipe from this restaurant is an exquisitely subtle dish of sweetbreads gaily garnished with sweet red pepper strips and fresh artichoke hearts.

1½ pounds sweetbreads
1 sweet red pepper
4 fresh artichokes
1 cup chicken stock
1 cup fresh pasteurized heavy cream
(not ultrapasteurized; see page 303)
Salt and freshly ground white pepper to taste

1. Soak sweetbreads in ice water for 6 hours, changing the water several times.
2. Meanwhile bake the pepper in a 400-degree oven for 12 to 15 minutes, or until skin can be easily removed, or toast it over a gas flame, turning frequently. To facilitate removal, place the partially cooked pepper in a plastic bag and close tightly. When cool enough to handle, cut into quarters and remove and discard skin, inside membranes, and seeds. Cut pepper into thin slices and set aside.
3. Clean the artichokes, leaving the hearts only. Slice the hearts and cook in boiling salted water for 5 to 8 minutes, or until fork tender. Set aside.
4. Drain the sweetbreads, cover with salted water, bring to a boil, and simmer for 10 minutes. Drain again and remove any fat or discolored bits from around the sweetbreads.
5. Place sweetbreads in a saucepan with the chicken stock, bring to a simmer, cover, and cook over low heat for 20 minutes. Remove the sweetbreads from the stock, add the cream, and boil rapidly until sauce is reduced to about 1½ cups.
6. Slice sweetbreads and add to the reduced sauce along with the artichokes and red peppers. Add salt and pepper to taste and heat to serving temperature.

☆ ☆   # MOUSSE DE BROCCOLI AU BEURRE CITRONÉ   ☆ ☆
(Broccoli with lemon butter)
SERVES 4

A lovely vegetable to serve as an accompaniment to the sweetbreads or with broiled chicken or fish.

1 1-pound bunch broccoli
Salt and pepper to taste
2 eggs
1 cup heavy cream, divided
2 tablespoons melted butter
2 tablespoons lemon juice
¼ pound (1 stick) cold sweet butter, thinly sliced

1. Wash broccoli and trim ends. Remove about a dozen florets and cut remaining stalks into chunks. Put into a saucepan of rapidly boiling, salted water and boil for 5 minutes. With a slotted spoon, remove the florets, chill quickly in cold water, and set aside for garnish. Broil remaining broccoli for another 3 to 5 minutes. or until fork tender. Drain, rinse in cold water, and drain again.

2. Empty cooked broccoli into container of an electric blender (it should almost fill it). Add the eggs and ¾ cup cream and blend on medium speed until well puréed, stopping to stir down sides of container once or twice if necessary. Season the purée to taste with salt and lots of pepper (freshly ground white is best).

3. Brush the insides of six 6-ounce timbale molds or custard cups with the melted butter and fill with the broccoli mixture. Place molds or cups in a shallow baking pan, fill pan ¾ full of boiling water, and place pan in a preheated 350-degree oven. Bake for 55 minutes to 1 hour.

4. Reheat the reserved florets in a little hot water.

5. Meanwhile in a small saucepan reduce lemon juice to about half its original quantity. Add the remaining 4 tablespoons heavy cream and bring to a boil. Gradually beat in the cold butter slices, a few at a time, and season to taste with salt and pepper. The sauce should never get hot enough to completely melt the butter. It should be just lightly creamy and warm.

6. To serve: Invert the molds onto individual plates and top with a spoonful of the sauce. Decorate with the broccoli flowers.

Laurent

111 East 56th Street
New York, N.Y. 10022   753-2729

There are some traditions that should never change and Laurent is one of them. Tucked into a midtown hotel, this is the place where some New Yorkers had their first haute cuisine meal, their first glass of champagne, and met their first authentic maître d'. This restaurant is a large, formal room that continues to serve traditional French cuisine at a time when nouvelle anything has made inroads at most other places. Actually many people prefer the bar. It's a wonderfully quiet place to hide before dinner, after work, or at the end of any day. Laurent is filled with quietly powerful people who dine on salmon, veal, or the daily specials, but tend to leave room for dessert.

☆ ☆ STEAK AU POIVRE FLAMBÉ À ☆ ☆ L'ARMAGNAC
SERVES 1

The steak au poivre at Laurent is flamed with Armagnac, and the sauce is enriched with a touch of crème fraîche.

1 14-ounce sirloin steak
Salt
Lightly pounded crushed black pepper (about 2 tablespoons)
1 ounce Armagnac
½ cup beef or veal gravy, homemade or bottled
2 teaspoons Dijon mustard
2 teaspoons butter
2 teaspoons crème fraîche (page 301)

141

1. Trim excess fat from steak and trim the ends so that the steak is somewhat square. Sprinkle steak lightly with salt and press the crushed black pepper into both sides with heel of the hand.
2. Cook the steak in a lightly oiled pan over very high heat until well browned on both sides.
3. Remove steak for a moment, pour excess fat from pan, and wipe the pan clean with paper towels.
4. Return steak to the very hot pan, pour the Armagnac over it, and set aflame. When the flame burns out and steak is cooked to taste, remove it to a warm platter and prepare the sauce.
5. To pan in which steak was cooked, add gravy and stir to blend it with the remaining juices in the pan. Add mustard and butter and stir well to blend. Stir in crème fraîche.
6. Spoon sauce over the steak and serve immediately.

☆ ☆   # PETITS POTS DE CRÈME AU CHOCOLAT   ☆ ☆

SERVES 8

Good things come in small packages, and this dessert is no exception.

2 cups heavy cream
8 ounces sweet chocolate, grated in blender
¼ cup sugar
6 egg yolks, lightly beaten
1 tablespoon vanilla

1. In a saucepan combine cream, chocolate, and sugar. Cook over low heat, stirring constantly, until thoroughly blended and the mixture begins to simmer.
2. Remove immediately from heat and slowly beat into the beaten egg yolks. Use an electric beater for this if possible.
3. Stir in vanilla.
4. Pour into little cream pots, cover with the tops, and chill.

Le Cirque

58 East 65th Street
New York, N.Y. 10021   794-9292

Quiet elegance best describes the atmosphere of this popular East Side restaurant with its subdued lighting and enchanting wall murals by artist Kenneth Stern. Under the direction of host Sirio Maccioni, the service is impeccable, police, and efficient. Inside the entrance is a mouth-watering display of desserts and pastries, and an hors d'oeuvre table graced with fascinating fish and vegetable pâtés, the creations of Le Cirque's talented young French chef, Alain Sailhac. An extensive menu includes oysters with Pernod, scallops salad, sautéed Black Forest mushrooms with herbs, fettuccine with white truffles, quenelles, goujonette of sole, noisettes of venison, and many grilled entrées. Expensive, but worth it. Reservations are necessary.

☆ ☆ ## SPAGHETTI PRIMAVERA À LE CIRQUE ☆ ☆

Serves 6 to 8 as an appetizer; 4 as a main course

There are many variations for spaghetti primavera. This is one of the best. If a vegetable is unavailable, don't be afraid to substitute another or leave it out entirely.

1 bunch broccoli
2 small zucchini
4 stalks asparagus, each 5 inches long
1½ cups green beans, trimmed and cut into 1-inch lengths
½ cup fresh or frozen snow peas

1 tablespoon peanut or vegetable oil
2 cups thinly sliced fresh mushrooms
1 teaspoon finely chopped hot fresh red or green chiles,
or about ½ teaspoon dried red pepper flakes
½ cup finely chopped parsley
6 tablespoons olive oil, divided
1 teaspoon finely chopped garlic, divided
3 cups ripe tomatoes, peeled and cut into 1-inch cubes
6 fresh basil leaves, chopped (about ¼ cup), or 1 tablespoon pesto
Salt and freshly ground pepper to taste
1 pound spaghetti or spaghettini
4 tablespoons butter
2 tablespoons fresh or canned chicken broth
½ to ¾ cup heavy cream
⅔ cup freshly grated Parmesan cheese
⅓ cup toasted pine nuts

1. Trim broccoli and break into bite-sized florets. Trim and discard ends of zucchini, cut lengthwise in quarters, then into 1-inch lengths. Cut asparagus stalks into thirds. Prepare green beans. Cook each of these vegetables separately in boiling salted water until tender but still crisp, about 5 minutes. Drain well, run under cold water, and drain again. Combine all in a large mixing bowl.

2. Cook snow peas for 1 minute if fresh, 30 seconds if frozen. Drain, chill as above with cold water, and drain again. Add to other vegetables.

3. Heat peanut or vegetable oil in a skillet and in it cook mushrooms for about 2 minutes, shaking skillet frequently. Add chiles and parsley, stir to combine, and pour over vegetable mixture.

4. In the same skillet heat 3 tablespoons olive oil. Add half the garlic, the tomatoes, and sweet basil. Cook for about 4 minutes, stirring gently and being careful not to crush the tomatoes. Sprinkle with a little salt and freshly ground pepper and set aside.

5. Bring 4 quarts lightly salted water to a boil in a kettle large enough to hold all ingredients. When boiling rapidly drop in the spaghetti and cook until it is just tender to the tooth or al dente. The spaghetti is ready when it still retains a slight resilience in the center. Drain and return spaghetti to the kettle. Add butter and toss until butter is melted. Add chicken broth, ½ cup cream, and cheese, tossing spaghetti quickly to blend.

6. While spaghetti is cooking, heat remaining 3 tablespoons olive oil in a kettle large enough to hold all vegetables. Add remaining garlic and the vegetable mixture and cook, stirring gently, over low heat, just long enough to heat vegetables thoroughly.
7. Add half the vegetables and liquid from the tomatoes to the spaghetti, tossing and stirring. Add remaining vegetables and tomato mixture and, if sauce seems too dry, the remaining ¼ cup cream. Sauce should not be soupy. Add pine nuts and give the mixture a final tossing. Serve in hot soup or spaghetti bowls.

☆ ☆   # MAIGRET DE CANARD AU GINGEMBRE ET CASSIS   ☆ ☆
(Duckling with ginger and cassis)
SERVES 2

Originally maigret de canard meant the breasts of ducklings force-fed to make them particularly fat and succulent. Present day cultures, however, demand the thinner, leaner meat of traditional ducklings. Broiling the breasts removes most of the remaining excess fat, and when served with this glorious sweet sour hot sauce, the imaginative combination of chef Alain Sailhac, they become a masterpiece of flavor and texture. The cooked breasts are sliced and served with the sauce on large serving plates, accompanied by snow peas and cooked wild rice.

1 5-pound duckling
Ginger and Cassis Sauce (see below)

1. To prepare the duckling: With a sharp knife, make a slit from vent to neck bone on either side of breast bone or keel. Gradually scrape away the meat from the bone and remove each breast in one piece along with the skin and any underlayer of fat. Refrigerate until ready to cook. (Note: Save the carcass for soup or boil it; remove meat from bones for salad or for spaghetti sauce.)
2. Make the sauce and set aside.

3. Twenty minutes before serving, arrange breasts skin side down on rack in broiling pan. Broil six inches from source of high heat for 5 minutes. Turn and broil for another 5 minutes. Turn again, reduce heat to medium, and broil for 5 minutes. Finally turn skin side up and continue to broil without letting the skin burn or overbrown for a final 5 minutes.
4. Slice breasts into thin strips and serve one breast per person with 2 to 3 tablespoons of the sauce spooned over.
5. Garnish plate with cooked snow peas and wild rice.

GINGER AND CASSIS SAUCE À LE CIRQUE

Enough for 3 ducklings or 6 servings

This sauce may be made in advance and reheated when needed. It will keep for months in the refrigerator in a tightly covered glass container. It's excellent served with broiled swordfish and with roast goose, of course.

½ cup sugar
Zest of 2 oranges and 1 lemon, minced or grated
2 shallots, minced
1 tablespoon green peppercorns, well drained
Juice of 4 oranges
Juice of 2 lemons
½ cup Madeira wine
2 tablespoons minced or shredded fresh ginger
4 tablespoons ginger preserves
4 tablespoons black currant jelly
½ cup demiglace of duck, or duck or meat gravy
4 tablespoons preserved black currant berries
Salt to taste

1. In a heavy saucepan caramelize the sugar, being careful not to let it burn. Add zest of oranges and lemon and stir for 2 minutes. Add shallots and peppercorns and cook, stirring, another 2 minutes.
2. Add orange and lemon juice and Madeira, and simmer for 10 minutes, stirring frequently.
3. Add ginger, ginger preserves, black currant jelly, and demiglace or gravy and cook for 15 minutes, stirring occasionally.
4. Add black currants and salt to taste, and cook for 5 minutes. Reheat when needed.

Le Cygne

55 East 54th Street
New York, N.Y. 10022   759-5941

For many years Le Cygne was a staple on the tour of "haute" restaurants in the city. Then it moved one door to the east and became modern—at least in its decor. The design and architecture are postmodern at their best. You feel as if you are in the private dining room of a luxury liner. The "all aboard" feeling is the same in the dining room upstairs but, unless you want a secluded lunch, the place to see and be seen is downstairs. The food, though, is still classic—with that special something that sets this restaurant apart from all the others. The fish dishes are varied and popular. The other specialty here, not to be missed, is the game. Reservations are a must and prices are high.

☆ ☆   **FILLETS DE ROUGETS**   ☆ ☆
AUX POIVRE ET VINAIGRE
(Red mullet with sour pepper sauce)
SERVES 4

A favorite entrée served at Le Cygne is this fillet of red mullet with a zesty sauce. This is not a dish with a paucity of calories.

2 red mullet fillets, each about 8 ounces
1 teaspoon French olive oil
1 teaspoon cracked black pepper, crushed
¾ cup fresh wine vinegar
2 cloves garlic, peeled, crushed, and minced
3 tablespoons Dijon mustard
3 tablespoons tomato purée
1½ cups muscadet or other good dry white wine
4 baby yellow squash, trimmed and sliced
4 teaspoons sweet butter, divided
1 cup sliced mushrooms*
1 cup fresh pasteurized heavy cream
(not ultrapasteurized; see page 303)
Salt and pepper to taste

1. Wash the fillets, making sure that all the scales have been removed, and use pliers to pull out any bones remaining in the flesh. Dry on paper towels, brush each side with olive oil, and sprinkle with the crushed pepper. Set aside.
2. In a saucepan bring the wine vinegar to a boil. Add garlic, mustard, tomato purée, and dry white wine and boil until liquid is reduced to about ½ cup.
3. Meanwhile prepare the garniture: Boil or steam the squash for 3 to 5 minutes, or until barely fork tender, and sauté in 1 teaspoon of the butter until lightly browned. Also sauté the mushrooms in a teaspoon of butter until lightly browned. Set aside and keep warm.
4. In a heavy skillet heat remaining 2 teaspoons butter and in it sauté the fillets, skin side down, for about 3 minutes. Turn over and cook for 2 minutes longer or until cooked through. Set fillets aside and keep warm.
5. Add cream to juices remaining in the pan and bring to a boil. Add the reduced sauce and correct the seasoning with salt and pepper. Boil rapidly until sauce is reduced to a heavy silky texture.
6. To serve: On a hot plate, spread a layer of the sauce. Place the fish on the sauce, skin side up, and put a spoonful of squash on one side, a spoonful of mushrooms on the other.

* Use wild mushrooms when possible (fresh, canned, or dried), such as morels, cepes or chanterelles. If dried they must be soaked in a small amount of warm water to cover for about ten minutes. The ones used at Le Cygne are called *trompette de la mort* and are occasionally found in California markets. They are undoubtedly available to the restaurant trade, but the home chef may have to search a bit to find them.

Lello Ristorante

65 East 54th Street
New York, N.Y. 10022 751-1555

This sophisticated Italian restaurant is a dream come true for Lello and Enzio Arpaia. Housed in a chic two-story brownstone, Lello features Northern Italian specialties as well as some Southern Italian dishes. In the beautifully appointed dining room tinted mirrors on padded mauve walls, thick Oriental carpets, and dimly lit crystal chandeliers create a serene atmosphere for serious dining.

   The restaurant's aim is to combine the high-caliber food, helpful and unobtrusive service, and elegant surroundings found in the best French restaurants.

☆ ☆ LELLO'S FUNGHI RIPIENI ☆ ☆
CON LUMACHE
(Mushrooms stuffed with garlicky snails)
Serves 4 as luncheon dish; 6 as appetizer

Although snails are considered a French dish, they are commonly used in Northern Italy. This recipe is Lello's creation and combines his two favorite foods—snails and mushrooms. Serve it as an appetizer or luncheon dish with hot Italian bread.

24 medium-sized fresh mushrooms, washed and dried
¾ pound (3 sticks) butter, divided, at room temperature
3 cloves garlic, peeled
1 tablespoon lemon juice
24 cooked canned snails
Salt and freshly ground pepper to taste
2 tablespoons white wine
2 tablespoons chopped fresh parsley

1. Remove stems from mushrooms and reserve for another purpose. Put ½ pound (2 sticks) butter into blender container with garlic and lemon juice. Blend to a smooth paste. Rinse and drain snails.
2. Sauté mushroom caps in 4 tablespoons of butter for 3 to 4 minutes on each side, or until golden. Arrange on rimmed jelly roll pan, hollow side up. Set aside.
3. In the same pan heat remaining 4 tablespoons of butter, add snails, and sprinkle with salt and pepper. Add the white wine. Sauté for 10 minutes. Fill each mushroom cap with a snail.
4. Preheat oven to 350 degrees.
5. Put 2 teaspoons of the garlic butter on the snail in each mushroom, and bake in the preheated oven for 10 minutes. Brown lightly under the broiler and sprinkle with parsley.

☆ ☆ ## LELLO'S CAPELLINI ☆ ☆
D'ANGELO CAPRESE
(Pasta with mixed seafood
in tomato sauce)
SERVES 4

This is a colorful pasta dish, easy to make in the home kitchen. To duplicate it, be sure to seek out the freshest seafood available. Chef Lello Arpaia prefers Fara San Marino pasta, which contains more durum wheat than most others, and little starch. Vermicelli No. 10 may be substituted for the capellini, if you like, and the meat from two small lobsters may be substituted for the crab meat.

5 medium shrimp, shelled, deveined, and chopped
4 Alaska king crab legs, shelled and chopped
6 fresh cherrystone clams, shucked and chopped
1 tablespoon chopped onion
1 tablespoon chopped shallots
1 tablespoon chopped garlic
1 stalk celery, cut into thin strips about ⅛ inch wide
and 1½ inches long
1 carrot, peeled and cut into thin strips about ⅛ inch wide
and 1½ inches long
1 small leek, white part only, cut into thin strips

¼ cup salad oil
¼ cup olive oil
2 tablespoons white wine
1 8-ounce can plum tomatoes, drained
(save liquid for the soup pot)
1 tablespoon chopped parsley
½ pound capellini pasta

1. Prepare shrimp, crab, and clams, reserving any juices, and combine. Peel and chop the onion, shallots, and garlic. Julienne the celery, carrot, and leek.
2. Put a large kettle (at least 2 quarts) of lightly salted water on to boil.
3. Meanwhile, in a skillet heat the two oils and sauté onion, shallots, and garlic for 3 minutes. Add other vegetables and sauté for about 6 minutes, stirring frequently. Add wine, shellfish, and any reserved juice, and continue to cook, tossing and shaking pan frequently for 6 minutes longer. Add plum tomatoes and squash them, mixing them into the other ingredients. Simmer while pasta is cooking.
4. Cook pasta in the rapidly boiling water according to package directions. Do not overcook; it should be al dente. Drain and empty into serving bowl.
5. Toss pasta with the seafood sauce and sprinkle with parsley.

☆　☆　　　# SCAMPI RIBELLI　　　☆　☆
(Broiled shrimp with mozzarella cheese)
SERVES 4

If all the ingredients for this colorful dish are prepared in advance, it takes no more than 8 to 10 minutes to finish. You will need four individual gratin dishes.

20 jumbo shrimp, shelled, deveined, and split lengthwise
½ cup vegetable oil
2 large cloves fresh garlic, finely chopped
½ stick (4 tablespoons) sweet butter
¼ cup dry white wine
Salt and freshly ground pepper to taste
8 slices (6 ounces) mozzarella cheese (fresh if possible)
½ cup Concasse of Tomatoes (see page 301)
2 tablespoons chopped parsley

1. Shell shrimp: The easiest, most efficient way to do this is to use a small pair of sharp scissors. Cut deeply through shell, including tail section. The shell will peel off easily. Rinse out vein under cold running water. Split shrimp almost in half lengthwise and press open flat. Refrigerate, covered, until needed.
2. In skillet heat oil, add garlic, and sauté, stirring occasionally until golden. Add shrimp and cook for 2 minutes, turning each shrimp once.
3. Drain off excess oil and add butter. Sauté for 1 minute longer. Sprinkle with wine, salt, and pepper.
4. Arrange 5 shrimp in each gratin dish and spoon a little of the pan sauce over them. Arrange 2 slices cheese on top of each portion, and broil about 6 inches from heat for 5 minutes or until cheese is melted and browned.
5. Remove dishes from broiler, top with a spoonful of tomatoes, and sprinkle with a little parsley.

Le Régence at the Hôtel Plaza Athénée

37 East 64th Street
New York, N.Y. 10021   606-4647/8

The first thing that strikes you about this restaurant is its soothing beauty. The pale aqua walls, the vaulted ceilings that enclose trompe l'oeil clouds, and the crystal chandeliers make this room perfect for those who enjoy eating in an elegant, peaceful restaurant. The menu makes it a restaurant for anyone who is interested in lavish food, and attentive service completes the picture. Hotel dining rooms were once places to avoid; restaurants such as this one have now made them places where diners around the city flock. The menu is a combination of classic French, plus the Gallic version of a low-cal special. In the main room, the tables are widely spaced and allow for quiet conversation, especially in the banquettes. The smaller side room is more intimate, but not as private.

☆ ☆ OEUFS BROUILLÉS AU CAVIAR ☆ ☆
(Scrambled eggs with caviar)
SERVES 2

This first recipe is as soothing and inviting as the room itself, a perfect luncheon dish for two on a bright spring day or a honeymoon breakfast.

1 cup fresh spinach, leaves only
1½ tablespoons soft sweet butter, divided
4 eggs, lightly beaten
4 quail eggs*
¼ cup heavy cream, fresh pasteurized, if possible (see page 303)
1 tablespoon beluga or sevruga caviar

1. Wash spinach leaves. Arrange them around the rims of two large ovenproof dinner plates. Brush them lightly with 1 tablespoon soft butter, then set aside.
2. In a 10-inch skillet heat ½ tablespoon butter. Add the beaten eggs and stir with a whisk over low heat so that they thicken and coagulate slowly and evenly. Remove the pan from the heat while the eggs are still very soft and moist.
3. Brush a 5- to 6-inch-diameter skillet or crêpe pan with butter and place over gentle heat. Break the quail eggs into it and let them just set without overcooking. Set aside.
4. Pour the cream into a small saucepan, bring to a boil, and reduce over high heat to half its original quality. If it is fresh pasteurized cream it will thicken and become syrupy.
5. Place the plates with the spinach leaves into a preheated 350-degree oven for 45 seconds to 1 minute until spinach is cooked. Remove from oven and place a 3½-inch ring or cookie cutter in the center of one plate. Spoon half the scrambled eggs into it. Transfer ring to the other plate and repeat.
6. Cut the quail eggs into neat shapes with a 1¼-inch ring. Arrange 2 quail eggs on each pile of scrambled eggs. Top each with a spoonful of caviar and pour the thickened cream around the eggs and over the spinach, in a thin stream. Serve immediately.

* Most restaurants have their own sources of special commodities like quail eggs. There are domestically raised quail available to the home cook if she wishes to seek them out. Your state game warden might help you locate a farm or hunting lodge where quail are raised and used in the training of hunting dogs. Where there are quail, there are eggs. Just make sure that your source can guarantee the eggs are fresh.

☆ ☆ # ESTOUFFADE D'AGNEAU ☆ ☆
(Braised lamb)
SERVES 4

Estouffade literally means smothering or suffocating. In this recipe the lamb is baked in a tightly sealed casserole for 3 to 4 hours, until it is so tender it falls off the fork, and melts in your mouth. A wonderfully easy dish. Combine all ingredients, seal the casserole, put it in the oven, and forget it! It's ready when you are. Serve it over buttered fettuccine or other pasta. A big tossed salad and an apple for dessert complete a nutritious meal.

3 pounds boneless leg of lamb, cut into 1½- to 2-inch pieces
1½ cups dry white wine
1 pint beef consommé
1 pint water
1 quart homemade brown gravy
Salt and freshly ground black pepper
1 teaspoon tomato paste
½ pound small onions, peeled
½ pound carrots, trimmed, scraped, and cut into small ovals
½ pound white turnips, peeled
6 ripe tomatoes, fresh or canned, peeled and diced
2 cloves garlic, peeled and thinly sliced
Zest of ½ orange, julienned
1 bay leaf
½ teaspoon dry thyme
3 sprigs parsley

1. Select a heavy enameled cast-iron pot with tight-fitting cover, about 8-quart capacity. Put the meat in the pot and add white wine, consommé, water, gravy, and salt and freshly ground black pepper. You won't need much salt because the consommé is salty.
2. Add remaining ingredients and cover. If the lid does not fit tightly place a round of parchment paper over the ingredients, or seal the lid with a paste made of 2 cups flour and about ¾ cup water. The purpose of this is to prevent the steam from escaping. You want it to rise to the paper or inner lid, condense, and fall back into the stew.
3. Bring the liquid to a simmer over direct heat, then transfer pot to a 350-degree oven. Cook for 2½ to 3½ hours. If you are not ready to serve, reduce oven temperature to 250 degrees and continue to cook until needed.

Le Saint Jean des Prés

112–114 Duane Street
New York, N.Y. 10007   608-2332

Located in an awesome space in TriBeCa, Le Saint Jean des Prés is the first American branch of an eleven-restaurant operation owned by Belgian Albert Michiels. From the omnipresent murals by Belgian artist Eric Boumal to the traditional Belgian pastry cart, Le Saint Jean des Prés could fit into Brussels as easily as it joins the ranks of lower Manhattan's restaurant renaissance. Perhaps the biggest factor is the authenticity guaranteed by the rotation of chefs Mr. Michiels brings to America from Belgium.

The menu, which is the same for lunch and dinner, includes classic Belgian fare such as chicken waterzooi, escargots in puff pastry, and a pâté maison, as well as veal scaloppine with Roquefort sauce, and fish and seafood specialties. Each dish is garnished with mixed salads common in Belgium but hard to find in this country. A very reasonable three-course prix fixe menu beckons regulars, including Belgians, who also come for the extensive Belgian beer stock. Reservations are recommended, and required on Saturday night. Le Saint Jean des Prés has seating for private parties of ten to sixty.

☆ ☆ **CHERRY TOMATOES STUFFED** ☆ ☆
WITH SHRIMP

SERVES 6

The first recipe sent by chef Pascal Fisette might be a delightfully colorful and cooling entrée on a hot day, though at Saint Jean des Prés it is offered as an appetizer.

½ pound raw shrimp
48 cherry tomatoes
1 cup mayonnaise
Chopped parsley
¼ cup lemon juice
Salt and pepper to taste
Lettuce leaves

1. Put shrimp into a saucepan with water to cover. Bring to a boil and simmer for no longer than 3 minutes. Set aside to cool. When cool enough to handle, shell, devein, and chop coarsely.
2. Meanwhile cut a thin slice from stem end of each cherry tomato and discard. With the tip of a teaspoon or a melon ball scoop, remove seeds, leaving a shell. Invert tomatoes on a rack to drain.
3. Combine mayonnaise, shrimp, parsley, lemon juice, and salt and pepper.
4. Stuff each little tomato with the filling and keep cold.
5. Serve 8 tomatoes per person on a bed of lettuce leaves.

☆ ☆ # DUCK WALNUT PÂTÉ ☆ ☆

A 3-pound loaf or terrine

The pâté maison is a rich duck pâté studded with walnuts and redolent of juniper berries. It's an easy one to make at home; all the ingredients are readily available. Serve with French bread or brioche.

1 pound duck meat
½ pound duck liver
¾ pound lean pork
1 medium onion, peeled and finely chopped
11 ounces dry white wine
¼ teaspoon dry thyme or 2 branches fresh thyme
2 eggs
1 teaspoon salt
½ teaspoon freshly ground pepper
½ pound sliced fatback
¼ pound shelled walnuts
2 bay leaves
10 juniper berries

1. A day in advance, grind duck meat, liver, and pork.
2. Sauté the onion in a nonstick pan until transparent. Add wine and thyme and bring to a boil. Remove from heat and let cool.
3. When cool, add to ground meat mixture along with eggs, salt, and pepper. Chill for 12 hours, or overnight.
4. Next day line bottom of a 6-cup terrine or loaf pan with half the slices of fatback. Pack half the pâté mixture into the prepared dish and stud with walnuts. Cover walnuts with remaining pâté mixture and cover the surface with remaining slices of fatback.
5. Place bay leaves and juniper berries on top. Set pan or terrine in a larger pan containing at least 1 inch hot water, and bake in a preheated 450-degree oven for 1 hour.
6. Cool before serving.

Le Veau d'Or

129 East 60th Street
New York, N.Y. 10022   838-8133

One of the most charming, intimate restaurants in the very heart of Manhattan is owned and operated by Gerard Rocheteau and chef Gerard Vidal. There is seldom a vacant table at this legendary establishment, so be sure to call for reservations in advance, otherwise you may find yourself among the many people crowded around the long narrow bar in the center of the room waiting to be seated.

☆ ☆   ## SCALLOPS VEAU D'OR   ☆ ☆
SERVES 4

We suggest scallops Veau d'Or for an appetizer, a beautiful dish of the utmost simplicity. At home it may be made in advance and takes only ten minutes to complete before serving. Use fresh pasteurized cream.

1½ pounds sea scallops
6 medium mushrooms
4 tablespoons soft sweet butter, divided
1 tablespoon chopped shallots
2 teaspoons paprika
½ cup dry white wine or vermouth
1 cup heavy cream (not ultrapasteurized; see page 303)
1 tablespoon flour
Salt, white pepper, and lemon juice
1 tablespoon chopped parsley

1. Wash scallops and cut them into quarters. Put them in a small saucepan and cover with boiling water. Return water to a boil and simmer scallops for 2 minutes only. Drain and set aside.
2. Wash mushrooms, trim, and slice. Set aside.
3. In a small saucepan melt half the butter. Add mushrooms and sauté for about 5 minutes, or until tender. Add shallots and paprika and stir in wine. Bring to a boil and boil until liquid is reduced by half.
4. Add cream and boil rapidly until sauce is the consistency of syrup.
5. While sauce is boiling combine flour with remaining 2 table-spoons butter to make a roux, or paste. Reduce heat and stir the roux into the sauce bit by bit.
6. Return scallops to sauce and simmer for 2 minutes.
7. Correct seasoning with salt, pepper, dash of lemon juice.
8. Divide scallops and sauce into four shells or ceramic dishes, and sprinkle each with a little of the chopped parsley.

☆ ☆   CASSOULET DE CARCASSONNE   ☆ ☆
(Baked beans with duck)
SERVES 8 TO 12

For a main course, nothing can top this famous French bean dish served with the house salad. A cassoulet is not a dish to be tackled by the inexperienced cook. It is a production and considered to be one of the great dishes of the world. But oh, those calories! This dish will take a good part of 2 days to complete, so don't plan to serve it to guests at the last minute.

Pork Stock for Cassoulet (see below)
1½ pounds white beans, preferably Great Northern
1 4½-pound duckling
Salt
½ cup tomato purée
6 ounces fresh unsalted fatback or fat pork
2 tablespoons finely minced garlic
Freshly ground black pepper
2½ pounds lean pork, cut into 1½-inch cubes
Cooked pork skin (see recipe for pork stock)
8 sweet Italian sausages (about 2 pounds) without fennel seeds
½ cup fine dry bread crumbs

1. A day in advance make pork stock. Also put beans in a large bowl and add cold water to cover the beans to a depth of about 2 inches. Let stand overnight.
2. A day in advance prepare the duckling. Cut duckling into pieces as follows: two legs, two thighs, and two breast halves. Cut each breast crosswise into three pieces of equal size. There should be a total of 10 pieces. Trim away and reserve all excess fat. Put pieces of duck into a bowl, sprinkle with 1 tablespoon salt, and refrigerate overnight.
3. Next day: Drain the beans and empty into a large 4-quart casserole. Add cold water to a depth of about half an inch above the top of the beans. Cover and bring to a boil on top of stove. Uncover and let boil about 5 minutes. Drain well.
4. Return beans to the casserole and add 5 cups pork stock. Bring to a boil. The beans must simmer slowly throughout the cooking period. Stir in the tomato purée.
5. Put the fatback and garlic into container of a food processor and process until a smooth paste is formed. Scrape this paste into the beans. Add salt and pepper to taste. Cover and simmer over low heat.
6. Put reserved scraps of duck fat into a large skillet and cook, stirring often, until rendered of their fat. Discard solids. Pour off and reserve all but 2 tablespoons of the duck fat. Set the fat aside.
7. Put the duck pieces in the 2 tablespoons duck fat remaining in the skillet and cook until golden brown on each side, about 5 minutes a side. Pour off all but ¼ cup of the fat. Set duck pieces aside.
8. To the fat remaining in the skillet add the pork, one batch at a time. Do not crowd the meat cubes or they will not brown. Brown one batch on all sides. As they brown transfer them to a bowl and continue browning the meat cubes until all are cooked, adding a little more fat to the skillet if necessary. Add the pork cubes and duck pieces to the cassoulet. Leave the fat in the pan and set aside.
9. Cut enough of the pork skin into ½-inch cubes to make 1½ cups. Add to the casserole.
10. As the cassoulet cooks, uncover occasionally and stir. When it has cooked for 2 hours, uncover and continue to cook.

11. Prick sausages all over with tines of a fork and add them to the fat in the skillet. Brown on one side, turn and brown lightly on the other side. Cover and cook for about 10 minutes or longer if necessary until sausages are thoroughly cooked through.
12. Preheat broiler to high heat, then turn to low.
13. Transfer the cassoulet to a heatproof casserole for serving. Arrange the sausages attractively on top and sprinkle with bread crumbs. Bring cassoulet to a boil on top of stove. Pour the reserved duck fat over the surface and place under broiler heat for about 20 minutes.

PORK STOCK FOR CASSOULET
2 QUARTS

1 pig's knuckle
½ pound fresh pork skin
3 sprigs parsley
½ bay leaf
1 small onion, peeled and stuck with 1 clove
6 peppercorns, crushed
12 cups water
Salt to taste

1. Combine all ingredients in a kettle and bring to a boil.
2. Simmer uncovered for 2 hours. Strain, reserving the pork skin for the cassoulet.

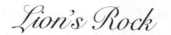

Lion's Rock

316 East 77th Street
New York, N.Y. 10021   988-3610

No matter how many times you read about it, until you actually see the garden at this place, you can't imagine what a paradox it is. Take one looming rock—part of the outcropping that runs under most of Manhattan—surround it with some beautiful plants, and then light it in the best theatrical sense, and you'll have an idea of what the patio at Lion's Rock looks like. The inside is a little less dramatic unless you find some drama in a stuffed lion's head over a fireplace, but inside or out what you get is a sense of comfort. This restaurant has been around for at least a decade and it has a loyal following, especially for Sunday brunch on a beautiful spring day. Brunch is your choice of eggs Benedict, huevos rancheros, a wide selection of omelets, or the house favorite—poached eggs in puff pastry with hollandaise sauce. At lunch and dinner there is a choice of salads and fish and meat dishes. The simpler the better is a good rule here.

☆ ☆ POACHED SNAILS IN BURGUNDY ☆ ☆ GARLIC BUTTER

SERVES 1

Kenneth Adams, manager of Lion's Rock, sent us this exciting appetizer created by its chef, Steven Christianson. The recipe may easily be doubled.

1 teaspoon minced garlic
1 teaspoon chopped shallots
6 tablespoons sweet butter, divided
5 canned French snails
2 shiitake mushrooms, sliced
1 ounce burgundy wine
1 teaspoon minced fresh parsley
4 toast points
1 sprig dill

1. Sauté garlic and shallots in 2 tablespoons of the butter for 1 to 2 minutes, being careful not to let the garlic burn.
2. Add snails and mushrooms and sauté for 2 to 3 minutes longer, shaking pan almost constantly.
3. Add burgundy and boil until wine is reduced by half. Then whip in remaining butter without letting the sauce boil. Add chopped parsley.
4. Place snails in center of plate, pour sauce over, and arrange toast points around the outside of the plate. Garnish with the sprig of dill.

☆ ☆ IRISH SEA SCALLOPS AND ROE ☆ ☆ BEURRE ROUGE WITH DILL

SERVES 1

At certain seasons of the year, the roe is found attached to the side of the scallop. Be careful not to discard it when washing the scallops.

7 sea scallops with roe attached
Flour to coat
Salt and pepper to taste
2 tablespoons clarified butter
2 ounces (1 serving) cooked fusilli pasta (see Note)
2 tablespoons lightly salted butter
Beurre Rouge (see below)
½ teaspoon chopped fresh dill

1. Wash scallops and drain well. Coat with flour mixed with salt and pepper and sauté in the hot clarified butter for about 1½ minutes on each side. Remove from pan and set aside.
2. Sauté the cooked fusilli in the lightly salted butter until warmed through.
3. Arrange fusilli in center of plate, place scallops around it, and spoon the beurre rouge over the scallops. Sprinkle with dill.

BEURRE ROUGE

2 tablespoons burgundy wine
1 teaspoon chopped shallots
½ tablespoon red wine vinegar
½ teaspoon minced garlic
1 tablespoon chopped parsley
3 tablespoons sweet butter
Salt and freshly ground black pepper to taste

1. Into a small saucepan combine burgundy, shallots, vinegar, garlic, and parsley. Bring to a boil and reduce liquid by half. Gradually whip in butter over low heat without letting the sauce boil. Season to taste with salt and pepper.

Note:

Fusilli is spaghetti twisted like a corkscrew in a long shape, quite different from the tight short spiral correctly know as rote, or "wheels." In Italian markets fusilli may be purchased plain or flavored with spinach or tomato. At Lion's Rock they mix all three flavors and colors.

Lou Siegel's

209 West 38th Street
New York, N.Y. 10018   921-4433

Since 1917, New York's garment center has been the neighborhood for what is now an institution: Lou Siegel's kosher restaurant. Edward Share took over the restaurant in 1979; today, his son Myles manages the bustling 350-seat operation. Local business people and shoppers come to Lou Siegel's for the traditional chopped liver, stuffed cabbage, gefilte fish, and boiled beef flanken. But the menu also features less usual kosher fare such as Long Island duckling and prime lamb chops. Clearly, patrons come here as much for the quality of the food as for the dietary restrictions of the restaurant. Homemade pies (chocolate cream is the hands-down favorite), pastries, and cakes are the stars of the dessert wagon. Wines are kosher: the house variety is Kedam Chablis, available by the glass or carafe.

☆ ☆   # STUFFED CABBAGE   ☆ ☆

10 STUFFED LEAVES

Lou Siegel's stuffed cabbage is one of the best in the city, if not *the* best. The chef offered a great method for removing leaves from a head of cabbage without tearing them (see below).

> *1 large head green cabbage*
> *·   1 cup tomato purée*
> *1 cup peeled whole tomatoes*
> *1 cup water*
> *1 medium onion, peeled and chopped*
> *1 apple, peeled and chopped*
> *½ cup golden raisins*
> *¼ cup sugar*
> *2 tablespoons apricot jam or marmalade*
> *1½ pounds ground beef*
> *¾ cup uncooked rice*
> *Freshly ground white pepper to taste*

1. Freeze cabbage head as described below. When it is thawed, carefully remove the large outer leaves (you'll need 10 of them for the rolls). Chop remaining cabbage and with it line the bottom of a heavy 4-quart pot or kettle.
2. To the chopped cabbage, add tomato purée, whole peeled tomatoes, water, chopped onion and apple, raisins, sugar, and jam or marmalade.
3. Combine the ground beef with the rice and pepper.
4. Put about 1/10 of the meat mixture in the center of each cabbage leaf, fold over the bottom, fold edges to center, and roll loosely.
5. Arrange stuffed leaves in the pot on top of the tomato mixture, and weight them down with an inverted heavy plate. Cover with the pot lid and bring to a boil. Remove cover and simmer for 1¾ hours, shaking pot and stirring occasionally.
6. Remove cooked cabbage rolls from pot and serve 2 per person with a large spoonful of the pot gravy over the rolls.

Note:
     Cut out core from cabbage and place the head in the freezer for the day. Remove from freezer in enough time to allow the leaves to thaw. The now wilted leaves may be easily removed.

Lutèce

249 East 50th Street
New York, N.Y. 10022   752-2225

For haute cuisine, impeccable service, and a pristine setting, New York's Lutèce is hard, if not impossible, to surpass. André Soltner, owner-chef since 1972, and his charming wife, Simone, personally oversee every detail, which makes Lutèce the epitome of a fine French restaurant. Each of the several rooms in this cozy restaurant, housed on two floors of a narrow brownstone, has its own individual charm. Be sure to take along plenty of cash or your credit card. Reservations are essential.

☆ ☆ ## BLANQUETTE DE SOLE ET ST. JACQUES ☆ ☆

SERVES 4

1½ tablespoons butter
2 tablespoons flour
1¼ cups boiling fish stock
A few stamens of saffron
½ cup fresh pasteurized whipping cream (not ultrapasteurized;
see page 303)
3 ounces (6 tablespoons) sweet butter
Julienne des legumes (see step 3)
1 pound sliced fillets of sole, free of bone
½ pound sea scallops, sliced
Salt and white pepper

168

1. In a medium saucepan melt the 1½ tablespoons butter, stir in flour, and mix to a smooth paste. Remove saucepan from heat and add fish stock and saffron. Whisk over medium heat until sauce is smooth and thickened, then simmer gently for 30 minutes, stirring occasionally.
2. Stir in the cream and gradually whisk in all but 1 tablespoon of the sweet butter. Set aside.
3. For the julienne des legumes, cut carrots, celery, and leeks into thin lengthwise strips, about ⅓ cup for each vegetable, for a total of 1 cup of mixed vegetables. Sauté the vegetables in the remaining 1 tablespoon sweet butter for about 5 minutes, or until barely tender.
4. Put the prepared fish and scallops into a 1½-quart flameproof gratin or casserole dish and strain the sauce over them. Add the cooked vegetables, bring to a boil, and cook over low heat for 4 minutes. Season with salt and white pepper and serve hot in the dish in which the fish was cooked.

☆ ☆   # COQ SAUTÉ À LA BIÈRE D'ALSACE   ☆ ☆

(Chicken sautéed in beer)

SERVES 4

This delightful dish is an easy one for the home chef to make. The chicken should be as fresh as possible. Fine noodles are the perfect accompaniment.

1 chicken, 4 pounds or more, cut into serving portions
Salt and pepper
3 tablespoons sweet butter
1 onion, peeled and chopped
1 clove garlic, peeled and chopped
1 bay leaf
2 cloves
3 cups beer
1 generous tablespoon butter
1 tablespoon flour
1 cup heavy cream
Pinch nutmeg
3 beaten egg yolks
Garniture of sliced truffles and sautéed mushroom caps (optional)

1. Sprinkle chicken pieces lightly with salt and pepper and sauté them in a large skillet in the 3 tablespoons butter over medium heat until golden on all sides.
2. Add onion, garlic, bay leaf, and cloves. Add beer and bring to a boil. Simmer the chicken for 20 to 30 minutes, or until drumsticks are tender.
3. Remove chicken to a serving platter and keep warm. Cook liquid remaining in the pan over high heat for 5 to 6 minutes, or until reduced one-third in quantity. Strain and reserve. You will have about 1 cup.
4. In a second saucepan melt remaining generous tablespoon butter, blend in the flour, and gradually stir in the reserved broth. Add the heavy cream and a pinch of nutmeg and thicken the sauce by whisking it into the beaten egg yolks.
5. Return sauce to saucepan and reheat gradually, whisking constantly. Be very careful that the sauce does not reach a boil or it will curdle.
6. Pour the sauce over the chicken and garnish, if you like, with truffles and sautéed mushroom caps. Serve with fine noodles.

☆　☆　　　　　# TARTE LUTÈCE　　　　　☆　☆

SERVES 6

Just one of the many fabulous creations of André Soltner, a man generally considered the finest chef in America.

Pâte à Tarte or Pâte Sucrée (see page 212)
8 Golden Delicious or Granny Smith apples
Juice of 1 lemon
¼ pound (1 stick) sweet butter
8 tablespoons sugar
½ cup heavy cream

1. Follow directions for making the pastry, or use your own favorite recipe. Roll it out into a flat disk 9 inches in diameter. Transfer to a baking sheet and bake in a preheated 375-degree oven for 12 to 15 minutes or until crisp and golden. Remove from oven and set aside. Leave oven on.

2. Peel, core, and slice the apples about ¾ inch thick. Squeeze lemon juice on them to prevent them from turning brown.
3. Put the butter and sugar in an ovenproof skillet over high heat and cook, stirring constantly, until sugar melts to a golden caramel color.
4. As the color deepens to a rich caramel, add the heavy cream and cook, stirring, for 2 minutes longer.
5. Add the apples and toss and mix until each slice is coated with the caramelized sugar. Cover the skillet with a piece of aluminum foil and place it in the 375-degree oven for 10 minutes.
6. Remove pan from oven. Remove apples with a slotted spoon and arrange them on the crust in a single circular layer beginning with the outer edge and working toward the center.
7. Heat the caramel remaining in the pan for 2 minutes and pour or drizzle it on top of the apples.

☆ ☆   # MOUSSE DE BANANES   ☆ ☆

SERVES 6

And still another light, delightful dessert from the generous chef. It's one you'll want to serve frequently at home.

6 bananas
Juice of 1 lemon
½ cup sugar
1 cup heavy cream

1. Cut the bananas in halves lengthwise. Remove the fruit without breaking the skins. Set aside 6 of the most perfect skins or "boats."
2. Purée the bananas by pushing through a sieve with a wooden spoon into a bowl. Mix the lemon and sugar into the purée. Chill.
3. Whip the cream until very thick and fold it into the chilled purée. Fit a pastry bag with a ½-inch star tube. Fill the bag with the mousse, secure the top, and pipe the mousse into the banana skins with a rotating motion of the wrist.

Manhattan Chili Company

302 Bleecker Street
New York, N.Y. 10014   206-7163

When aspiring actor Michael McLaughlin realized he was getting better reviews and more applause for his food than for his acting, he followed his calling. A native of Colorado, McLaughlin managed the Silver Palate store on Manhattan's West Side and also coauthored the store's best-selling cookbook. Then, with Bruce Sterman and Luba Pincus, McLaughlin ventured into the restaurant business, offering popular Tex-Mex fare in a refreshing adobe-pink and green setting.

Not surprisingly the focus is on chili, at least six different kinds. McLaughlin says the most ordered variety is "Numero Uno," a beef and pork combo enlivened with sweet chile, cinnamon, oregano, cumin, and cocoa. Other popular dishes include guacamole, homemade salsa (a blend of hand-chopped tomato, cilantro, and jalapeño hot peppers) with chips; and nachos, tortilla chips topped with McLaughlin's own blend of cheeses, refried beans, and fresh chipotle chiles, roasted to smoky perfection.

Desserts include fresh orange cheesecake and margarita pudding. And speaking of margaritas, they're available in two forms here, both made from ground whole lime peels, to balance the drink's innate sweetness: frozen for those who prefer their margaritas refreshingly slushy, or straight up the way the purists enjoy them. Beer is also in demand and McLaughlin stocks several brands. He also features a variety of California wines.

☆ ☆   # SEVICHE   ☆ ☆

Serves 8 to 10 as an appetizer;
5 to 6 as a main course

There are many versions of seviche, the dish of raw, marinated seafood, some of which McLaughlin thinks are unpleasantly sour, masking the sweet taste of the fish. He avoids this by discarding the lime juice after it has "cooked" the fish and replacing it with a light jalapeño vinegar and olive oil dressing.

1½ pounds very fresh sole or flounder fillets
¼ pound bay scallops
¼ pound large shrimp, shelled and deveined
¾ cup fresh lime juice (from 4 to 5 limes)
¼ cup liquid drained from vinegar-packed canned jalapeños
(labeled "en escabeche")
2 tablespoons good quality olive oil
¾ cup finely chopped cilantro, also called fresh coriander
or Chinese parsley
2 or 3 firm, ripe tomatoes
½ cup finely diced red onion
Salt (optional)
2 heads of romaine lettuce

1. A day in advance, trim fish fillets, discarding any tough or bony bits. Cut the flesh into ½-inch cubes. Rinse the scallops and drain well. Cut the shrimp crosswise into thirds.
2. In a medium-sized glass or ceramic bowl combine the seafood and the lime juice. Cover and refrigerate overnight, stirring once or twice.
3. Next day, drain the marinated seafood and return it to the bowl. Stir in jalapeño liquid, olive oil, and cilantro, and return the seviche to the refrigerator.
4. Just before serving, halve the tomatoes, squeeze out liquid and seeds, and dice. Stir tomatoes and diced onion into seviche and season with salt if you wish, although the dish doesn't need it.
5. To serve, separate the romaine into leaves, reserving the coarse, dark leaves for another use. Line plates with several of the pale green or yellow inner leaves and mound the seviche on the leaves. Spoon any accumulated juices from the bowl over the seviche and serve at once, offering guests a pepper mill.

☆ ☆ ABILENE CHORAL SOCIETY AND ☆ ☆
MUSIC GUILD CHILI

SERVES 8

In other words, a gourmet chili for tenderfeet and other genteel types. Mild enough for a baby.

3 pounds ground beef, preferably coarse or "chili-grind" (see Note)
1 tablespoon salt or to taste
6 tablespoons olive oil, divided
2 medium yellow onions, peeled and coarsely chopped
(about 4 cups)
3 large stalks celery, coarsely chopped
4 medium cloves garlic, peeled and minced
1 35-ounce can Italian-style plum tomatoes,
crushed and well drained
4 cups chicken stock or broth
1½ cups dry red wine
4 tablespoons mild pure chili powder (see Note)
1½ tablespoons dry sweet basil
1 tablespoon ground toasted cumin (see Note)
½ teaspoon cayenne pepper (optional)
2 large red bell peppers, cored and diced
2 large green bell peppers, cored and diced
2 16-ounce cans red kidney beans, drained
2 to 3 tablespoons cornmeal as thickener (optional)

1. Set a large flameproof casserole over medium heat. Add the beef and salt and cook uncovered, stirring often, until the meat loses all pink color, about 20 minutes. Do not brown.
2. Meanwhile, in a large, heavy skillet, heat 3 tablespoons olive oil. Add the onions, celery, and garlic. Cover and cook over moderate heat, stirring occasionally, until translucent and very soft, about 20 minutes.
3. Scrape the onion mixture into the casserole with the meat. Add the tomatoes, chicken stock, red wine, chili powder, basil, cumin, and cayenne pepper, if desired.
4. Meanwhile, in a large skillet, heat the remaining 3 table-spoons olive oil. When it is very hot add the diced red and green peppers and cook, tossing and stirring, for about 5 min-utes, or until the peppers are lightly browned.
5. Correct seasoning of chili, and add the sautéed peppers. Con-tinue to simmer, stirring occasionally, for 30 minutes.

6. Add the drained beans to the chili. To thicken the chili further, if you wish, stir in the cornmeal 1 tablespoon at a time. Do not degrease until absolutely necessary; much of the chili's flavor and heat are concentrated there. The cornmeal will bind the melted fat into the chili, making it invisible. Simmer another 5 minutes before serving. Like all chilis, this one tastes better the next day. So plan ahead if you can.
7. To serve, reheat until steaming, stirring frequently. Ladle chili into deep heavy bowls and serve with an array of appropriate garnishes—sour cream, shredded Cheddar and jack cheeses, chopped onions, tomatoes, scallions, avocado, jalapeños, and so on.

Note:

Chili-ground beef: This is meat ground as coarsely as that for Italian sausage. In some parts of the country it is found in supermarkets alongside the regular-grind beef, while in other areas health authorities have deemed it unsafe, since chips of bone can potentially pass through the holes of the larger blade. To us the gamble is worth it, since the coarse beef makes a chili of superior texture. Order in advance from a reputable butcher and make it very clear you want the meat well trimmed before he begins grinding. An alternative is to buy top round and dice it fine yourself. With a good knife and a chopping board, it takes only a few minutes.

Supermarket chili powders often contain cumin, oregano, garlic powder, and other flavorings you may not want. Buy a good, plain chili powder, which leaves you in control of whatever else seasons your chili. Our personal favorite is produced by the Santa Cruz Chili and Spice Company, Box 177, Tumacocori, AZ 65540. The mild powder marketed by the Pecos River Spice Company is also a good choice and is widely available.

Whole cumin seeds are available from spice companies and some supermarkets. Toast them in a small cast-iron skillet over low heat, stirring constantly, until they are a deep brown color. (To prevent burning, use at least ½ cup seeds.) Store them in an air-tight jar and grind them as needed, measuring after grinding.

Maxwell's Plum

1181 First Avenue (at 64th Street)
New York, N.Y. 10021   628-2100

Maxwell's Plum is an institution. In the sixties it was famed as a meeting place for singles. In the seventies it was known as a great place to take children. And in the eighties it is still a wonderful place to watch the scene on the Upper East Side. The restaurant is usually noisy and crowded, so don't plan any quiet or intimate conversations here, just eat, drink, and be merry. Shish kabob served atop a generous serving of rice is one of the most popular entrées. It's also a spectacular dish to serve at home. At Maxwell's Plum it is served with a broiled tomato and a lemon basket filled with parsley.

☆ ☆ MAXWELL'S PLUM SHISH KABOB ☆ ☆ WITH RICE ISTANBUL

SERVES 4

1 medium onion, peeled and sliced
3 cloves garlic, peeled and crushed
1 stalk celery, chopped
¼ teaspoon cumin seed
¾ cup cider vinegar
½ cup lemon juice
½ cup vegetable oil
1 teaspoon salt
½ teaspoon coarsely ground pepper
2½ to 3 pounds boned lamb from the leg
2 large sweet onions, peeled and quartered
4 medium mushroom caps
4 green peppers, halved, seeded, and quartered
Rice Istanbul (see below)

1. A day ahead make a marinade by combining in a glass or enamel bowl the sliced onion, garlic, celery, cumin, vinegar, lemon juice, oil, salt and pepper.
2. Cut the lamb into 1¼-inch squares, add to the marinade, cover, and refrigerate for 24 hours, turning lamb pieces several times.
3. Next day blanch the onion quarters in simmering water for 5 minutes. Drain.
4. Thread a mushroom, then a pepper, then an onion section on long skewers alternately with 5 pieces of the marinated lamb.
5. Broil the kabobs 4 inches from source of heat for 5 minutes. Turn, baste with some of the marinade, and broil for another 5 minutes. Turn and baste again and broil for 5 minutes longer. Do not overcook the lamb. It should be slightly pink on the inside.
6. Serve with rice Istanbul and garnish each plate with a broiled tomato and parsley.

☆ ☆   # RICE ISTANBUL   ☆ ☆
SERVES 4

This is really a pilaf and is the correct accompaniment to the lamb dish, which originated in Armenia, where pilafs and pilaus are daily fare.

1 chicken liver
2 teaspoons butter
1 large onion, peeled and chopped
2 tablespoons vegetable oil, divided
2 tablespoons blanched, slivered almonds
2 tablespoons golden raisins
2 cups converted raw rice
3 cups water
¼ teaspoon aniseeds
½ teaspoon salt
¼ teaspoon cayenne pepper
Pinch saffron stamens
2 tablespoons melted butter
2 tablespoons diced pimiento

1. Sauté chicken liver in the 2 teaspoons butter in a heatproof skillet or casserole. Remove the liver and chop it finely.
2. To the butter remaining in the dish add 1 tablespoon oil and sauté the onion until lightly brown. Add almonds and sauté until almonds are brown.
3. Add chicken liver, raisins, and rice. Mix well, pour in water, and add aniseeds, salt, cayenne pepper, saffron, and the remaining 1 tablespoon oil.
4. Bring the water to a full boil, stir once, cover tightly and put into a preheated moderate 350-degree oven for 30 minutes, or until all the water is absorbed and rice is tender. Or it may be cooked over direct heat if you have a tight-fitting cover for the dish. Reduce heat to very low and simmer for 30 minutes.
5. Remove from heat and spoon into serving dish or platter. Pour melted butter over the top and garnish with the pimiento.

Mitali West

296 Bleecker Street
New York, N.Y. 10014 989-1367

In the late seventies, Mitali joined the ranks of reasonably priced Indian restaurants on East 6th Street in the East Village; several years later, Mitali West opened on the corner of Bleecker Street and 7th Avenue. Both restaurants specialize in Northern Indian food, milder and more meat-oriented than that of the Southern region of India. Although Mitali West is a bit more lavish than its parent operation, the two menus are very similar.

Owners Abu Ahmed and his uncle work with their North Indian chef to offer an extensive array of traditional preparations including dansak curry (lamb, beef, chicken, or ground meat simmered with lentils); dakhee (marinated quail stuffed with meat and almonds); and murgha tikka muslam (chunks of tender chicken in a creamy, almond-studded sauce).

To begin your meal try the meat or vegetable samosas, little turnovers that are dipped in a sweet and sour sauce. Desserts, such as kheer (a creamy rice pudding with dried fruits and rose water), rasmali (cardamom-scented cottage cheese balls cooked in milk with rose water), and firni (cornstarch pudding with coconut and rose water), are all fitting endings to a multiflavored meal, especially accompanied by a cup of spiced tea.

Although Indian beer is sold at Mitali West, light beer and Japanese Kirin are more popular choices among diners. A California Chablis is also available by the glass or carafe.

☆ ☆   # MURGHA TIKKA MUSLAM   ☆ ☆
SERVES 6

This is a fascinating recipe. A boneless chicken is marinated in herbs and spices and barbecued over charcoal. When cooked, it is then cut into cubes and sautéed for a few minutes with cream and almonds. Everyone, familiar or unfamiliar with Indian cooking, seems to agree that it's a truly delicious dish.

1 boned roasting chicken (4 pounds boned), or an equal amount of boneless chicken parts
1 large onion, peeled and finely minced or ground
½ teaspoon salt
1 teaspoon paprika
2 tablespoons minced fresh ginger
1 whole head of garlic, smashed and peeled
1 tablespoon turmeric
¼ teaspoon red chili powder
1½ tablespoons ground coriander, preferably freshly ground
¼ tablespoon ground cumin, preferably freshly ground
¼ teaspoon powdered cinnamon
¼ teaspoon ground cardamom
4 tablespoons lemon juice
½ tablespoon ground nutmeg
1 cup vegetable or olive oil
8 ounces plain yogurt
1 stick (4 ounces) butter, clarified (Indian ghee)
1 cup dairy sour cream
1 cup blanched, sliced almonds
1 tablespoon minced fresh coriander or parsley

1. Have your butcher bone the chicken for you if you do not know how. There is no better time than now, however, to try this culinary feat, which is not difficult providing you have a sharp boning knife. And in this recipe it doesn't matter if you botch the job since the chicken is going to be cut into chunks, not re-formed into its original shape.
2. Put all remaining ingredients except the butter, sour cream, almonds, and coriander in a large bowl. Mix thoroughly and place the boned chicken in it to marinate for 6 hours, turning and spooning the marinade over it occasionally.

3. Cook the chicken in a charcoal grill for 10 minutes on each side or roast it in a preheated 450-degree oven for 20 minutes.
4. Remove chicken from heat and, when cool enough to handle, chop into bite-sized cubes.
5. In a large skillet melt the butter and add the cubed chicken. Spoon a little of the marinade over it and sauté for about 4 minutes, stirring frequently and adding more of the marinade if needed.
6. Add the sour cream and almonds and cook, stirring, for about 5 minutes longer.
7. Serve in a casserole or oblong serving dish garnished with the chopped coriander or parsley.

☆ ☆   # KHEER   ☆ ☆

SERVES 2 TO 3

A famous Indian dish made from milk, rice, and dried fruits, flavored with cardamom and rose water.

4 tablespoons converted raw rice
1 cup milk
1 tablespoon chopped nuts
1 tablespoon mixed dried fruit and peel, chopped
1 tablespoon raisins
6 tablespoons sugar
1/2 teaspoon freshly ground cardamom or whole seeds
1/2 teaspoon ground pistachios
2 tablespoons rose water

1. Rinse the rice in several changes of cool water, then cover with water and soak for 10 minutes.
2. Meanwhile simmer the milk in a saucepan with the nuts, dried fruits, and raisins. When boiling, gradually add the rice and cook, stirring, until the mixture becomes thick.
3. Stir in sugar and cardamom and cook over low heat for 4 to 5 minutes, stirring occasionally. Serve in sherbet glasses, hot or cold, as preferred, topped with pistachios and rose water.

Odeon

145 West Broadway
New York, N.Y. 10013   233-0507

Although this place looks like an upscale cafeteria, one glance at the menu will convince you that the food is far from steam tables filled with soggy vegetables and glutinous gravy. Here there is a mix of nouvelle and modern American cuisine, and traditional steak frites or sautéed calf's liver. Odeon is about as close as New York gets to an oversized French bistro. During lunch you'll find the Wall Street crowd in early, neighborhood people later, while the dinner hour attracts people from all over town. Come for late supper and pick up the next day's New York Times *on your way out, compliments of the establishment. The food is delicious— homemade ravioli with wild mushrooms is a favorite, as are most of the specials. For dessert leave room for the chef's chocolate cake or a luscious crème brûlée.*

☆ ☆ **SALMON IN PUFF PASTRY WITH** ☆ ☆
SPINACH AND CAVIAR
SERVES 4

This first recipe from Odeon will show the quality of the menu offerings. It's an entrée that is much in demand.

¾ pound puff pastry
1 pound skinless, boneless salmon fillet
Butter to coat baking sheet
Salt and pepper
Shallot Sauce (see below)
2 tablespoons butter
1½ pounds fresh spinach, cleaned and washed
2 ounces American sturgeon caviar
½ cup chopped chives
Parsley for garnish

1. Preheat oven to 350 degrees.
2. Roll out pastry into a rectangle approximately 12 inches by 16 inches and ¹⁄₁₆ inch thick. Prick all over with tines of a fork, transfer to a baking sheet, and let rest for half an hour. Then bake in the preheated oven for 35 minutes, or until golden brown.
3. Cut salmon into 8 thin escalopes of 2 ounces each, making them as wide and flat as possible. Place them on a lightly buttered baking sheet, sprinkle with salt and pepper, and place under a hot broiler for about 1 minute, or just until they lose their raw look. Set aside.
4. Prepare the sauce and keep warm.
5. Cut pastry into 8 equal squares, approximately 3 by 3 inches.
6. Melt the 2 tablespoons butter and in it sauté the spinach for about 4 minutes, stirring and tossing frequently, until cooked through. Season lightly with a little salt and pepper.
7. To serve: Place a square of puff pastry on each of 4 warm plates. Divide half the spinach into 4 equal portions and place on top of the pastry squares. Put a piece of salmon on top of the spinach. Stir the caviar and chives into the shallot sauce and pour a spoonful of the sauce over each piece of salmon on the four plates.
8. Garnish with parsley and serve immediately.

SHALLOT SAUCE

ABOUT 1 CUP

2 shallots, peeled and minced
1 tablespoon butter, plus 6 ounces (1¼ sticks)
½ cup white wine
¼ cup heavy cream (not ultrapasteurized; see page 303)
Juice of ½ lemon
Pinch of cayenne

1. Cook the shallots in the 1 tablespoon of butter until translucent but not brown. Add the wine and boil until wine is reduced to almost nothing.
2. Add the cream and boil again, reducing until sauce is thick and bubbly.
3. Remove sauce from the heat and gradually whisk in the 6 ounces of butter, a bit at a time. If the sauce cools, return it to the heat until warm but not hot. You don't want the butter melted, just soft and fluffy. Continue whisking until all the butter is incorporated, then whisk in the lemon juice and cayenne. Set aside.

☆ ☆   # CRÈME BRÛLÉE   ☆ ☆
SERVES 8

This favorite dessert is flavored with Amaretto.

1 quart heavy cream
1 vanilla bean, split
10 egg yolks
½ cup granulated sugar
2 tablespoons (1 ounce) Amaretto
8 teaspoons superfine sugar

1. In a saucepan bring the heavy cream to a boil with the vanilla bean. Cover and remove from the heat. Let the vanilla bean steep in the cream for 20 minutes, then remove.
2. Beat egg yolks with the sugar until sugar is dissolved and the mixture is thick and pale in color. Gradually beat in the hot cream.
3. Let the cream cool, then stir in the Amaretto.
4. Fill 8 porcelain custard molds to the top with the cream mixture. Arrange the filled molds in a metal pan filled ¾ full of hot water. Place in a preheated 250-degree oven on the lower rack and bake for about 45 minutes or until the custard is just set.
5. Remove creams from the oven, cool, and refrigerate.
6. When the cream is cold, sprinkle 1 teaspoon sugar over the top of each custard, coating the entire surface. Place under broiler until the sugar caramelizes. Watch carefully that the sugar does not burn. Serve immediately or refrigerate until ready to serve.

Oyster Bar & Restaurant

Grand Central Station (lower level)
New York, N.Y. 10017   490-6650

For years the Oyster Bar in Grand Central Station was accepted as one of the great seafood places in New York City. Then, gradually, it seemed to go downhill and fall into disrepair, and eventually it closed. Many people were sad to see its demise, but accepted it in the spirit that, like railroads themselves, it had had its day.

Jerry Brody, however, was willing to stake his reputation and his money to disprove this. He restored the restaurant's decor and reestablished the original menu, complete with dozens of varieties of clams, the famous oyster stew, and the popular fried clams. Jerry has happily proved that people will seek out a good restaurant, even if it's off the beaten track or in the basement of a railroad station.

 ☆ ☆ ## OYSTER STEW ☆ ☆

1 SERVING

The oyster stew here is the best in New York and is so simple to make you can enjoy it at home or anyplace where fresh oysters are available. The only trick is not to overcook the oysters.

9 freshly shucked oysters with their liquor
2 tablespoons clam broth
1 tablespoon plus 1 teaspoon butter
¼ teaspoon paprika
⅛ teaspoon celery salt
1 tablespoon Worcestershire sauce
1 cup half and half
Paprika

1. Put all ingredients except the teaspoon butter into a saucepan and bring to a simmer. Watch carefully and remove from the heat the moment the edges of the oysters begin to curl.
2. Pour into a warm soup plate and top with the teaspoon butter and a sprinkling of paprika. Serve piping hot.

☆ ☆ # FRIED CLAMS ☆ ☆
SERVES 4

Here's how to make light, crispy, thinly breaded, delicious fried clams. Nothing could be easier, provided you have a good clam shucker.

4 dozen soft-shell clams, such as Ipswich or steamers
4 tablespoons flour
1 egg
2 tablespoons milk
1½ cups unsalted soda cracker crumbs
Salt
Pepper
Vegetable oil for frying

1. Scrub clams with a stiff brush to remove sand. Open with a very sharp knife or a clam opener, reserving the clam liquor for another use.
2. Drain clams on paper towels, then coat lightly with flour and shake off excess.
3. In a shallow dish beat egg and milk. Dip clams, one at a time, first into the egg mixture, then into cracker crumbs seasoned with salt and pepper. Shake off excess crumbs and place clams on paper towels until all are coated. Fry immediately.
4. Heat vegetable oil in a deep skillet to a depth of 2 inches. An electric frying pan is excellent. Heat oil to 350 to 375 degrees, or until a cube of bread turns golden in 1 minute.
5. Fry clams a few at a time for about 3 minutes or until golden. Remove with a slotted spoon, drain on paper towels, and serve immediately with lemon wedges and tartar or cocktail sauce.

☆ ☆ DIJON DRESSING FOR MUSSELS ☆ ☆ OR FRIED FISH

ABOUT 2 CUPS

This savory sauce is perfect with mussels but can be served with any breaded or fried fish.

> *1 egg yolk*
> *1 hard-cooked egg, chopped*
> *3 tablespoons Dijon mustard*
> *¼ teaspoon freshly ground black pepper*
> *½ teaspoon salt*
> *Pinch sugar*
> *1 tablespoon minced onion*
> *2 teaspoons minced shallots*
> *1 clove garlic, minced*
> *2 teaspoons dry oregano*
> *1 teaspoon dry sweet basil or a few drops of pesto (see page 301)*
> *2 teaspoons finely chopped parsley*
> *1 cup olive oil*
> *3 tablespoons dry white wine*
> *3 tablespoons white vinegar*

1. In a small bowl combine egg yolk with hard-cooked egg, mustard, pepper, salt, sugar, onion, shallots, garlic, and herbs.
2. In a large measuring cup combine olive oil, white wine, and vinegar. Gradually beat oil mixture into egg and herb mixture until it thickens and holds together.

Parma Restaurant

1404 Third Avenue (between 79th and 80th streets)
New York, N.Y. 10021   535-3520

You may wonder why this restaurant is so busy. The decor is non-existent, the atmosphere could be called harried, and the menu is simple. It's basically a neighborhood Italian restaurant and the patrons come for the food, no surprises, no frills, just good pasta, fish, and old-time reliables like spinach with garlic or roasted peppers. So even though the dress code is casual, the noise level high, and there is usually a wait, this is where people go for a good Italian meal.

☆ ☆ ## ROASTED FRESH PEPPERS ☆ ☆

SERVES 6

6 very ripe red peppers
½ cup olive oil
2 cloves garlic, peeled and halved

1. Preheat broiler. Place peppers on their sides on a broiler pan and broil 2 inches from source of heat for 15 to 20 minutes, turning as often as necessary, until skins are charred all over.
2. Remove peppers from broiler and immediately enclose them in a paper bag until cool. When cool, slip off the thin skins and remove stems, seeds, and ribs.
3. Cut peppers into thin strips and put into a bowl with the oil and garlic.
4. Cover and let remain at room temperature for several hours. When you serve them, pass a pepper grinder.

Note:
Some people marinate the peppers in a vinaigrette sauce, or add 1 tablespoon red wine vinegar and a favorite herb such as bay leaf, oregano, thyme, or dill to the oil.

☆ ☆ # PASTA QUATTRO GUSTI ☆ ☆
(Pasta with meat sauce and four cheeses)
SERVES 4

Meat Sauce (see below)
1 pound favorite pasta
½ cup heavy cream
¼ cup grated Parmesan cheese
¼ cup shredded fontina cheese
¼ cup shredded Swiss cheese
¼ cup shredded mozzarella cheese
Freshly ground pepper to taste

1. Make meat sauce and keep at a slow simmer.
2. Meanwhile cook pasta according to pasta directions. When barely tender or al dente, drain into serving bowl. Pour the meat sauce over the pasta, add the cream, the four cheeses, and pepper and toss well. Serve with additional Parmesan cheese if desired.

MEAT SAUCE
ABOUT 3 CUPS

2 medium onions, chopped
2 cloves garlic, peeled and minced
1 stalk celery, chopped
2 tablespoons cooking oil
½ pound ground lean beef
1 1-pound can imported tomatoes, drained
4 tablespoons tomato paste
1 bay leaf
½ teaspoon rosemary
1 cup dry red wine or beef bouillon
Salt, coarsely ground black pepper, and cayenne to taste

1. Cook onions, garlic, and celery in the oil over medium heat until onion is golden. Add the meat and cook, stirring, until meat loses all its red color.
2. Crush and add tomatoes, tomato paste, bay leaf, rosemary, and red wine, and simmer, stirring occasionally, for 30 minutes.
3. Season to taste with salt, pepper, and cayenne.

Petaluma

1356 First Avenue (at 73rd Street)
New York, N.Y. 10021   772-8800

Petaluma County, in Northern California, is the inspiration behind this new restaurant on Manhattan's Upper East Side. Elio Guaitolini and his partners, Ann Isaacs and Vertucci Gennaro, transformed the site of the old Czechoslovak Praha restaurant into a spacious peach expanse with a sky blue ceiling—a breezy setting for the light nouvelle American food with Italian overtones prepared by chef Tom Repetti.

Appetizers at Petaluma, Mr. Guaitolini's second restaurant (he also owns Elio's on Second Avenue and 84th Street) include seafood sausage served with saffron butter sauce, baked goat cheese salad, and fried polenta with a daily special sauce. For entrées, a great majority of Petaluma diners order the grilled fish or meat that sizzles over mesquite in the middle of the restaurant. Baby chicken, duck, ribs, and at least three varieties of fresh fish take on the smoky flavor that's become so popular. A wood-burning stove turns out special pizzas and calzone, also favorite items.

Desserts return to the more homespun: Apple pie, strawberry shortcake, and lemon tarts share star billing with freshly prepared ice creams and sorbets. Wines, listed on the back of the midnight blue menu, are reasonably priced, reflecting the owners' philosophy that Petaluma should fulfill the need of sophisticated diners who want light fare at reasonable cost. Perhaps to keep prices low, Petaluma does not honor credit cards, so be sure to take along some cash.

☆ ☆ RADICCHIO, WHITE BEAN, AND ☆ ☆
TUNA SALAD

SERVES 4

The first recipe from Ann Isaacs is a delightful bean salad or appetizer with red onion and tuna.

½ cup giant dried lima beans or white navy beans
1 head radicchio
1 4-ounce slice fresh tuna fish
1 tablespoon plus 1 teaspoon olive oil
1 small red onion, peeled and thinly sliced
1 stalk celery
3 tablespoons lemon juice, or to taste
Salt and freshly ground pepper

1. A day in advance, cover beans generously with cold water
   and let them soak overnight. Next day, drain, cover again generously with cold water, and bring to a boil. Simmer for about
   40 minutes, or until beans are tooth tender, adding more
   water if needed to keep them covered at all times. When
   cooked, drain and set aside to cool.
2. Wash radicchio leaves and drain well.
3. Brush tuna fish with 1 teaspoon of olive oil and cook on a
   very hot grill for about 3 minutes or until cooked on one side.
   Turn and cook for 3 to 4 minutes or until cooked through.
   Cool fish to room temperature, then flake the flesh, discarding
   any bone or skin.
4. Combine beans, tuna fish, red onion, celery, and the radicchio leaves. Toss with remaining olive oil and lemon juice
   and season with salt and pepper to taste.

☆ ☆   # BLUE-CORN BLINIS   ☆ ☆

MAKES 15 BLINIS OR 4 TO 5 SERVINGS

1 cup blue cornmeal
1 cup all-purpose flour
½ teaspoon salt
½ ounce fresh yeast
1 cup scalded milk at room temperature
2 large eggs, separated
⅔ cup crème fraîche, whipped (see page 301), plus
approximately 5 teaspoons for garnish
American sturgeon, salmon, and whitefish caviar

1. Mix the cornmeal, flour, and salt.
2. In another bowl, mix the yeast with the warm milk.
3. In a third bowl, beat together the egg yolks and the créme fraîche.
4. When the yeast is thoroughly incorporated into the milk, add the crème fraîche/egg-yolk mixture and work into a thick batter. Let sit one hour to proof.
5. Beat the two egg whites till stiff and add them to the batter. Let it sit another ½ to 1 hour to ensure that the cornmeal is soaked. The mixture is very dense and will need the extra time.
6. In a lightly buttered Teflon pan, cook the blinis one at a time in 1-ounce portions. Carefully rotate the pan to evenly distribute the batter. The finished blinis will be the diameter of silver dollars. Stack them as you cook them.
7. Top each blini with ½ teaspoon of each kind of caviar and about 1 teaspoon of crème fraîche. Serve immediately.

Petrossian Delicacies Restaurant and Boutique

182 West 58th Street
New York, N.Y. 10019   245-2214

When Christian Petrossian and his cousin Armen do anything, they do it with style, perfection, and flair. Since the 1920s the name Petrossian has been synonymous with caviar in Parisian circles; today, the family-run company is the only one allowed by the Russian government to select its caviar from the Caspian Sea. (The Petrossians also sell their own wild salmon, smoked over a secret blend of woods, and buttery foie gras from the Périgord.) So it comes as no surprise that the Petrossian Delicacies Restaurant and Boutique, which opened in the fall of 1984 in the historic Aldwyn Court Building, is the ultimate showcase for the company's products.

A salmon pink and gray color scheme sets the stage for granite floors, leather stools at the caviar bar, burled-wood walls, original thirties bronze sculptures, Lalique wall sconces, Erté mirror etchings—even a mink banquette or two. Tables are set with pale gray linens woven with the Petrossian ship emblem, Christofle silverware, and Limoges china especially created for the Petrossians.

Whether your favorite caviar is sevruga, ossetra, or beluga, it will be served as the purists like it, with crustless toast and unsalted butter (pressed caviar is served with blini, yeast-raised buckwheat cakes). But the young chef, Michel Attalo, also presents a tempting array of entrées including fillet of beef with shallots and sherry vinegar, foie gras salad, and boneless breast of chicken served with a julienne of leeks.

The "chariot" or dessert cart features individual lemon mousse or strawberry tarts, a pear tart, and an intense chocolate mousse cake, sure to satiate even the most fanatic chocolate addict.

Champagne and vodka are the only truly appropriate accompaniments for caviar, and Petrossian serves more than two dozen varieties of champagne or Stolichnaya vodka. Sauternes and other white and red wines are also available.

☆ ☆   # SUPRÊMES DE POISSON À LA JULIENNE DE LÉGUMES   ☆ ☆

(Fish Fillets with
Vegetables)
SERVES 4

An elegant fish dish to be so humbly named.

2 large skinless, boneless fish fillets of red snapper, salmon, or
striped bass (about 2 pounds total)
2 to 3 large ripe tomatoes (1¾ pounds), cored and peeled
4 tablespoons shallots, divided
1 large black truffle, sliced paper-thin (optional)
¼ pound shiitake mushrooms
6 tablespoons minced parsley, divided
¼ teaspoon dried thyme
Salt and pepper to taste
Butter to grease baking dish
1½ tablespoons Dijon or other good prepared mustard
¾ cup Petrossian Fish Stock (see below)
½ cup dry white wine or vermouth
½ cup (1 stick) butter, sliced

1. Carefully remove any bones from the fillets. Wash and dry with paper towels.
2. Place tomatoes, cored side down, on a flat surface and cut off the thick outside flesh on all sides. Scrape seeds from inner portion. Cut flesh into long strips. You should have about 2 cups. Empty into a medium bowl.
3. Add half the shallots and truffle to tomatoes.
4. Cut mushrooms into thin slices, then slice into strips. Add to tomatoes with half the parsley, the thyme, and salt and pepper to taste, and toss lightly.
5. Preheat oven to 400 degrees.
6. Butter a baking dish large enough to hold the fish fillets in 1 layer without crowding. Scatter with the remaining 2 tablespoons shallots. Arrange fillets, dark side down, in the dish and brush each fillet with the mustard, coating them evenly.
7. Pile tomato mixture equally on each fillet and pour the fish stock and wine around the fish.
8. Bake in the preheated oven for about 10 minutes, or until fish loses its transparency.

9. Transfer fillets to a warm serving platter and cover with foil to keep warm.
10. Pour sauce and vegetables remaining in baking dish into a saucepan and reduce liquid over high heat to ½ cup. Gradually add the butter to the simmering sauce, stirring constantly and rapidly with a wire whisk.
11. When all butter has been added, remove from the heat and stir in remaining parsley. Serve the sauce over the fish.

PETROSSIAN FISH STOCK

2 CUPS

¾ pound fish bones
1 small onion, coarsely chopped
1 stalk celery, coarsely chopped
½ cup dry white wine
2 cups water
Salt to taste
12 crushed peppercorns
1 bay leaf
½ teaspoon dry thyme

1. Combine all ingredients in a saucepan, bring to a simmer, and simmer for 20 minutes. Strain.

☆ ☆ # CHOCOLATE MOUSSE CAKE ☆ ☆

SERVES 8 TO 12

One of those delectable melt-in-your mouth confections that no one can resist.

Butter to coat pan
1 cup all-purpose flour
¹⁄₁₆ teaspoon baking powder
¼ cup cocoa
4 eggs
½ cup sugar plus 2 tablespoons
10 ounces (squares) semisweet chocolate, melted
1½ cups heavy pasteurized cream (not ultrapasteurized;
see page 303)
1 cup cold strong coffee
Sifted cocoa
Confectioner's sugar

You need two pans for this cake: an 8-inch round cake pan in which cake is baked, and a 9-inch springform pan in which to assemble cake and filling.

1. Coat the bottom and sides of an 8-inch round cake pan with butter and lightly flour it. Set aside.
2. Preheat oven to 325 degrees.
3. Sift together the flour, baking powder, and cocoa.
4. In a mixing bowl combine the eggs and ½ cup sugar. Place bowl over simmering water in the lower pan of a double boiler, being sure the bottom of the bowl does not touch the water, and whip (use an electric beater if possible) until egg mixture becomes light in color and thick, like soft ice cream.
5. Remove bowl from heat and gently fold the dry ingredients into the egg mixture with a rubber spatula or large kitchen spoon. Mix only until blended.
6. Pour batter into prepared cake pan and bake for about 30 minutes, or until surface of cake springs back when lightly touched with a finger, and starts to pull away from sides of pan.
7. When cooked, remove cake from pan and cool completely on a wire rack.
8. Prepare filling: Melt chocolate over very low heat in a bowl over simmering water. Set aside to cool. Whip the cream over a bowl of ice until it forms firm peaks (or blender whip) and gently fold in the melted and thoroughly cooled chocolate until just blended.
9. Combine coffee and remaining 2 tablespoons sugar and set aside.
10. To assemble the mousse cake: Split the chocolate cake into 2 layers. Place half the cake, cut side up, in the center of the 9-inch springform pan. Brush with coffee-sugar mixture to moisten. Cover with half the chocolate cream.
11. Place remaining layer of cake on top, brush with coffee, and top with the remaining cream.
12. Carefully smooth top of the cake and place in the freezer for 1 hour or until firm.
13. To unmold, wrap a hot, damp towel around the pan to loosen the cake, and open the pan.
14. Dust cake with sifted cocoa and finish with a topping of sifted confectioner's sugar.

Pig Heaven

1540 Second Avenue (between 80th and 81st streets)
New York, N.Y. 10028   744-4887

Every person who professes to thrive on three lettuce leaves and a sliver of low-fat cheese harbors a secret desire to pig out at least once in a while. There's no better way to do it than with some old-fashioned messy pork spareribs. Pig Heaven mixes just about every Chinese-style pork or seafood dish you can think of with some down-home-style vegetables and some rib-sticking puddings. Don't come to Pig Heaven if you need peace and quiet, but do come to have fun. It's also a place where kids are welcome and can have a good time.

☆ ☆
PIG HEAVEN'S BREAD AND BUTTER PUDDING WITH ORANGE SAUCE
☆ ☆
SERVES 6

One of the most popular puddings served.

24 to 25 slices good-quality white bread
1 stick (½ cup butter) at room temperature
¼ cup confectioner's sugar, plus additional for garnishing
1 teaspoon cinnamon
6 cups milk
1 vanilla bean
7 egg yolks
3 whole eggs
¾ cup granulated sugar
Orange Sauce (see below)
Candied Orange Peel (see below)

1. Butter bread and toast buttered side only, in oven or under broiler heat. Remove from stove and cut off crusts. Cut slices in half diagonally.
2. Butter sides and bottom of a 10 x 3 inch round cake pan with a little of the butter. Arrange 6 triangles of toast around sides of pan, toasted side toward the center and points up. Continue to line the pan with concentric layers, round and round, until only a small center hole is left and 2 triangles of toast remain. Fill this center with 2 remaining triangles. The toast points should be almost vertical.
3. Combine the confectioner's sugar and cinnamon and sprinkle over bread lining the pan.
4. In a saucepan heat milk and vanilla bean to simmering.
5. Meanwhile with a whisk or in an electric beater beat egg yolks, eggs, and granulated sugar until mixture is pale and thickened. Gradually and slowly pour in the hot milk. Skim off all the froth on the surface and slowly pour the egg mixture into the center of the bread-lined pan. The toast points will float up and remain dry.
6. Fill a baking or roasting pan large enough to accommodate the pudding pan, and place in a preheated 400-degree oven. Fill pan half full of boiling water. Carefully put bread pudding into the pan, and bake in the hot oven for 55 to 60 minutes, or until custard is set but still retains its elasticity when tested with a fingertip.
7. When done, remove to room temperature. Dust liberally with additional confectioner's sugar, slice into wedges, and serve with Orange Sauce and Candied Orange Peel.

ORANGE SAUCE

1 quart fresh orange juice
¼ cup cornstarch moistened with
a couple of tablespoons of water
Sugar to taste

1. Bring orange juice to a boil and cook until it is reduced by about ⅓. Stir in cornstarch and water mixture, and sugar to taste. Simmer a few minutes until sauce thickens.

CANDIED ORANGE PEEL

1. Remove the orange rind from a large orange with a vegetable peeler, being careful not to include any of the bitter white pith. Put peel in small saucepan with ½ cup water and ⅓ cup sugar and boil until candied. Chill and use as a garnish.

Pinocchio

170 East 81st Street
New York, N.Y. 10020   650-1513

Owner-chef Sal Petrillo comes from a restaurant family. His father and brothers all had places in the Village, but Petrillo decided he wanted his kids to go to uptown schools so he opened an uptown restaurant to be near his home. The first version of Pinocchio was a tiny storefront; Petrillo then took over the space next door. You'll find opera posters on the walls and more than one Petrillo on hand. The food is definitely not nouvelle Italian, but more traditional Italian fare. Desserts include zabaglione and strawberries in cannoli cream. Check out the special wine list—one of Sal's sons is the house expert. Reservations are necessary and so is your pocketbook or checkbook. No credit cards are accepted.

☆ ☆ # PAGLIA E FIENO GENOVESE ☆ ☆
(Pasta with veal and vegetables)
SERVES 4

Most of this dish can be prepared in advance; even the pasta can be cooked ahead and reheated in the broth. Just be sure not to overcook it the first time.

8 ounces egg fettuccine
8 ounces spinach fettuccine
4 ounces veal scaloppine
4 ounces thinly sliced prosciutto
2 tablespoons olive oil
4 tablespoons sweet butter
1 medium onion, minced
½ cup minced celery
1 cup minced carrots
1 cup shelled fresh peas or frozen petits pois
1 cup strong chicken broth
2 cups freshly grated Parmesan cheese
Freshly ground pepper

1. Cook fettuccine in a generous amount (6 to 9 quarts) lightly salted rapidly boiling water until *barely* tender. Rinse immediately and thoroughly in cold water; set aside.
2. Cut veal and prosciutto into strips about 1 inch wide.
3. In a large sauté pan or skillet heat oil and butter until butter is melted and mixture is hot. Add meat and onion and sauté over medium heat until both are cooked, about 10 minutes.
4. Add celery, carrots, and fresh peas to pan; cook, stirring occasionally, for about 10 minutes longer. If using frozen peas, add them about 5 minutes after you add the celery and carrots.
5. Add pasta and about half the chicken broth and heat thoroughly, tossing pasta gently.
6. Empty pasta onto a large warm serving platter and sprinkle with half the cheese. If too dry, quickly heat a little more butter and broth in a small pan and pour over the pasta.
7. Add remaining cheese and ground pepper to taste.

☆ ☆ # MOSCOVITA DI CIOCCOLATA ☆ ☆
(Chocolate mousse)
SERVES 6

8 ounces semisweet chocolate bits
7 ounces milk chocolate, chopped into small pieces
¼ cup water
¼ cup sugar
4 egg yolks
2 ounces Neapolitan espresso coffee
2 ounces brandy
2 ounces coffee liqueur
1½ cups heavy cream

1. Put chocolate bits and pieces into container of an electric blender, cover, and blend on high speed until chocolate is finely ground.
2. Heat water and sugar in a small saucepan until sugar is completely melted and syrup is boiling. Add hot syrup to ground chocolate, cover, and blend again on high speed for 30 seconds.
3. Add egg yolks one at a time, blending briefly after each addition, then add coffee, brandy, and coffee liqueur and blend until mixture is smooth, stopping to stir down if necessary. Set aside to cool to room temperature.
4. Whip 1 cup of the cream and fold the chocolate mixture into the cream until uniformly blended. Pour into 6-ounce ramekins, cover with plastic wrap, and freeze.
5. About 2 hours before serving, remove moscovita from freezer. Whip remaining cream and top each serving with a spoonful or "rosette" of the whipped cream (see page 302).

The Polo in the Westbury Hotel

840 Madison Avenue (at 69th Street)
New York, N.Y. 10022   535-9141

Several years ago this restaurant underwent a renovation and a rebirth. Before, it was a lackluster hotel restaurant set in the middle of one of the most opulent areas of Manhattan. Today, the horse prints are still on the wall and are indicative of the understated elegance that the management has tried to bring to this place. The food is a blend of classic French cooking and lighter nouvelle cuisine. For example, at lunch a light chicken salad and a hot lobster salad are so popular that to remove them from the menu might cause a small revolution. For those who prefer the more classic menu there's foie gras in abundance and game dishes galore. You won't find celebrities here, just those with the time and money to dine luxuriously.

☆ ☆ L'ÉVENTAIL DE VOLAILLE ☆ ☆
AUX NOIX
(Chicken with walnuts and vegetables)
SERVES 2

One of this restaurant's most popular entrées is a chicken breast fanned out on a plate and surrounded by literally every vegetable in season. Such a spectacular dish is easy for a restaurant, but the home cook would do better to settle for more of a few favorite vegetables. Prepare and cook them in advance; reheat by dipping them briefly into boiling water.

The garniture:
4 baby carrots, peeled and cooked
2 small zucchini, cooked and sliced
12 snow peas, steamed briefly
1 cooked artichoke bottom, halved and sliced into small strips
1 cooked red beet, sliced into small strips
8 cooked asparagus tips
2 cooked tomatoes, chopped
2 florets broccoli, cut into bite-sized pieces
1 yellow squash, cooked and sliced
2 mushrooms, peeled and sautéed in a little oil
2 white turnips, cooked and sliced
2 pears, poached in red wine and sliced

1 chicken breast, halved, boned and skinned
2 teaspoons olive oil
½ cup sherry vinegar
2 tablespoons sweet butter
2 tablespoons chopped walnuts
1 tablespoon chopped parsley
Salt and pepper to taste

1. Prepare the garniture first. Cook each vegetable separately al dente. They must *not* be overcooked. Arrange them and the pears around the circumference of 2 warm serving plates and keep warm.
2. Sauté the chicken breasts in olive oil for about 5 minutes on each side or until golden brown. Slice each breast thinly and fan the slices out in the middle of the garnished plates.
3. To the skillet in which the breasts were cooked add the sherry vinegar and boil briskly until vinegar is reduced to half its quantity. Gradually whisk in the butter. Just before all the butter is melted and the sauce is slightly thickened, spoon it over the breasts and sprinkle with walnuts, parsley, and a little salt and pepper. Or offer the pepper grinder at the table.

☆ ☆ # CHOCOLATE GANACHE CAKE ☆ ☆
SERVES 12

This sinfully rich cake topped with curls of shaved chocolate is one of the luxurious desserts offered at the Polo.

Chocolate Genoise (see below)
Rum Syrup (see below)
Ganache Filling and Topping (see below)
4 ounces bitter chocolate, shaved into curls

1. Slice the cake into three layers. Moisten each layer with rum syrup. Put the layers together with ganache filling, using about ¾ (3 cups) of the filling. Use remaining cream to cover top and sides.
2. Sprinkle top and sides with shaved chocolate. Chill for several hours before serving. Serve in small slices.

CHOCOLATE GENOISE
1 8-INCH CAKE

4 ounces semisweet chocolate
4 tablespoons strong coffee
Oil for pan
Wax paper
4 large eggs, at room temperature
½ cup sugar
½ cup unsifted all-purpose flour

1. Melt chocolate with coffee over simmering water, stirring occasionally until mixture is smooth. Set aside.
2. Oil bottom of a round cake pan 8 inches in diameter and 2 inches deep. Line bottom with wax paper and oil the paper.
3. Beat eggs and sugar until mixture is thick, pale in color, and takes some time to level out when beater is withdrawn. Use an electric beater if possible and beat on high speed for about 10 minutes, or place the bowl containing the sugar and eggs over (but not touching) hot water and beat vigorously with a rotary beater.
4. Sift flour twice and fold into the beaten eggs, a little at a time. Fold in melted chocolate.

5. Pour and scrape the foamy batter into the prepared pan and bake in a preheated 350-degree oven for 35 minutes, or until a cake tester comes out clean.
6. Let stand for only a few minutes, then run knife around edge of pan and turn cake out onto a wire rack to cool.

RUM SYRUP

ABOUT 2 CUPS

1½ cups water
¾ cup sugar
2 teaspoons lemon juice
½ cup dark rum

1. In a saucepan combine water and sugar. Boil rapidly for 5 minutes. Remove from heat and stir in lemon juice and rum.

CANACHE FILLING

1 QUART

½ pound Lindt brand bittersweet chocolate with vanilla
1 pint (2 cups) fresh pasteurized heavy cream
(not ultrapasteurized; see page 303)

1. Chop chocolate into small pieces with a large knife and put into a mixing bowl.
2. Bring cream to a boil, watching carefully that it does not boil over, and pour into the chocolate. Stir cream and chocolate together with a hand whip until chocolate is melted and mixture is smooth.
3. Set chocolate cream in refrigerator or an ice water bath and stir about every 3 to 5 minutes, or until mixture is cooled to below room temperature (60 to 65 degrees).
4. Using an electric beater or a balloon whip, beat for 1 to 3 minutes, to the soft ribbon stage. Chill in refrigerator for at least 1 hour before using.

Primavera Ristorante

1578 First Avenue (between 81st and 82nd streets)
New York, N.Y. 10028   861-8608/9

When Primavera moved about half a block uptown only one thing changed. It became more attractive. The storefront restaurant moved into larger, more luxurious quarters appreciated by both its faithful crowd of regulars and newcomers. On Sundays everyone wants the baby goat, a house specialty. On other days veal dishes are favored. Mushrooms—a different kind for each season —are a popular appetizer, as is the carpaccio with a sprinkling of Parmesan. Pastas are homemade and so are the stuffed tortellini. Primavera is open only for dinner and you'll get an idea of the crowd it attracts when you see the limos lined up outside, especially on a Sunday.

☆ ☆ TORTELLINI DELLA NONNA ☆ ☆
SERVES 4

Tortellini are little rings of homemade pasta filled with different types of filling.

Pasta Dough (see below)
Tortellini Filling (see below)
4 slices prosciutto, chopped
4 tablespoons butter
½ cup cooked peas
1 cup heavy cream
½ cup freshly grated Parmesan cheese
Salt and pepper to taste

1. Place a heaping ½ teaspoon of filling on each pasta square and fold into a triangle. Press edges together, then wrap the triangle around a finger to form a ring, and seal ends. Place on a cloth, cover with a towel, and let dry for about 1 hour before cooking.
2. Cook the tortellini in a large quantity of rapidly boiling salted water until just barely tender, or al dente. Drain.
3. In a large skillet sauté the prosciutto in the butter for 2 minutes. Add the tortellini, peas, cream, and cheese and cook over low heat until well blended. Add salt and pepper to taste and serve very hot.

PASTA DOUGH FOR TORTELLINI

Dough for enough tortellini to serve 4

2 cups flour
1 teaspoon salt
2 eggs
2 tablespoons salad oil

1. Put flour into a bowl with the salt and make a well in the center. Into the well put eggs and oil and stir with a fork until well mixed and a soft dough is formed.
2. Turn out on floured board and knead for 5 to 7 minutes.
3. Roll out the pasta dough very thinly and cut into 1½-inch squares.

TORTELLINI FILLING

4 tablespoons butter
5 ounces turkey breast, sliced
3 ounces mortadella, cubed
3 ounces cooked ham, cubed
2 eggs
¼ cup grated Parmesan cheese
Salt and pepper

1. In a skillet melt the butter and in it sauté the turkey breast for about 10 minutes on each side or until tender and cooked through. Add the mortadella and ham and cook, stirring, for 1 minute.
2. Put the meat mixture through a meat grinder or mincer twice or process in a food processor until finely chopped and well blended.
3. Beat the eggs, adding the Parmesan cheese, and mix with the ground meat. Season to taste with salt and pepper.

☆ ☆ # SCALOPPINE ALLA ZINGARA ☆ ☆
SERVES 4

One of the most popular entrée dishes at Primavera is a scaloppine of veal flavored with grated black truffle.

12 thin slices veal from the leg
6 mushrooms, sliced
2 slices prosciutto, chopped
½ cup butter
½ cup white wine
½ cup cooked peas, fresh when possible
Salt and pepper to taste
1 black truffle

1. Pound the veal slices between two pieces of wax paper until very thin, and trim into even ovals.
2. Sauté the mushrooms and prosciutto in the butter until lightly browned. Add the veal slices and cook until golden on each side. Add the wine and cook over high heat until sauce is reduced to about half its original quantity.
3. Add the peas, salt, and pepper.
4. Serve on individual serving plates with a little of the sauce spooned over each portion and grate a little of the truffle over each serving.

The Coach House
Black Bean Soup (page 50) and Striped Bass Adriatic (page 48)

Photographs by Lou Manna

Andrée's Mediterranean Cuisine
Bouillabaisse (page 15)

John Clancy's
Lobster à l'Americaine (page 111) and Lemon Meringue
Pie (page 113)

Cafe des Artistes
Pot-au-Feu (page 38)

Petaluma Restaurant
Radicchio, White Bean, and Tuna Salad (page 191) and
Blue-Corn Blinis (page 192)

Lutèce
Tarte Lutèce (page 170) and Blanquette de Sole et St. Jacques (page 168)

Lello Ristorante
Funghi Ripieni con Lumache (page 149) and Scampi Ribelli (page 151)

The Quilted Giraffe
Phyllo Tarts with Radish, Cucumber, and Sour Cream
(page 215) and Caviar Beggars' Purses (page 213)

Odeon
Salmon in Puff Pastry with Spinach and Caviar (page 182)

Petrossian
Suprêmes de Poisson à la Julienne de Légumes (page 194)
and Chocolate Mousse Cake

"21" Club
Chocolate Pots de Crème (page 272) and Roast Baby
Pheasant, Sauce Périgourdine (page 270)

Windows on the World
Beef Medallions with Braised Shallots in Red Wine Sauce
(page 292) and Hazelnut Dacquoise (page 295)

☆　☆　　　　# CARPACCIO　　　　☆　☆
SERVES 4

This is so different from the carpaccio recipe given by the Rainbow Room that we couldn't resist including it.

1 pound fillet of beef
1 teaspoon capers
3 green olives
1 small shallot
6 leaves fresh sweet basil
4 to 5 drops Worcestershire sauce
2 drops Tabasco
2 anchovy fillets
2 tablespoons mayonnaise
4 lemon shells (optional)

1. Trim all fat from the beef fillet, wrap in foil, and freeze for 30 minutes. This will make it easier to slice. Slice paper-thin with the grain, using an electric slicer if you have one. Place the slices on a serving plate and set in a 150-degree oven, just to take the chill off, while making the sauce.
2. Put remaining ingredients except the lemon shells into the container of an electric blender and blend until smooth. Serve in scooped-out lemon halves on individual plates.

Quatorze

240 West 14th Street
New York, N.Y. 10014   206-7006

If you long for authentic Parisian bistro fare, consider a trip to Greenwich Village instead; it's closer and cheaper and you won't be disappointed. Peter Meltzer and Mark DiGiulio's Quatorze is reminiscent of those cozy places Parisians frequent when they want honest, satisfying food at reasonable prices. Quatorze's bracing red enameled, paneled entrance is as authentic as any you'll find in France. The tiled floor, marble bar, and the newspapers stored on poles are proof that Meltzer and DiGiulio have created a down-to-earth bistro.

That's not to say the food is humdrum. Classic dishes such as choucroute garnie (braised sauerkraut with smoked pork and sausage), cassoulet, and roast duckling with green peppercorn sauce are prepared and served with panache. Although French in design and intent, the menu is almost entirely in English. Oysters are always available; whatever varieties are in season may be ordered by the piece. Other appetizers include smoked chicken breast with horseradish cream and the Quatorze specialty: chicory with bacon and hot vinaigrette. For dessert, many opt for either the plate-sized apple tart on a sheet-thin butter crust, the flourless chocolate regal cake, or silky crème caramel. Reasonably priced French wines are available.

☆ ☆ CHICORY AND BACON SALAD ☆ ☆ QUATORZE

SERVES 1

1 small shallot, peeled and chopped
1 tablespoon Dijon mustard
1¼ tablespoons red wine vinegar
5 tablespoons olive oil
Pinch salt, if necessary
Freshly ground black pepper

⅓ pound slab bacon, cut into ½-inch cubes
8 ½-inch cubes French bread, crusts removed
3 cups washed and drained curly chicory

1. In a small bowl combine the shallot, Dijon mustard, and red wine vinegar.
2. With a small wire whisk, slowly beat in the olive oil, salt, and pepper. Set aside.
3. In a small heavy saucepan cook the bacon cubes until nicely browned on all sides. Remove bacon cubes with a slotted spoon and set them aside. Pour off and discard all but 3 table-spoons of the bacon drippings. Add the bread cubes to the skillet and sauté until golden on all sides.
4. Return the bacon to the pan and heat rapidly with the bread cubes until very hot, stirring constantly.
5. Remove skillet from the heat and to it add the dressing all at once. Watch it carefully, as the dressing will spatter.
6. Pour the dressing, bacon, and bread cubes over the prepared chicory and serve immediately.

☆ ☆   APPLE TART QUATORZE   ☆ ☆

1 7-inch tart, serves 1 or 2

Serve, if desired, with crème fraîche flavored with a little Curaçao or Benedictine.

Pâte Sucrée or Pâte à Tarte (Tart Pastry) (see below)
1 Granny Smith apple, peeled, cored, and sliced
⅓ cup sugar
¼ cup butter
Apricot Glaze (see below)

1. Roll out Pâte Sucrée into a round no thicker than 1/16 inch (the thinner the better) and 7 inches in diameter. Fit it onto the removable bottom of a 7-inch fluted tart pan. Reassemble the pan.
2. Cover the pastry with overlapping very thin slices of apple arranged in concentric circles. Cover with plastic wrap and chill up to 2 hours in the refrigerator.
3. Preheat oven to 450 degrees. Unwrap the tart and sprinkle the apples with the sugar and dot with the butter.
4. Bake in the hot oven for 20 minutes, or until apples are lightly colored. Watch carefully that the tart does not burn.

5. Remove from the oven and brush surface of the apples with warm apricot glaze.
6. Remove the rim of the pan and slide the tart off the bottom of the pan onto a serving plate. Serve immediately.

PÂTE SUCRÉE OR
PÂTE À TARTE (TART PASTRY)

Enough pastry for 2 7-inch apple tarts
Double quantities for 4 tarts

1 cup flour (no need to sift)
1 egg yolk
½ tablespoon sugar
½ cup (1 stick) cold butter, but not out of freezer, sliced
1 to 2 tablespoons water

1. Measure flour into a mixing bowl and make a well in the center. Into the well put the egg yolk, sugar, butter, and 1 tablespoon water. With fingers of one hand, knead these center ingredients, adding the other tablespoon water if necessary, and gradually working in remaining flour to make a dough that can be gathered together into a ball.
2. Wrap dough in plastic wrap and refrigerate for 30 minutes. The dough will be easier to handle, but it's an unnecessary step if you are expert at handling doughs. Using a pastry cloth and cloth-covered rolling pin will also make your job easier.
3. Spread pastry cloth on work surface and rub generously with flour. Also flour rolling pin. Press ball of dough into a flat circle with heel of the hand, and sprinkle lightly with flour.
4. Begin rolling dough out into a circle, rolling from center to outer edge all around the circle. Turn the circle of dough occasionally to keep both sides floured. Continue to roll until dough is less than ⅛ inch thick. Transfer pastry to the bottom of a 7-inch fluted tart or quiche pan with removable bottom. Trim away overhanging pastry and reroll to use for a second tart base, turnovers, or tiny tarts.

APRICOT GLAZE

Enough glaze for 1 7-inch tart

½ cup apricot jam or jelly
2 tablespoons hot water

1. Combine jam or jelly and water in a small saucepan and stir over low heat until mixture boils.

The Quilted Giraffe

955 Second Avenue (between 50th and 51st streets)
New York, N.Y. 10022 753-5355

This restaurant's worldwide reputation makes it tough to get a reservation. When you phone The Quilted Giraffe, a recorded message answers just about every question you may have, including where to park. Once your call is answered you're treated to the calm, efficient service that continues throughout your meal. Host and owner Barry Wine is very proud of his restaurant, and he's tried to work out every detail to make your evening a serene, delicious experience. There are twelve at work in the kitchen; timers are set to assure a party of a minimum wait between courses, and every dish within a course is delivered at the same time to a table. Considering what happens in other places, this is no mean feat. As for the food, if a surfeit of truffles, caviar, and foie gras appeals to you, you'll find them here. You'll also encounter a luscious confit of duck, veal, and fish dishes, and a chocolate soufflé that may finish you before you finish the meal. The tab is steep—plan on $100 per person—the atmosphere muted, and if you hope to find any of the beautiful people you'll probably be disappointed. This is a place to eat, not to be seen or make the scene.

☆ ☆   CAVIAR BEGGARS' PURSES   ☆ ☆
12 CRÊPES

It will take a wealthy beggar to make this appetizer.

12 Crêpes (see below)
12 long chives
4 tablespoons beluga caviar
1½ tablespoons crème fraîche (page 301) or sour cream
¼ cup clarified butter (page 301)
2 lemons, thinly sliced

1. To prepare the crêpes: Trim the crêpes to a diameter of 4½ inches. Hold the chives under the hot water from the tap for 10 minutes, or until limp.
2. Lay the crêpes out on a work table. Spoon 1 teaspoon of caviar into the center of each. Spoon a small teaspoon of crème fraîche or sour cream onto each mound of caviar.
3. If you are right-handed, place a crêpe in the palm of your left hand and with the right hand, gather the part of the crêpe around the caviar up like a little leather pouch and tie it near the top with a chive. Trim away any excess chive.
4. Heat the clarified butter until just warm and dip each "purse" into it to warm the crêpe ever so slightly. Serve each on a slice of lemon.

Note:

   If you make these early in the day, refrigerate them in a tightly sealed container, and remove them an hour before serving to let them reach room temperature.

CRÊPES

Approximately 40 6-inch crêpes

Crêpes may be made in quantity, so you can make a big batch and freeze them for future use. To freeze: Simply stack them between layers of wax paper, put in a sealed container, and place in the freezer. To use within a day or so, wrap stacked crêpes in foil or plastic, and refrigerate until about 1 hour before serving.

1 cup unbleached or pastry flour
1¾ cups milk
4 eggs
¼ teaspoon salt
1 tablespoon melted butter
Additional melted butter for cooking crêpes

1. Combine all ingredients except butter for cooking in blender container or bowl and blend or beat with a rotary beater or whisk until smooth, about 30 seconds. Strain the batter into a bowl or jug and let stand at room temperature for at least 1 hour.
2. Heat a 6-inch crêpe pan over medium heat until a drop of water sizzles on the surface. Using a paper towel moistened with a bit of melted butter, grease the pan lightly and quickly.

3. Into the hot greased pan pour just enough batter to coat the bottom with a thin layer: As you pour with jug or bowl held in the right hand, immediately rotate and tilt pan with left hand to swirl the batter quickly and evenly, then pour out any excess batter. Cook the crêpe until it is lightly browned on one side, then carefully flip it over. Cook for about 15 seconds and empty out onto a strip of paper towel or wax paper. If not using crêpes immediately, wrap them carefully in plastic to keep them from drying out. See note on freezing.

☆ ☆ ## PHYLLO TARTS WITH RADISH, ☆ ☆ CUCUMBER, AND SOUR CREAM

Makes 4 large tarts

An interesting version of the more common cheese-filled triangles so frequently served as an hors d'oeuvre.

½ cucumber, peeled, seeded, and finely chopped
4 radishes, finely chopped
½ teaspoon chopped hot fresh or canned jalepeño pepper
½ cup dairy sour cream
2 teaspoons toasted sesame seeds
½ teaspoon salt
Pepper to taste
1 teaspoon lemon or lime juice
4 sheets phyllo pastry
Melted butter for brushing phyllo
3 tablespoons finely chopped or crushed walnuts

1. Combine cucumber, radishes, hot pepper, sour cream, and sesame seeds. Season to taste with salt and pepper and lemon or lime juice. Set aside.
2. Spread out one sheet of the phyllo pastry and brush lightly with melted butter. Put about one quarter of the filling in the center and sprinkle with nuts. Gather the pastry up around the filling in folds as you would crumple newspaper around a ball.

3. Brush a second sheet with butter and place the first "package" upside down in the center of it. Gather the pastry up around it as in step 2. Assemble remaining tarts in the same fashion. Place the tarts on a baking sheet brushed with butter and refrigerate until ready to bake.
4. Bake in a preheated 375-degree oven for 15 to 16 minutes, or until golden brown and crisp. Serve warm.

☆ ☆ # GRILLED CHICKEN WITH AIOLI ☆ ☆
SERVES 4

If you are a garlic lover—and who isn't?—you'll love this dish.

4 tablespoons olive oil
4 tablespoons sesame oil
¼ cup finely chopped garlic
½ cup peeled, finely chopped fresh gingerroot
1 large chicken cut into 8 pieces
Salt and pepper to taste
Aioli Sauce (see below)
8 small boiled potatoes
4 teaspoons finely chopped parsley

1. In a large skillet combine the olive and sesame oils, garlic, and ginger. Cook over low heat for about 10 minutes to reduce the harshness of their flavors.
2. Spread this savory marinade in a shallow glass dish and arrange the pieces of chicken on top. Sprinkle lightly with salt and pepper, cover with transparent film, and refrigerate for at least 3 hours, better still overnight, turning the pieces several times during this period.
3. To cook: Place chicken on a broiler rack skin side down and broil about 5 inches from source of heat for 10 minutes. Brush with the marinade, turn, and broil for 10 minutes longer. Brush with more marinade, turn, and broil for another 5 to 10 minutes.
4. Serve two pieces of chicken per person. Garnish with 2 boiled potatoes. Spoon a little of the sauce sparingly over the grilled chicken and sprinkle potato and chicken with chopped parsley.

AIOLI SAUCE FOR GRILLED CHICKEN OR FISH
ABOUT 1 CUP

All ingredients must be at room temperature

1 egg yolk
1 teaspoon lemon juice
1 tablespoon olive oil
2 tablespoons sesame oil
2 tablespoons peanut oil
2 tablespoons heavy cream
2 cloves garlic, minced
Salt and cayenne pepper to taste

1. In a small bowl put egg yolk and lemon juice. Start whisking them together. Very slowly, as in the making of mayonnaise, whisk in oils, cream, garlic, salt, and pepper. Store in refrigerator but bring to room temperature before serving.
   To Make in a Blender: Use 1 whole egg instead of 1 yolk. Put it in the blender container with the garlic and 1 tablespoon lemon juice. Combine the oils, increasing the peanut oil to 4 tablespoons. Pour ¼ cup of the combined oils into blender container with the egg, salt, and cayenne pepper. Turn blender on low speed. Immediately remove inner cap of cover and pour in remaining oil in a heavy stream. Blend in cream.

☆ ☆ ## CHOCOLATE SOUFFLÉ FROM ☆ ☆
THE QUILTED GIRAFFE
SERVES 6

Recipes for chocolate soufflé are a dime a dozen, but this one is unique. You'll need extra egg whites for it, so begin saving them a few days in advance. You'll need a total of 2 cups, or the whites from 16 eggs—10 eggs plus those separated from the 6 yolks in this recipe. You will also need individual 12-ounce soufflé dishes, bowls, or extra large coffee cups.

6 ounces (1½ sticks) sweet butter
9 ounces (squares) bittersweet chocolate
Soft butter and sugar for the soufflé dishes
2 cups egg whites, at room temperature
½ cup sugar
6 egg yolks
⅔ cup lukewarm water
1 pint coffee ice cream
1 cup heavy cream, blender-whipped (see page 303)

1. Cut butter and chocolate into small pieces and put them together in a bowl or saucepan over simmering water to melt.
2. While chocolate is melting, brush the insides of the soufflé bowls with a thin coating of soft butter. Coat the bowls with sugar. To do this easily, simply half-fill the first bowl with sugar and swirl it to coat sides entirely, then pour sugar into the next bowl and on and on until the remaining sugar is finally emptied back into its original container.
3. Preheat oven to 425 degrees.
4. Put egg whites and ½ cup sugar in large bowl of an electric mixer. Beat on high speed until mixture is glossy and moderately stiff. Empty into a large mixing bowl and set aside.
5. Put egg yolks in the same bowl used to beat the egg whites, add lukewarm water, and beat on high speed for 10 minutes. Fold in cooled melted chocolate-butter mixture. Thoroughly fold in ⅓ of the beaten egg whites. Pour chocolate mixture into remaining egg whites and fold together lightly until no large lumps of meringue remain.
6. Ladle the finished soufflé mixture into the prepared bowls and bake in the hot oven for 7 to 10 minutes, or until well puffed. Immediately upon removing them from the oven, drop a scoop of coffee ice cream into each center and cover with a heaping tablespoon of the whipped cream. Serve immediately.

☆ ☆ ## CHERRY SOUP WITH SHERBETS ☆ ☆

SERVES 4 TO 6

In Scandinavian countries fruit soups are frequently served either as a first course or as a dessert. This unusual "soup" falls into the dessert category. A refreshing finale on a hot summer eve.

1 pound dark, sweet cherries, stemmed but not pitted
1 quart water
½ cup sugar
¼ cup honey
2 cups fruity red wine such as a zinfandel
½ cinnamon stick
3 cloves
Zest of 1 lemon, 1 lime, and 1 orange
Lemon Sherbet (see below)
Strawberry Sherbet (see below)
Candied Lime Zest (see below)

1. Wash the cherries and put them in a stainless or enameled pot with the water, sugar, and honey. Bring to a simmer very slowly, uncovered, watching carefully that they do not boil and burst open. Simmer for 10 minutes. Remove from heat, cool, and refrigerate in their cooking liquid.
2. While the cherries are cooking combine the wine, cinnamon stick, cloves, and citrus zests in another pot. Bring wine to a boil and boil for 10 minutes, or until reduced by half its volume. Strain out the spices and zests and add the liquid to the poached cherries in the refrigerator.
3. To serve, spoon some cherries and their "soup" into a serving bowl. Add one scoop of each of the sherbets and sprinkle the sherbets with lime zest.

LEMON SHERBET

ABOUT 1 QUART

¾ cup sugar
1¼ cups warm water
2 cups lemon juice
Pinch of salt

1. Dissolve the sugar in the warm water. Add the lemon juice and salt. Freeze in an ice cream maker according to directions for the maker.

STRAWBERRY SHERBET
ABOUT 1 QUART

2 pints strawberries, hulled
1 cup water
½ cup sugar
Pinch salt
A few drops lemon juice

1. Put all ingredients into a blender and purée them thoroughly. Using a wooden spoon force the purée through a fine sieve and freeze in an ice cream maker according to directions.

CANDIED LIME ZEST

To prepare the candied lime zest, first cut the green rind off the limes with a vegetable peeler. This helps to avoid getting any of the bitter pith that lies beneath. It is also the most efficient method. Put the zest into a pot of cold water and bring quickly to a boil. Pour off the water and repeat this process three times, starting each time with fresh cold water. This will remove the excess bitterness from the zest. After the final blanching, add 1 cup fresh water and ¼ cup sugar. Simmer gently for 45 minutes. The candied zests will keep best in their cooking syrup.

Raga

57 West 48th Street
New York, N.Y. 10020   757-3450

For the most part Indian restaurants concentrate on food and leave the decor to other ethnic eating establishments. Not here, however. Here the atmosphere is dark and mysterious, but it is also filled with plush chairs, comfortable carpeting, and a lounge area that makes you think you've walked into the wrong place. But pause, take a drink, sample the hot hors d'oeuvre, and only then go in for dinner. You have discovered one of the best Indian restaurants in the city. Dishes such as lobster Malabar and tandoori chicken are traditional and as spicy as you wish or dare, and you can always compromise by tentatively trying some of the spiced condiments served on the side. For dessert, cool your palate with sophisticated and soothing mango ice cream.

☆ ☆ # MURG HYDERABADI ☆ ☆
(Curry of chicken)
SERVES 4

The first recipe from this restaurant is a superb anise-based chicken curry from the royal kitchen of the nizam of Hyderabad.

2 young whole chickens, cleaned and washed
⅔ cup shredded fresh ginger
1 cup vegetable oil, divided
2 cups chopped onions
8 cloves garlic, peeled
½ teaspoon turmeric
1 tablespoon aniseeds
Seeds from 6 cardamom pods
4 sticks cinnamon
8 cloves
4 bay leaves
1½ cups seeded, chopped, cooked tomatoes
1½ cups plain yogurt
1 cup water
Salt to taste
Chopped green coriander or parsley
Cooked rice

1. Cut the chickens into 8 pieces each: 2 legs, 2 thighs, 2 wings, and 2 breasts. Set aside.
2. Peel and shred enough fresh ginger to measure ⅔ cup.
3. In a deep skillet or chicken fryer heat 4 tablespoons of oil and in it cook the onions until they are well browned. Set aside.
4. Put ginger, garlic, turmeric, and aniseeds into container of an electric blender. Heat remaining ¾ cup oil to cooking temperature (350 degrees). Turn blender on medium speed, remove inner cap of cover, and gradually pour in the hot oil. Replace cap, switch to high speed, and blend all ingredients to a smooth paste. Add the paste to the onions and cook, stirring, for about 5 minutes.
5. Add the cardamom seeds, cinnamon sticks, cloves, and bay leaves and continue to cook, stirring, for another 3 minutes.
6. Add tomatoes and yogurt and stir. Add chicken, water, and salt to taste and bring to a simmer. Cover and cook for about 20 minutes, or until chicken is tender.
7. Sprinkle with chopped coriander or parsley and serve with cooked rice.

☆ ☆   # GOBI MASALA   ☆ ☆
(Spicy cauliflower and tomatoes)

This second curry, redolent of garlic and ginger, appeals to vegetarians. Its fire is tamed by fresh tomatoes. Like all curries, it needs rice to enhance its individual characteristics.

1 large cauliflower
6 tablespoons vegetable oil
1 tablespoon cumin seeds
1 tablespoon minced fresh ginger
2 teaspoons finely chopped garlic
1 teaspoon ground red pepper
1 teaspoon ground coriander
½ teaspoon garam masala (see Note)
Salt to taste
4 tomatoes, peeled and cut into sections
½ cup water
Chopped fresh coriander or Italian parsley

1. Cut the core from the cauliflower and discard it along with any discolored leaves. Separate the head into florets and set aside.
2. In a large skillet or chicken fryer, heat the oil until very hot. Add cumin seeds. The oil should be hot enough to crack the seeds. Stir in ginger and garlic. Add the cauliflower and remaining spices and cook over high heat, stirring constantly, for 2 to 3 minutes.
3. Add tomatoes and water, reduce heat, and cook, stirring constantly, for 2 to 3 minutes.
4. Cover and cook for about 10 minutes longer, or until cauliflower is barely tender to the fork.

Note:
Garam masala is available at markets carrying Indian and Ceylonese spices. Or, if preferred, substitute cayenne pepper.

The Rainbow Room

30 Rockefeller Plaza
New York, N.Y. 10112 757-9090

The Rainbow Room atop Rockefeller Plaza has been one of the great tourist restaurants in New York City for many years. Like the Rockettes, it is on the schedule of "musts" for visitors from all over the world. From its windows are some of the best views in town. The large dining room with its Art Deco overtones is one of the best places to dine and dance—that's the operative word. There are few places in Manhattan where you can enjoy good food and, between courses, get up and whirl around the dance floor. The Rainbow Room's menu is traditionally French with few of the frivolous combinations of nouvelle cuisine. It features such classics as rack of lamb sardalaise, chateaubriand bouquetière, and roast Long Island duckling à l'orange. Its only nods to "keeping up with the times" are wild mushrooms and puréed vegetables, and a côte de boeuf au poivre vert for two. Its appetizers, soups, and salads are fairly orthodox, and its selection of desserts is provocatively tempting. The menu is à la carte, and expensive, but the view and the charming ambience, combined with the excellence of its food, makes it memorable. Reservations are necessary.

☆ ☆ # CARPACCIO ALLA HARRY ☆ ☆

SERVES 6

Carpaccio alla Harry would make an excellent luncheon or supper dish, served with good French bread and a salad.

15 anchovy fillets
1 teaspoon prepared English mustard
2 small gherkins
¼ cup drained capers
½ cup finely chopped onion
3 tablespoons Worcestershire sauce
Juice of 2 lemons
Leaves from 1 bunch parsley
⅔ cup olive oil
2 tablespoons red wine vinegar
Freshly ground black pepper to taste
12 thin slices lean beef (use top butts)

1. Put all ingredients except the beef slices in container of an electric blender. Cover and blend on medium speed to make a dressing with a coarse but creamy consistency.
2. Arrange two slices of beef on each dinner plate. Pour 4 to 5 tablespoons of the dressing over them and serve with sliced French bread.

☆ ☆ ### ROAST FILLET OF BEEF ☆ ☆
WELLINGTON
SERVES 4 TO 6

Oysters or clams on the half shell or prosciutto and melon would be suitable appetizers to serve before the elegant fillet.

2½ pounds well-trimmed beef fillet
2 tablespoons melted butter
1 4-ounce can Strasbourg liver pâté
½ tablespoon minced onion
3 tablespoons minced mushrooms
Chilled Pie Pastry (see below)
2 eggs, lightly beaten

1. Preheat oven to 400 degrees. Place fillet on a rack in a shallow roasting pan and brush with the melted butter.
2. Roast fillet in the preheated hot oven for 15 minutes. Remove and let cool.
3. Combine the pâté, onion, and mushrooms to a paste and spread over the cool fillet.
4. Roll out the chilled pastry into a rectangle large enough to enclose the fillet. Brush edges with beaten egg, place fillet in center, cover with the pastry, and seal the edges. Slash top of pastry decoratively to allow the steam to escape.
5. Transfer fillet to a baking sheet and brush top and sides with beaten egg. Return to preheated oven and bake approximately 30 to 35 minutes, or until pastry is golden brown.

PIE PASTRY

2 cups sifted all-purpose flour
½ teaspoon salt
1 cup butter
⅓ cup ice water

1. In a large bowl combine flour and salt. Cut in butter with pastry cutter or two knives until mixture looks like cornmeal.
2. Add as much of the water as needed to gently press dough into a ball. Wrap in wax paper and chill thoroughly before rolling out.

Romeo Salta

30 West 56th Street
New York, N.Y. 10019   246-5772

Small, seating only eighty people in its two rooms, Romeo Salta's has been a favorite Northern Italian restaurant of the great and near great for at least thirty years. Grace Kelly, before she became Princess Grace of Monaco, lunched there frequently when learning to ride sidesaddle in Central Park for her role in The Swan. The restaurant was founded by Romeo Salta, now retired, but his personal collection of paintings graces the walls of the front room with its cozy banquettes lining both sides. Son Salvatore now manages the restaurant and says its popularity is still due to the good food, good service, and the intimate, attractive atmosphere. The menu is extensive, with a minimum per person of $16.00. Bonifato, either white or red, is an excellent house wine. Reservations should be made in advance.

☆ ☆ # FETTUCCINE "LISA" ☆ ☆
SERVES 4 OR 5

The first recipe from Romeo Salta's is a creamy spinach-flavored noodle dish with just a whisper of sweet basil.

1 large clove garlic, peeled and lightly smashed
¼ cup salad oil
1 10-ounce package frozen chopped spinach, defrosted
½ cup chicken broth
1 tablespoon chopped fresh basil or 1 teaspoon pesto
1 tablespoon chopped parsley
½ cup freshly grated Parmesan cheese, divided
10 tablespoons whipped ricotta
½ teaspoon salt
Freshly grated white pepper
⅔ cup heavy cream (see page 303)
1 pound imported egg fettuccine
Additional grated Parmesan cheese for garnish (optional)

1. Sauté garlic in oil in a large skillet until golden. Discard the garlic, reserving the oil.
2. Squeeze out excess moisture from spinach and add to the oil. Cover and sauté the spinach for about 5 minutes.
3. Add chicken broth, sweet basil or pesto, parsley, half the Parmesan, the whipped ricotta, salt, and pepper. Mix with a wooden spoon, and gradually stir in the heavy cream in a thin stream. Cook, stirring, over low heat for 2 minutes, or until sauce is smooth and thickened.
4. Cook the fettuccine in boiling salted water for the minimum amount of time suggested on the package. It should not be overcooked. Drain.
5. Empty fettuccine into an oven casserole, add half the spinach mixture, and toss well. Pour remaining spinach mixture on top and sprinkle with remaining Parmesan.
6. Place casserole in a preheated 350-degree oven for about 1 minute or until cheese is golden. Serve with additional grated cheese.

☆ ☆ # SCALOPPINE "MARGHERITA" ☆ ☆
SERVES 2

This main course veal dish with dried cepe or porcini mushrooms uses a fresh cheese called mascarpone, which is available only in Italian markets or specialty cheese stores. Its shelf life is brief, so it is seldom found in the average market. A suitable substitute is sour cream.

4 thin slices boneless leg of veal, or scallops, about ½ pound
Flour to coat meat
1 ounce dry porcini mushrooms or fresh cepes if available
1 tablespoon olive or salad oil
Salt and freshly ground pepper to taste
¾ cup dry white wine
4 tablespoons mascarpone cheese or sour cream
Parsley sprigs for garnish

1. Pound the slices of veal between two pieces of wax paper until paper-thin, and coat both sides lightly with flour. Soak the mushrooms, if dry, in 1 cup lukewarm water for ten minutes. Drain well.
2. Brush excess flour from veal and sauté the slices in the oil until golden brown on both sides, about 2 minutes per side. Sprinkle with a little salt and pepper.
3. Gradually add the wine and cook until all but about 2 tablespoons are absorbed by the meat.
4. Add the mushrooms and cook for 5 minutes.
5. Add the cheese or sour cream and mix well with the mushrooms, pan juices, and meat. Cook for another 2 to 3 minutes.
6. Place scaloppine on a serving dish and pour the cream sauce and mushrooms on top. Garnish with parsley.

Rosa Mexicano

1063 First Avenue (corner of 58th Street)
New York, N.Y. 10022   753-7407

It is said that there are at least 2,000 recorded Mexican dishes, but until recently New Yorkers were able to sample only a few of them. Rosa Mexicano was one of the first restaurants that set out to let customers know there was more to Mexican food than tacos and enchiladas.

Jammed from the day it opened, the restaurant offers a wide choice of Mexican dishes plus a sampling of more familiar Tex-Mex favorites. Guacamole, made to order at your table, will forever change your mind about what this avocado appetizer should taste like. Other appetizers include fresh mushrooms with a Mexican green tomato sauce, roasted green chiles filled with sardines, and oysters sautéed and served in a marinade of chiles and spices. Rosa Mexicano has an effusive charm that reminds you of typical places in Mexico where you could easily lose an entire afternoon eating and talking.

☆ ☆   ## GUACAMOLE   ☆ ☆

SERVES 6

Here is how to make Rosa Mexicano's famous guacamole at home. Just be sure you buy the black-skinned avocado from California. Those grown in Florida contain too much moisture and not enough flavor for guacamole. You'll need a mortar and pestle.

1 teaspoon chopped fresh coriander
1 heaping tablespoon minced onion
¼ teaspoon chopped chile serrano, or to taste
⅛ teaspoon salt
1 just ripe avocado
An additional 2 tablespoons chopped onion
3 tablespoons chopped ripe tomato
An additional tablespoon chopped coriander
Chopped jalapeño or serrano pepper to taste
Salt to taste

1. Into mortar put the teaspoon coriander, 1 heaping tablespoon minced onion, ¼ teaspoon chopped chile serrano, and the salt. Mash with the pestle until mixture becomes a very soft paste.
2. Slice the avocado in half lengthwise and discard the pit. In each half of the avocado make slices in the flesh ½ inch apart both horizontally and vertically. Using a teaspoon scoop out the squares of avocado into the paste and stir into the mixture.
3. Add remaining ingredients and blend well without mashing the avocado too much. Serve with corn chips or crackers.

☆ ☆   # Platanos Rellenos   ☆ ☆
(Meat-stuffed plantains)
SERVES 6

Plantain is a tropical fruit similar to the banana but larger and firmer, making it better for cooking purposes. Sometimes when they are still green they are cut into 1-inch pieces, flattened with the fist into round chips, and deep-fried as a snack or an hors d'oeuvre. As they ripen the skin gradually turns black.

2½ pounds ripe tomatoes
4 tablespoons vegetable oil
1 medium onion, peeled and chopped
1 clove garlic, peeled and minced
2 heaping teaspoons raisins, soaked in warm water and drained
10 pitted green olives, quartered
Pinch each oregano and thyme
1 bay leaf
Salt and freshly ground pepper to taste
½ pound coarsely ground sirloin steak

6 plantains, black-ripe
6 egg whites
5 egg yolks
Oil for deep-frying
Tomato Broth (see below)

1. Core and peel the tomatoes. If they are vine-ripened, the skin will strip off easily, otherwise dip them one at a time into a saucepan of simmering water for 15 seconds. Strip off skin and core the tomatoes deeply to remove seeds. Chop coarsely and set aside.

2. In a skillet heat vegetable oil and in it sauté onion and garlic until the onion is translucent but not brown. Raise the heat and add tomatoes, raisins, olives, and spices. Sauté for 10 minutes, then add the meat and continue to cook for another 10 minutes, stirring often to blend all the ingredients well. Set aside to cool.

3. Meanwhile cut each plantain into 3 or 4 cylinders and scoop out the center of each, leaving from ¼ to ⅜ inch of the flesh next to the skin, making each cylinder into a hollow tube. Fill these tubes with the meat mixture, then very carefully slit the skin lengthwise and discard it.

4. Beat egg whites until they stand in soft peaks. With same beater, beat egg yolks until thick and pale in color. Fold the egg yolks into the beaten egg whites.

5. Dip each filled plantain cylinder into the egg mixture and fry in deep oil, heated to 350 degrees, turning occasionally, until lightly browned on all sides. Drain on paper towels and serve with tomato broth.

TOMATO BROTH

2 tomatoes, peeled
1 small onion, peeled
1 garlic clove, peeled and sliced
3 tablespoons vegetable oil
1 to 1½ cups chicken broth
Salt and pepper to taste

1. Into container of an electric blender put the tomatoes, onion, and garlic. Cover and blend on medium speed until vegetables are coarsely chopped.

2. In a saucepan heat oil. Add blended ingredients and stir and cook over medium heat for 10 minutes. Add chicken broth and simmer for 10 minutes longer. Correct the seasoning with salt and pepper to taste and serve with the plantains.

Saigon

60 Mulberry Street
New York, N.Y. 10013   227-8825

In addition to Hunan, Szechwan, and Cantonese cuisines, China-town is the setting for two Vietnamese retaurants. One of them is Saigon. Tucked behind Manhattan's courthouses and the district attorney's offices, Saigon serves many of the city's judges and lawyers. The clientele, mostly American, come to enjoy authentic cuisine prepared and proudly served by the Dao family. Saigon is indeed a family affair; even the Daos' son-in-law mans the kitchen.

Vietnamese cuisine is lighter and less oily than Chinese, probably due to French influence. A typical lunch or dinner might include barbecued shrimp on sugarcane, steamed pork roll, and chicken with lemon grass. Although there's no bar, Saigon offers a complete assortment of cocktails as well as Partager wine.

☆ ☆   ## VIETNAM SPRING ROLLS   ☆ ☆
ABOUT 20

2 dried black fungus or tree ears
8 water chestnuts, chopped (⅓ cup)
¼ pound fresh shrimp
1 ounce package soy bean vermicelli or threads
¼ pound ground or finely chopped lean pork
1 carrot, trimmed, scraped, and finely shredded
1 teaspoon minced garlic
¼ teaspoon sugar
¼ teaspoon salt
Freshly ground pepper to taste
1 egg yolk
1 teaspoon water
½ pound rice paper, about 24 (rounds 4 inches in diameter or 4-inch squares)
½ cup vegetable oil for frying

1. Put dried mushrooms into a bowl containing enough warm water to barely cover them. Soak for 20 minutes.
2. Chop the water chestnuts, and shell, devein, and coarsely chop the shrimp.
3. Pour hot water over the soy bean noodles, drain, and chop. Drain liquid from mushrooms, squeezing out any excess, and finely chop the mushrooms.
4. Combine ground pork (it may be chopped in a food processor) with the mushrooms, water chestnuts, shrimp, noodles, carrot, garlic, sugar, salt and pepper. Blend well. You can do this best with your hands.
5. Beat egg yolk with the 1 teaspoon water and set aside.
6. How to wrap a spring roll: Rice paper is quite fragile, so work with only 4 sheets at a time and keep the remaining stack of rice paper covered with a barely damp cloth. Have on hand a basin of lukewarm water. The wrapping takes patience, but basically it is very simple. Immerse one sheet of rice paper at a time into the warm water, then quickly spread it out flat on a worktable. Spread all four sheets on the table, without letting them touch. Fold over the bottom third of each round or square. Put about 2 teaspoons of the filling in the center of the folded side; fold one side over the filling, then the other side, and press into a rectangle. Roll the filled rice paper from the bottom third to top, completely enclosing the filling. To seal the roll, brush the end with a little of the egg yolk mixture.
7. To fry: Pour about ½ inch oil into a small skillet and heat it to frying temperature (360 degrees). Fry a few rolls at a time, without crowding them or letting one touch another, for 7 to 10 minutes, adjusting heat to moderate or low if they begin to burn. When they are crisp and golden brown they are ready to serve.
8. Serve 2 to 3 spring rolls as an appetizer, 4 to 6 for a main course. Garnish each serving with scallion "flowers" (see Note), fresh parsley, coriander, or mint, and cucumber slices.

Note:

To make scallion flowers, trim scallions to about 4 inches in length. Place flat on a chopping board and slice the white and part of the green, about 2 inches of the scallions, lengthwise as thinly as possible, keeping the scallion intact at the green end. Drop into lightly salted water and refrigerate until ready to use. They will open into little white and green brushes.

☆ ☆ CHICKEN WITH LEMON GRASS ☆ ☆

SERVES 2

This recipe from Kenneth Dao, owner-chef of Saigon, calls for fresh lemon grass. It is available year round in Chinese and Vietnamese markets. In appearance it is similar to our green onions or scallions but its flavor is that of fresh lemons. In this recipe only the bulbous root end is used and it should be finely chopped or ground. Generally only one blade of lemon grass is used in a recipe, the equivalent of the grated rind of 1 lemon, but here a bunch of lemon grass is called for. Vietnamese markets are also a source for the fish sauce or nuoc mam used in this and other Vietnamese dishes.

> *2 chicken legs and thighs or 4 thighs, about 1½ pounds*
> *2 teaspoons peanut oil*
> *1 teaspoon minced garlic*
> *⅓ cup water*
> *1 teaspoon honey*
> *2 teaspoons sugar*
> *1 teaspoon soy sauce*
> *½ teaspoon nuoc mam (fish sauce)*
> *A good sprinkling of freshly ground pepper*
> *1 bunch fresh lemon grass, bulb end only,*
> *or sliced zest and juice of 1 lemon*

1. Bone chicken legs by scraping away flesh and skin from bone until bone can be pulled out. Reshape the meat and cut it into 12 small cubes.
2. In a small skillet heat the oil with garlic. Stir and add the water, honey, sugar, soy sauce, nuoc mam, and pepper. Cook, stirring, for about 10 minutes.
3. Add the lemon grass or lemon juice and zest and the chicken and cook until the pieces of chicken turn a pale brown.
4. Serve with cooked rice.

Note on how to preserve rind of citrus fruit:
  Zest of a lemon or orange is the colored covering over the pith. It is most easily removed with a potato peeler. If you're smart, you'll never squeeze a lemon or orange without first removing the thin skin. Put it on paper towels and set it into an oven with a pilot light or the warming oven of an electric stove. In a few days it will be crisp and dry and can be blended in your electric blender and stored in a glass jar. To speed the process, after using your oven for baking or roasting, let it cool till it's just hot to the hand and set the rind in at that time to dry.

Salta in Bocca

179 Madison Avenue (between 33rd and 34th streets)
New York, N.Y. 10016   684-1757

Fulvio Tramontino came to this country from the Friuli region of Italy to pursue his trade of mosaic art. Today, his mosaic designs grace the walls of the restaurant he owns and has operated since 1976. As with many midtown spots, Salta in Bocca is busy with local business clientele at lunch, catering to a more diverse crowd at dinnertime. The 75-seat restaurant specializes in Northern Italian cuisine such as the dish that gives the place its name, tender veal scaloppine sautéed with prosciutto, sage, and wine and served on a bed of spinach; straw and hay, egg and spinach noodles tossed with cream, butter, peas, and prosciutto; and costoletto fiorentina, bone-in veal chop stuffed with ricotta cheese, prosciutto, and spinach, sautéed with white wine. Popular appetizers include a gratinéed dish of roast peppers, anchovies, and mozzarella cheese, named for former New York Times *restaurant critic Mimi Sheraton, and a sampler plate of juniper-flavored prosciutto, smoked beef, and cacciatorini (small salami), served with only oil and lemon to drizzle over the beef.*

Desserts such as tiramisù, chocolate hazelnut cake, and Italian pastries and cookies will soon come from Mr. Tramontino's new venture, Dolci on Park, a cafe and pastry shop. In honor of his birthplace, Mr. Tramontino features many wines from the Friuli region, along with others from elsewhere in Italy and California.

☆ ☆   # PEPERONI MIMI   ☆ ☆
SERVES 4

This is so easy that any good cook can add it to a repertoire of table appetizers.

4 red or green sweet bell peppers, preferably red
Salt and pepper to taste
1 tablespoon olive oil
1 large clove garlic, peeled and minced
½ pound mozzarella cheese (fresh if possible), sliced very thinly
1 tablespoon minced parsley
1 ounce anchovy fillets

1. Roast peppers over the top of a gas flame or under a broiler, charring the skin on all sides.
2. Enclose peppers in a paper bag to cool a little, then peel off skin. Cut peppers open on one side, discard the seeds, and arrange peppers in a little oiled baking dish. Sprinkle each with a little salt (remember the anchovies are salty) and pepper, olive oil, and garlic.
3. Cover the peppers with slices of mozzarella and bake in a 375-degree oven or place 3 inches from broiler heat for about 6 minutes, or until the cheese is melted and bubbly.
4. Sprinkle with parsley and arrange an anchovy or two on top. Serve immediately.

☆ ☆   # SALTIMBOCCA   ☆ ☆

SERVES 4

A warning from the chef to be careful not to oversalt this dish, as the prosciutto is usually salty enough for the entire dish.

12 thin slices veal from the leg for scaloppine
12 fresh sage leaves or 1 teaspoon dry sage leaves
12 thin slices Italian prosciutto
Flour to coat
1 pound fresh spinach, washed and stems removed
4 tablespoons olive oil
8 tablespoons (1 stick) butter
½ cup dry white wine
Freshly ground pepper and salt if necessary

1. Pound veal slices between 2 pieces of wax paper until very thin. Place 1 sage leaf on top of each slice and a slice of prosciutto on top of each sage leaf. Use toothpicks to hold the layers of meat together. Coat each side lightly with flour and set aside briefly.
2. In a large saucepan simmer the spinach in lightly salted water for 5 minutes. Cover and set aside.
3. In a large skillet heat oil and butter together until very hot and in it sauté the prepared meat over quite high heat for 2-3 minutes or until golden brown on each side. Total cooking time is 5 to 6 minutes.
4. Now add the white wine, freshly ground pepper, and salt (careful).
5. Drain the spinach and arrange in the skillet alongside the saltimbocca and cook for 1 minute. Serve 3 saltimbocca to each person with a spoonful of pan sauce on top and a serving of spinach on the side.

Sardi's

234 West 44th Street
New York, N.Y. 10036   221-8440

Smack in the middle of the theater district is Sardi's, New York's most celebrated spot for theater personalities and theatergoers. The wood-paneled walls are closely packed with caricatures of stars and other illustrious actors, directors, writers, and producers. Most caricatures are on the second floor, which is more private; both floors are usually crowded for both lunch and dinner. Downstairs you're apt to see actors and actresses at lunch or late in the evening when the shows are over.

One goes to Sardi's to see and be seen, and for homestyle American and Italian dishes, simply cooked from good ingredients— such homely dishes as broiled lamb chops, chicken hash, crab meat salad, and a variety of pasta dishes, with fruit, pound cake, and their famous cheesecake for dessert. Service is good, and if you tell the waiter that you're going to the theater, he'll get you out in time for the curtain.

☆ ☆   SUPREME OF CHICKEN SARDI'S   ☆ ☆

SERVES 6 TO 8

Supreme of chicken is a dish that is easy to duplicate in the home kitchen. It is usually made for two at Sardi's, but with a large gratin dish it may be prepared well in advance for 6 to 8 servings and baked at the last minute.

> **A 5- to 6-pound chicken, ready to cook**
> **6 medium-sized potatoes (about 2¼ pounds)**
> **¼ cup soft butter**
> **¼ cup hot milk**
> **Salt and pepper to taste**
> **1 egg yolk**
> **16 to 18 stalks asparagus**
> **1 quart Sauce Supreme (see below)**
> **½ cup freshly grated Parmesan cheese**

1. Roast chicken in a 400-degree oven for 1½ hours, or until it tests done. Cool and take meat off the bones in as even slices as possible. Set aside.
2. Peel potatoes and boil in lightly salted water until very tender. Drain, shake over the heat for a few seconds to dry them, then empty into the bowl of an electric mixer. Beat in butter, hot milk, salt and pepper to taste, and the egg yolk. Set aside.
3. Break off tough lower part of the asparagus stalks and steam the stalks until just fork tender. Drain and empty into a bowl of cold water to stop the cooking. Drain again and set aside.
4. Make Sauce Supreme (see below) and keep warm.
5. Arrange the sliced chicken meat in the center of a 12-inch oval gratin dish, or you may use two 9-inch round or oval dishes instead, and place half the asparagus stalks on one side and half on the other, with the tips extending slightly over the side of the dish. With a pastry bag fitted with a large fluted pastry tube, pipe potatoes parallel to the asparagus stalks in attractive peaks. Spoon the sauce over the chicken and sprinkle with the Parmesan cheese.
6. Bake in a preheated 400-degree oven for about 20 minutes, or until golden and sauce is bubbling.

SARDI'S SAUCE SUPREME

1 QUART

8 tablespoons (1 stick) butter
½ cup flour
1 quart hot milk
2 ounces sherry
Dash each salt, white pepper, and Worcestershire sauce

1. In a large saucepan melt butter, add flour, and whisk for about 1 minute, or until the roux (butter and flour mixture) is smooth and bubbling. Remove saucepan from heat and add milk, sherry, and seasonings while whisking.
2. Return saucepan to heat and cook, whisking, until sauce is smooth and thickened.

☆ ☆   # SARDI'S CHEESE CAKE   ☆ ☆

Serves 12 or more

There are many claims of the best cheesecake at restaurants, but none can truly beat this one. It's hard to believe it is so easy to make.

Crumb Crust:
½ cup fine dry bread crumbs or 1 cup graham cracker or
zwieback crumbs
3 tablespoons melted butter
2 tablespoons sugar
Soft butter to butter pan

1. Combine crumbs, melted butter, and sugar. Generously butter an 8- by 2- or a 9- by 2-inch round cake pan and coat with the prepared crumbs. Set aside.

Cheese Mixture

1. In the bowl of an electric mixer blend the cream cheese, cornstarch, flour, and vanilla until smooth. Add the sugar and the grated lemon rind and blend well. Add eggs, one at a time, blending until smooth after each addition. Add the sour cream in two additions. Last, beat in the cream or milk.
2. Pour the cheese mixture into the prepared pan, set the pan into a larger pan containing ½ inch boiling water, and bake in a preheated 475-degree oven for 25 minutes.

3. Lower oven temperature to 325 degrees, and continue to bake for about 35 minutes longer, or until cake tests done.

Cheese mixture	For 8-inch pan:	For 9-inch pan:
Cream cheese at room temperature	1 pound	1½ pounds
Cornstarch	3 tablespoons	5 tablespoons
Flour	3 tablespoons	5 tablespoons
Vanilla	1 tablespoon	1 tablespoon
Sugar	¾ cup	⅞ cup
Grated rind of	1 lemon	1 lemon
Eggs	2	3
Sour Cream	1 cup	1½ cups
Light cream or milk	½ cup	⅔ cup

☆ ☆   SARDI'S DEVILED ROAST BEEF   ☆ ☆
BONES

SERVES 2

A dividend recipe from Sardi's that many celebrities request. We couldn't resist it. So when you treat yourself to a standing rib roast, don't you dare give the bones to the dog!

2 teaspoons dry English mustard
½ cup water
4 roast beef bones from a cooked standing rib roast
¾ cup bread crumbs
4 tablespoons Deviled Sauce (see below)

1. Blend mustard and water. Dip bones into the mixture, covering them well (use a brush if necessary), then roll in bread crumbs.
2. Arrange bones in a shallow baking dish and broil until brown and hot, turning occasionally, or for about 7 minutes. Serve with Deviled Sauce.

DEVILED SAUCE

1¼ CUPS

½ cup sherry
¼ cup Dijon mustard
1½ cups Brown Sauce (see below) or bottled beef gravy

1. In a small saucepan heat the sherry and simmer until it is
   reduced to about half its quantity. Stir in mustard and simmer
   for 5 minutes. Add brown sauce and simmer for 5 minutes
   longer. This sauce will keep in the refrigerator for a week to
   10 days and may be reheated when needed.

BROWN SAUCE

1½ CUPS

1½ tablespoons butter
2 tablespoons flour
1½ cups beef consommé
¼ cup sherry
1 bay leaf
⅛ teaspoon commercial caramel coloring (optional)

1. In a saucepan melt butter. Add flour, and stir over moderate
   heat for 1 to 2 minutes, or until the flour mixture or roux is a
   golden brown.
2. In another saucepan heat consommé until simmering.
3. Remove roux from heat, pour in the hot consommé, return to
   heat, and stir rapidly until the sauce is smooth and thickened.
4. Add sherry and bay leaf and simmer for 15 minutes. Add caramel coloring to give the sauce a nice rich color, but only if
   necessary.

Scarlatti

34 East 52nd Street
New York, N.Y. 10022   753-2444

*Just when it seemed as though Manhattan could not handle an-
other Italian restaurant, along came Scarlatti, and it's jammed
every day. The crowds could be in part a result of its midtown
location and experienced management and staff. It's not large—
two small rooms, one opening onto the other—and not very con-
ducive to intimate dining, especially during lunch. But in the evening, it is much quieter, and if you're in the area it's a good place
to have a meal of your traditional Italian favorites.*

☆ ☆ ## MALFATTI CON CARCIOFI ☆ ☆
(Pasta with artichoke hearts)
SERVES 4

The first recipe from this restaurant is a homemade pasta dish with
well-seasoned artichoke hearts.

3 tablespoons olive oil
4 medium artichoke hearts, cleaned, quartered, chokes removed
3 pitted black olives, quartered
4 cloves garlic, chopped
2 anchovies, chopped
1 tablespoon small capers
1 pound homemade pasta dough (see page 275)
Freshly ground pepper to taste

1. On a lightly floured board, roll out dough until very thin. Cut
   into 2-inch strips and cut the strip into 2-inch squares. These
   are malfatti.
2. In a saucepan large enough to hold the artichoke hearts in a
   single layer, heat the olive oil. Add the hearts and sprinkle

244

with the olives, garlic, anchovies, and capers. Sauté over low heat until artichoke hearts are tender, but not brown, about 20 minutes.

3. Meanwhile cook the malfatti in a large quantity of rapidly boiling salted water for 3 to 5 minutes. Be careful not to over-cook. Drain pasta and empty into a mixing bowl. Add arti-choke mixture and pepper, and toss until all ingredients are evenly mixed. Serve on hot plates.

☆ ☆ # POLLO CIPRIANI ☆ ☆
(Breast of chicken garnished with shrimp)
SERVES 4

2 boneless chicken breasts, halved, with skin on
Flour to coat chicken
½ cup olive oil
1 clove garlic, peeled and minced
2 tablespoons butter
2 large shrimp, peeled, deveined, and coarsely cut
½ cup sliced mushrooms
½ cup dry white wine
4 tomatoes, peeled, seeded, and chopped
½ cup brown sauce or gravy
Salt and freshly ground pepper to taste
¼ cup chicken stock or broth
2 tablespoons crème fraîche (page 301)
Cooked fresh asparagus for garnish

1. Wipe chicken breasts with a damp cloth and coat lightly with flour.
2. In a large skillet over medium heat, heat oil and garlic. Add chicken breasts and cook for about 4 minutes on each side. Reduce heat and cook for another 5 minutes, or until golden brown. Do not overcook. Transfer chicken to plate and keep warm. Discard oil and garlic and, in the same skillet, melt the butter. Add shrimp and cook for 30 seconds or until pink.
3. Add mushrooms and sauté for another 3 to 4 minutes. Add wine and boil over medium heat until reduced by half.
4. Add tomatoes and brown sauce, salt and pepper, and simmer for 3 minutes. Return chicken to the skillet. Add the chicken broth and simmer for 2 minutes, basting breasts until hot.
5. Transfer chicken to a warm plate. Add the crème fraîche, in-crease heat, and stir rapidly until sauce is well blended. Pour over the chicken and garnish with asparagus.

Shun Lee Palace

155 East 55th Street
New York, N.Y. 10022   371-8844

This is a rarity—an elegant Chinese restaurant, with widely spaced tables and attractive decor and table settings. What's more, many consider the food at Shun Lee Palace to be the best served north of Chinatown.

Although Chinese food is very popular in New York, it is still prepared in few home kitchens. The dishes that follow were created by Shun Lee Palace's owner, the urbane Michael Tong, whose personality and style are reflected in the special "class" of this establishment. Each recipe makes a complete meal for four people.

Be sure to do all of the chopping well in advance of cooking, or you may find yourself frantic at the last minute. Once the initial preparation has been made, however, most Chinese dishes can be cooked in less than 5 minutes. Serve with rice.

☆ ☆   ## ORANGE BEEF   ☆ ☆
SERVES 4 TO 6

The first recipe from Chef Tong makes flank steak as tender as tenderloin.

1½ pounds flank steak
⅔ cup plus 3 tablespoons water
½ teaspoon baking soda
¼ teaspoon salt
3 tablespoons dry sherry or shao hsing wine, divided
1 egg white
3½ tablespoons cornstarch, divided
4 cups plus 2 tablespoons peanut, vegetable, or corn oil

2 scallions, cut into ½-inch lengths (about ⅓ cup)
3 tablespoons dried orange peel (see Note)
3 thin slices fresh ginger, cubed
1 fresh sweet red pepper, cut into ½-inch squares
1 long thin fresh hot pepper, seeded and chopped (optional)
2 tablespoons soy sauce
2 tablespoons sugar
1 teaspoon sesame oil
¼ cup chicken broth or consommé
10 dried small hot pepper pods

1. Put meat in freezer for about 1 hour, or until ice crystals form; it will be easier to slice. Place flank steak on a flat work surface and, holding a very sharp knife parallel to the beef, slice it in half widthwise. Cut each thin slice into very thin strips, about ¼ inch wide. There should be about 4 cups, loosely packed.
2. Place beef in mixing bowl and add ⅔ cup water mixed with the baking soda. Refrigerate for at least 1 hour or overnight. When ready to cook, rinse beef thoroughly under cold running water. Drain and pat dry.
3. To the meat add salt, 1 tablespoon of the wine, and the egg white. Stir in a circular motion until egg white is bubbly. Add 1½ tablespoons cornstarch and 2 tablespoons oil. Stir to blend. Set aside.
4. Combine scallions, dried orange peel, fresh ginger, sweet and fresh hot peppers. Set aside.
5. Combine remaining 2 tablespoons wine, soy sauce, sugar, remaining 2 tablespoons cornstarch blended with remaining 3 tablespoons water, sesame oil, and chicken broth. Stir to blend. Set aside.
6. Heat remaining 4 cups oil in a wok or skillet and when it is smoking hot (450 degrees) add the beef. Cook, stirring, about 45 seconds. Scoop out meat with a slotted spoon onto absorbent paper, continuing to heat oil in wok. Return meat to wok and fry over high heat for about 15 seconds, stirring constantly. Drain once more. Return meat a third time to the hot oil and fry, stirring, another 15 seconds. The purpose of this process is to make the meat crisp on the outside but keep the juices within.

7. Very carefully drain oil from wok or remove wok from heat and let cool in a safe place. Measure 2 tablespoons of the hot oil used in beef frying into a clean wok or skillet and add hot pepper pods. Stir over high heat until peppers are blackened, about 30 seconds. Discard peppers, leaving the oil in the pan.
8. Add to the hot oil the pepper-scallion-ginger-orange peel mixture and stir. Add beef and stir constantly for about 15 seconds. Add wine mixture, stirring for another 15 seconds, or until ingredients are piping hot and meat is well coated with the sauce.

Note:

Dried orange peel is available in many stores and supermarkets, but it is so easy to make yourself that there is little reason to buy it. Using a vegetable peeler, remove the peel from a large orange, leaving as much of the white pith as possible. Cut peel into small pieces, scatter on a baking sheet, and place in a 200-degree oven until dry, about 30 minutes. Chop into small pieces and store in a tightly closed container.

☆　☆　　　　# CHICKEN SOONG　　　　☆　.☆
(Cubed chicken in lettuce leaves)
SERVES 4 TO 6

1 head iceberg lettuce
1 large boned chicken breast, skinned, about 1 pound
1 egg white
½ teaspoon salt
2 tablespoons cornstarch
2 long green chiles, hot or mild, or ½ cup drained chopped green chiles
10 to 12 water chestnuts, canned or preferably fresh
½ cup diced celery
1 tablespoon finely diced carrot
1 teaspoon chopped fresh ginger
2 teaspoons or more finely chopped garlic
1 tablespoon finely chopped scallions
2 teaspoons shao hsing wine or dry sherry
½ teaspoon soy sauce
½ teaspoon chili paste with garlic or 1 teaspoon chili powder
1 teaspoon sugar
1 teaspoon water
2 cups peanut, vegetable, or corn oil
½ teaspoon sesame oil

1. Core lettuce and separate it into leaves; pile leaves on a platter and keep cold.
2. Place chicken breast on a flat surface and, holding a sharp kitchen knife almost parallel to cutting surface, cut breast into thinnest possible slices. Stack slices and cut into shreds. Cut shreds into tiny cubes. There should be about 1 cup.
3. Put chicken into a small mixing bowl. Add egg white, salt, and 1 tablespoon of the cornstarch. Blend well, then refrigerate 30 minutes or longer.
4. Core the chiles, discarding seeds. Split chiles in half, then shred them. Cut the slices into small cubes. There should be about ½ cup.
5. Slice water chestnuts thinly, then cut into cubes. There should be about ½ cup.
6. Combine chiles, water chestnuts, celery, carrot, and ginger. Set aside.
7. In another bowl combine garlic and scallions. Set aside.
8. Combine wine, soy sauce, chili powder or chili paste, and sugar. Set aside.
9. Combine remaining 1 tablespoon cornstarch and water. Set aside.
10. Heat peanut oil in wok or skillet and when very hot add chicken and, stirring constantly to separate the cubes, cook for 1½ minutes. Remove chicken with a slotted spoon to absorbent paper to drain. Set aside.
11. Measure 2 tablespoons of the oil into a clean wok or skillet and when hot, add celery and water chestnut mixture. Cook, stirring, for about 30 seconds. Return chicken and cook, stirring, for 30 seconds or until chicken is piping hot. Add wine and soy mixture and sesame oil. Stir cornstarch mixture until smooth and add. Combine, stirring rapidly for about 30 seconds. Transfer chicken mixture to a warm platter.
12. Serve the chicken mixture with the lettuce on the side. Let each person help himself, adding a spoonful of the chicken mixture to a lettuce leaf and folding it before eating.

☆　☆ # HUNAN LAMB ☆　☆

SERVES 4 TO 6

This recipe from Michael Tong uses lean lamb from the leg but meat from a large lamb shank may also be used. If you prepare the meat a day in advance and refrigerate it until cooking time, you're one step ahead.

1¼ pounds very lean lamb, cut from the leg or a large lamb shank
¼ teaspoon salt
2 small egg whites
2½ tablespoons cornstarch, divided
4 cups plus 3½ tablespoons peanut, vegetable, or corn oil
30 scallions
3 large cloves garlic
2 tablespoons shao hsing wine or dry sherry
2 tablespoons water
2 tablespoons soy sauce
½ teaspoon sugar
1 tablespoon red wine vinegar
½ teaspoon sesame oil
⅓ cup chicken broth

1. In advance or the day before, place lamb on a flat surface and, using a sharp knife, cut it against the grain into ¼-inch-thick slices. If desired the lamb may be partly frozen to facilitate slicing.
2. Place lamb slices in a mixing bowl and add salt and egg whites. Stir until egg whites become a bit bubbly. Stir in 1½ tablespoons cornstarch and 1½ tablespoons oil. Refrigerate until needed, preferably overnight, but at least 1 hour.
3. Trim root ends of scallions and discard any discolored parts of the green shoots. Flatten by pounding lightly with flat side of a cleaver and cut into diagonal one-inch lengths. You should have about 4 cups.
4. Peel and coarsely chop garlic. Set aside.
5. Combine wine, remaining tablespoon cornstarch blended with the water, soy sauce, sugar, vinegar, sesame oil, and chicken broth. Stir to blend and set aside.
6. In a wok or skillet heat the 4 cups oil until almost smoking hot, or 450 degrees. When very hot add the lamb, stirring to separate the slices. Cook, stirring constantly, for 45 seconds, no longer. Remove meat from oil with a slotted spoon and drain on absorbent paper.
7. In another wok or skillet heat the remaining 2 tablespoons oil and when very hot add scallions and garlic and cook, stirring and tossing, for about 30 seconds. Add lamb, stirring, and the vinegar mixture. Cook, tossing and stirring, until sauce is slightly thickened.

☆ ☆   # Mandarin Shrimp   ☆ ☆

SERVES 4 TO 6

The last entrée in this Chinese feast complements the other three. Again we need 2 woks or skillets or one of each.

10 giant shrimp or scampi, about 1¼ pounds
4½ tablespoons dry sherry or shao hsing wine, divided
2 egg whites
4 cups plus 1½ tablespoons peanut, vegetable, or corn oil
½ teaspoon salt
2½ tablespoons cornstarch, divided
2 scallions, white part only, trimmed and shredded
5 very thin slices fresh ginger, shredded
2 tablespoons water
2 tablespoons soy sauce
2½ tablespoons white vinegar
2 tablespoons sugar
½ teaspoon sesame oil
⅓ cup chicken broth
10 snow peas
10 slices water chestnuts, preferably fresh
½ cup loosely packed fresh coriander leaves or parsley

1. Peel shrimp, split in half, and devein.
2. Put shrimp in a medium-sized mixing bowl and add 1½ tablespoons wine, egg whites, and 1½ tablespoons oil. Stir until whites become bubbly. Add half the salt and 1½ tablespoons cornstarch. Stir to blend.
3. Prepare scallions and ginger and set aside.
4. Combine remaining 3 tablespoons wine, remaining 1 tablespoon cornstarch blended with the water, soy sauce, vinegar, sugar, sesame oil, and chicken broth.
5. Heat remaining 4 cups oil in a wok or skillet and add shrimp, one at a time. Cook about 1 minute, then add snow peas and water chestnuts and cook for another 10 seconds. Scoop out with slotted spoon, leaving oil in wok, continuously heating. Return shrimp to the oil and cook another 30 seconds. Remove again to drain thoroughly, and combine with snow peas and water chestnuts.
6. Put about 1 tablespoon of the hot oil in another wok or skillet and add scallions and ginger, stirring constantly. Cook about 5 seconds. Add shrimp and vinegar mixture. Toss and stir until piping hot and shrimp are evenly coated. Serve garnished with coriander.

Sistina

1555 Second Avenue (between 79th and 80th streets)
New York, N.Y. 10021   861-7660

Sistina's discreet brass nameplate against bleached oak—unreadable from across the street—is the mark of a self-confident, elegant restaurant. Inside, the simple and sophisticated atmosphere is the result of soft, flattering colors. Every table seats at least four. The menu is entirely in Italian, with specialties from all regions of Italy, including Sicily and Sardinia. The pastas are all made in the house, and a seasonal array of Italian delicacies, from white truffles to fresh porcini mushrooms, is on display.

In the best tradition of Italian restaurants, Sistina is a family affair, with the Bruno brothers (formerly of Lusardi's) and their cousin Alberto dei Montecchi in the roles of active owners.

☆ ☆ # SPAGHETTI ALLA ROSSANA ☆ ☆
SERVES 4

The first recipe from Sistina's chef is an easy dish of contrasting flavors and textures.

5 cloves garlic, peeled
½ teaspoon salt
6 leaves of fresh sweet basil, shredded, or substitute 1 tablespoon
pesto (page 301) for 1 tablespoon of the olive oil
2 tablespoons skinned almonds
2 tablespoons pine nuts
1 pound fresh tomatoes, or 2 cups canned tomatoes
or tomato purée
1 pound spaghetti
½ cup freshly grated pecorino cheese
½ cup freshly grated Parmesan cheese
2 tablespoons olive oil or to taste

1. Put garlic, salt, basil, almonds, and pine nuts in a mortar and pound with the pestle until mixture is a fine consistency.
2. Peel the tomatoes and purée them in container of an electric blender.
3. Transfer tomato purée to a medium saucepan and stir in the mixture from the mortar. Cover and simmer over medium heat for 25 minutes.
4. Boil the spaghetti in a large quantity (1 gallon) lightly salted water until just barely tender (al dente), following directions on package. Drain spaghetti and empty into serving bowl.
5. Pour the tomato sauce over the spaghetti and toss with the cheeses and olive oil. Serve on warm plates and pass additional cheese, if desired.

☆ ☆ # PANZEROTTI ALLE ALGHE ☆ ☆
MARINE FRUTTI
SERVES 6

This recipe with its exotic ingredients presents many cooks with a challenge. One advantage is that the panzerotti may be prepared ahead of time and frozen.

3 cups water, divided
1 pound spinach, washed
1 pound alghe or kelp (available in oriental markets as kombu,
an edible sea lettuce)
6 scampi
6 shrimp
6 scallops
1 pound cherrystone clams
2 pounds pasta dough, frozen or homemade (see page 275)
1 egg, lightly beaten
3 tablespoons olive oil
2 tablespoons chopped fresh parsley
2 anchovies, chopped
Pinch cayenne pepper or to taste
1 clove garlic, peeled and minced
1 cup white wine
3 red ripe tomatoes, peeled and chopped
Reserved broth from fish
Chopped parsley
2 tablespoons finely chopped sweet basil

1. Make the pasta filling: In a medium saucepan bring the water to a boil. Add spinach and alghe. Cover and simmer over medium heat for 10 to 15 minutes. Drain well and set aside.
2. In a large saucepan bring 2 cups water to a boil. Add the scampi, shrimp, scallops, and clams, cover, and simmer over low heat for 10 minutes, or until clam shells are opened and shrimp are done but not overcooked. Drain and reserve the broth. Shell clams and shell and devein the shrimp and scampi. Add them, along with the scallops, to spinach mixture and chop all together until finely minced.
3. Roll out pasta dough into a thin sheet and cut into 3-inch circles. Put 1 tablespoon of the filling on one side of each round and brush edge of pasta dough with beaten egg. Fold over once, making half-moon shapes, and pinch edges or crimp with prongs of a fork. These are called panzerotti. They may be made ahead of time and frozen.
4. Make the sauce: In a medium skillet, heat olive oil. Add parsley, anchovies, cayenne, and garlic and cook, stirring constantly, for 3 to 4 minutes. Add white wine, tomatoes, and the broth from the fish and simmer for 15 to 20 minutes, or until sauce is slightly thickened.
5. Drop the panzerotti into the simmering sauce and let them cook for 5 minutes. Remove them with a slotted spoon. Serve with the sauce and garnish with chopped parsley and basil.

Texarkana

64 West 10th Street
New York, N.Y. 10011   254-5800

Louisiana native Abe de la Houssaye and his wife, Alène, weren't newcomers to the restaurant world when they opened their Gulf Coast restaurant, Texarkana, in 1982; their first restaurant, La Louisiana, was already three years old. Perhaps practice makes perfect. From the decor to the food, Texarkana transplants Greenwich Village diners down South.

The dusty rose walls of Texarkana seem an appropriate backdrop for the knotty wood bar ornamented with desert relics and cacti. Blues and jazz fill the air, as does a pleasant smoky smell from the dining room barbecue pit.

One of the house specialties, mesquite-burnished suckling pig, is prepared on the pit. Each diner gets a piece from each part of the animal, accompanied by a cornbread dressing containing chopped jalapeño peppers. Other specialties include stone-barbecued steaks, prime ribs, and veal; a half chicken, boned and fried; "Cajun popcorn" (fried crayfish tails); and fresh Louisiana crab cakes served with the house tartar sauce and cayenne mayonnaise.

The sweet tradition of southern cooking is upheld at Texarkana. Black-bottom pie, strawberry-rhubarb pie, and pecan pie are a few of the offerings. Wines include those of regular and limited availability, priced accordingly.

☆ ☆ NEW ORLEANS ITALIAN SALAD ☆ ☆
SERVES 6

This delicious mushroom salad, without the lettuce, will keep in the refrigerator for a week.

½ pound button mushrooms, halved or quartered
1 3-ounce can pimientos, chopped
½ cup chopped, pitted black olives
½ cup chopped, pitted green olives
1 teaspoon oregano
1 teaspoon basil
½ teaspoon salt or to taste
1 teaspoon freshly ground white pepper
1 tablespoon lemon juice
1 cup olive oil
½ cup red wine vinegar
1 head romaine lettuce
1 head Boston lettuce

1. In a large bowl combine all ingredients except the lettuce, mixing well. Refrigerate and let marinate overnight.
2. When ready to serve, wash and break lettuce into 3-inch pieces. Arrange in individual bowls. Stir the mushroom mixture and spoon it over the lettuce with some of the marinade as dressing.

☆ ☆ ## CRAB CAKES LA LOUISIANA WITH CAYENNE MAYONNAISE ☆ ☆

SERVES 4

Different from most crab cakes, these are extremely delicate, crisp on the outside, moist and tender within.

1 cup plus 6 tablespoons flour
6 tablespoons butter
2 cups heavy cream
1 large onion, minced
1 pound fresh lump crab meat
½ teaspoon salt, or to taste
1 teaspoon cayenne pepper
2 tablespoons paprika
3 eggs
2 cups milk
4 cups vegetable oil for frying
Cayenne Mayonnaise (see below)
Lemon wedges for garnish

1. Make a thick cream sauce by mixing 6 tablespoons each of flour and butter in a saucepan over low heat for about 15 minutes, stirring, until mixture turns a light brown color and gives off a nutty aroma.
2. Remove the saucepan from the heat and let sit for a minute, then add the cream. Return to the heat and cook, stirring vigorously, until sauce is very thick and smooth. Reduce heat to very low and let the sauce cook for 20 minutes. Remove from heat to cool.
3. Add onion and crab meat and mix well. Refrigerate for at least 1 hour, or overnight.
4. When ready to cook, remove crab mixture from refrigerator and shape it into rather large balls about 2 inches in diameter, using about 6 tablespoons for each ball.
5. Mix the 1 cup flour with salt, cayenne, and paprika. Set aside. Then beat eggs and milk. Dip the crab balls into the flour mixture, then into the egg and milk mixture, then again into the flour.
6. Heat the vegetable oil to 375 degrees and deep-fry the crab balls for about 3 minutes, or until they are nicely browned. Carefully remove from the oil with a slotted spoon. Drain on absorbent paper and serve with cayenne mayonnaise and lemon wedges.

CAYENNE MAYONNAISE

ABOUT 2 CUPS

2 tablespoons wine vinegar
1 teaspoon dried hot pepper flakes
2 egg yolks
1 tablespoon white or cider vinegar
1½ cups vegetable oil
1 teaspoon lemon juice
½ teaspoon salt
½ teaspoon white pepper

1. In a small saucepan combine wine vinegar and hot pepper flakes. Bring to a boil and boil until vinegar is reduced to one-third its original quantity. Empty into a small mortar and work with a pestle until mixture is puréed, or press through a fine sieve. Set aside.

2. In a small bowl beat together the egg yolks and white or cider vinegar. While beating constantly, slowly drip in about two-thirds of the oil.
3. Beat in lemon juice, salt, and pepper and gradually whisk in remaining oil.
4. Stir in pepper purée and mix well.

☆　☆　　　# DIRTY RICE　　　☆　☆
SERVES 4

An unfortunate name for a dish as good as this one of rice, chicken livers, and vegetables.

2 tablespoons butter
1 cup ground chicken giblets and livers
1 small onion, finely chopped
2 stalks celery, finely chopped
1 sweet bell pepper, red or green, finely chopped
1 teaspoon salt, or to taste
1 teaspoon freshly ground pepper
4 cups freshly cooked white rice

1. In a sauté pan heat buttter. Add ground giblets and livers and chopped vegetables and cook until the chicken giblets and livers have lost all their red color.
2. Add salt and pepper and the hot rice and toss until well mixed.
3. Serve as accompaniment to the crab cakes and the Italian salad, or as a main course for two.

Thailand

106 Bayard Street (between Baxter and Mulberry streets, off Canal)
New York, N.Y. 10013   349-3132

Prasit Tangchakkrachai's forty-plus-table restaurant, slightly off the beaten track in Chinatown, but almost always crowded, began as a seven-table operation. As popularity grew, so did the space. Today, Mr. Tangchakkrachai's wife oversees the management of their second restaurant, Pongsri Thai, at 244 West 48th Street.

There is some crossover between Chinese and Thai cuisines, but certain flavorings and combinations are uniquely Thai. Coconut milk, lemon grass, and special chili sauces enliven many of the dishes on Thailand's reasonably priced menu. Two popular original Thai recipes (with no Chinese influence) are fried shrimp cakes with cucumber sauce, and fried whole fish topped with hot and spicy chili sauce. Other popular dishes include pad thai, noodles tossed with dried shrimp, peanuts, eggs, and bean sprouts; hot and sour shrimp and mushroom soup; chicken and coconut milk soup; roast duck curry; and spicy barbecue beef stick with peanut and cucumber sauces. Although sweets are traditionally served as snacks rather than after a meal, you'll find the fresh coconut and cassava root mixture prepared by Mr. Tangchakkrachai's sister-in-law, Pontip, pleasantly chewy and not overly sweet.

Wine is served by the carafe or glass. Thai beer and Heineken are also available and may be better choices to balance the fiery food. Incidentally, the condiments served on the table are incendiary. Use them with care! The cucumber sauce will calm an overheated palate.

☆ ☆ FRIED FISH TOPPED WITH HOT ☆ ☆
SPICY CHILI SAUCE

SERVES 2

Typical of the best of Thai cooking is this whole fried fish with
spicy sauce.

Hot oil for deep-frying
1½-pound whole red snapper or sea bass, cleaned, scaled, and
washed
½ cup salad oil for shallow-frying
1 small hot red pepper, seeded and chopped
2 teaspoons minced garlic
2 teaspoons minced onion
2 teaspoons minced celery
2 teaspoons sugar
2 teaspoons minced cilantro or Chinese parsley
½ cup chicken broth
½ teaspoon fish sauce (nam pla)
1 teaspoon cornstarch

1. Heat oil in a wok to a sufficient depth to cover the fish when
    it is submerged. When oil reaches a temperature of 370 de-
    grees, gently and carefully lower the whole fish into it and fry
    for about 5 minutes on each side, or until golden, turning
    once. Remove to serving platter and keep warm.
2. In a skillet heat the ½ cup oil and in it stir-fry the red pepper,
    garlic, onion, and celery for a few seconds. Add sugar, cilan-
    tro, chicken broth, and fish sauce and simmer for about 5 min-
    utes. Stir in cornstarch moistened with a little water or stock.
    As soon as sauce thickens, pour over fish on serving platter
    and serve piping hot.

☆ ☆   # MEE KROB   ☆ ☆

(Crispy noodles with shrimp)

SERVES 2

3 ounce package cellophane noodles
Oil for deep-frying
8 ounces bean curd
½ cup peanut oil
1 egg, lightly beaten
3 tablespoons minced onion
4 medium shrimp, shelled, deveined, and minced
3 tablespoons sugar
1 tablespoon nam pla (fish sauce)
½ cup chicken stock or broth
2 tablespoons vinegar
2 teaspoons cornstarch moistened with 2 teaspoons water

1. Fry noodles in oil heated to 375 degrees. It will only take a minute for them to puff and become crisp. Remove with a slotted spoon or spatula to paper towels to drain.
2. Fry bean curd until lightly brown, remove, cool, and shred. Set aside.
3. Heat just enough of the oil in an 8-inch skillet to coat the bottom. Pour in the egg and swirl pan to coat it as evenly as possible with a thin layer of beaten egg. When set on one side, turn with a spatula, and cook the other side. Turn out, let cook for a few moments, then roll like a jelly roll and cut into thin slices. Set aside.
4. In a saucepan heat remaining oil and in it stir fry the onion until lightly brown. Add shrimp, sugar, fish sauce, chicken stock, and vinegar. Combine cornstarch and water and stir into the shrimp mixture. Cook, stirring, until sauce is thickened.
5. Pour shrimp and sauce over noodles, add egg and bean curd, and mix lightly. Serve immediately.

Tre Scalini

230 East 58th Street
New York, N.Y. 10022   688-6888

Everyone in New York has a favorite Italian restaurant and it seems that most of them are located on East 58th Street. Almost from the day it opened one of the most popular has been Tre Scalini. Its elegant atmosphere and equally beautiful food keep customers coming back week after week. Work your way through the homemade pasta, the succulent veal—enjoy some of the best cuisine Northern Italy has to offer.

☆ ☆ FARFALLE TRE SCALINI ☆ ☆
SERVES 4

Farfalle are made of egg pasta dough in the shape of butterflies or bows. Farfallette are little butterflies, farfalloni are big butterflies. If you are unable to find any size in your market, egg noodles may be substituted.

1 ounce dried porcini mushrooms
½ cup oil
2 tablespoons chopped shallots
½ cup sliced prosciutto (about 3 ounces)
2 ounces or ¼ cup firmly packed ground veal
2 ounces or ¼ cup firmly packed ground chicken
2 ounces or ¼ cup firmly packed ground beef
1 cup dry white wine
1 cup brown gravy
1 cup peeled, mashed tomatoes
1 pound farfalle
2 tablespoons grated Parmesan cheese
2 tablespoons butter
Salt and freshly ground pepper to taste

1. Soak the dried mushrooms in tepid water to barely cover for 10 minutes. Drain and chop.
2. Heat oil in a saucepan and in it sauté shallots until transparent. Add prosciutto, veal, chicken, beef, and mushrooms and cook, stirring frequently, for about 10 minutes, or until meat has lost all red color.
3. Add white wine, gravy, and tomatoes, bring to a simmer, and cook for 20 minutes, stirring frequently.
4. Cook pasta in boiling salted water until just tender or al dente, following directions on package. Drain and empty into a serving dish. Add the sauce, cheese, butter, and salt and pepper to taste. Toss until well blended.

☆ ☆ # ABBACCHIO ALLA TRE SCALINI ☆ ☆
(Lamb chops with prosciutto)
SERVES 4

Boned lamb chops wrapped in veal are cooked in butter and served with a delicate white wine sauce. Serve with buttered baby carrots.

8 loin lamb chops, boned
16 slices dried porcini mushrooms, soaked in water to barely cover for 10 minutes
Salt and pepper to taste
8 thin slices veal, pounded until very thin
2 eggs, lightly beaten
1 cup flour
8 tablespoons butter, divided
½ cup chopped shallots
8 medium mushrooms, washed, trimmed, and sliced
½ cup dry white wine
½ cup brown gravy
Chopped parsley for garnish

1. With a heavy cleaver pound lamb chops until they are flattened and thin. Arrange 2 slices of porcini mushroom on each lamb chop, and sprinkle with a little salt and pepper. Then wrap each chop in a slice of veal to cover it completely.
2. Dip the veal-covered chops into egg, then coat on both sides with flour, and press edges of veal together to seal them. Refrigerate until time to cook.
3. In a large shallow pan heat half the butter (4 tablespoons) and in it brown the meat until golden on both sides.

4. In another large skillet or shallow pan, heat remaining 4 tablespoons butter and in it sauté the shallots and fresh mushrooms until shallots are transparent and mushrooms are cooked, about 5 minutes. Sprinkle with a little salt and pepper, add white wine and brown gravy, and bring to a boil.
5. Add chops with any pan juices and simmer in the sauce for 10 minutes, basting frequently and turning once.
6. Correct seasoning and serve, sprinkled with parsley.

☆ ☆ # SOUFFLÉ CAPPUCCINO ☆ ☆
SERVES 4

At the restaurant, this delicate dessert is served in extra-large pottery cups.

> *9 medium eggs*
> *2 cups milk*
> *⅔ cup sugar*
> *⅔ cup sweet butter*
> *6 tablespoons flour*
> *2 ounces Kahlúa or other coffee-flavored liqueur*
> *Butter and sugar to coat the cups or ramekins*
> *½ cup confectioner's sugar*

1. Separate eggs, putting the whites into one large bowl and the yolks into another.
2. Heat milk and sugar until scalding, and stir until sugar is dissolved.
3. In a saucepan melt the butter and stir in flour. Cook, stirring, until the butter and flour form a smooth paste. Remove from heat and let the roux cool a little. Then add sweetened milk all at once, and whisk briskly until sauce is smooth and thickened. Return to heat and stir in lightly beaten egg yolks with a little of the hot sauce. As soon as egg yolks are blended well into the sauce remove from heat and let cool.
4. Beat egg whites to soft peaks. Mix a large spoonful of egg whites thoroughly into the egg yolk mixture, then lightly fold in remaining whites. Fold in the Kahlúa.
5. Butter 4 individual 12-ounce cups or ramekins and sprinkle each with a little sugar. Spoon soufflé mixture into the cups, filling them about ¾ full.
6. Place the cups or dishes on a baking sheet and bake in a preheated 375-degree oven for 20 minutes, or until soufflé mixture rises to top of cups.
7. Remove from oven, dust tops with confectioner's sugar, and serve immediately.

24 Fifth Avenue

24 Fifth Avenue (at 9th Street)
New York, N.Y. 10011   475-0880

With almost twenty years of kitchen experience (and he's only thirty-three), chef Michel Fitoussi already has a history. Once chef of the ultraopulent Palace Retaurant, he's known for his inventive cooking and superb desserts. So well known, in fact, that most of his clients make the trek from midtown to enjoy such specialties from his handwritten menu as sweetbread-filled ravioli; fresh pasta with basil; sautéed mushrooms; duck with grapefruit sauce; and at least six to twelve daily fish specials grilled and served with sauce on the side.

Mr. Fitoussi hails from the Haute Savoie region of France. His seventy-seat restaurant is bathed in a soothing pink decor, with flowers everywhere—fresh ones on the marble-topped bar; in paintings; even etched on frosted glass panels that break the space into intimate eating areas. On weekends, all brunch entrées include Mr. Fitoussi's homemade brioches, croissants, and preserves. If you come at around 11:00 A.M., the breads will still be hot from the oven.

Mr. Fitoussi is also justifiably renowned for his desserts. Marzipan ice cream with chocolate almond cookie leaves is another favorite. 24 Fifth's wine list is divided between California and France, weighted toward the latter, with a price range that runs the gamut from an inexpensive Côtes du Rhone to a pricey Cristal champagne.

☆ ☆ LONG ISLAND DUCKLING WITH ☆ ☆
GRAPEFRUIT

SERVES 4

Blanched green beans and strips of blanched leek are tied in bundles to garnish M. Fitoussi's duckling. Preparation begins four days in advance.

2 Long Island ducklings, about 5 pounds each
2 grapefruit
¼ cup sugar
⅓ cup red wine vinegar
3 cups Veal or Duck Stock (see below)
Salt and pepper
Blanched vegetables in season, such as green beans, asparagus, broccoli florets, or julienne of carrot, zucchini, or white turnip, tied into bundles with strips of blanched leek

1. Keep ducklings in refrigerator, uncovered, for 4 days to dry out the skin.
2. On the day you plan to serve, preheat oven to 500 degrees. Cut tails and excess neck skins from ducks, along with all excess fat. Discard or reserve as desired. Tuck wing tips under and place ducklings breast up on a rack in a roasting pan. Roast for about 1 hour, or until well browned and crisp.
3. Meanwhile, with a sharp paring knife remove a thin slice from top and bottom of each grapefruit and discard. Then peel the grapefruit rind in long strips. Cut between the membrane of each fruit into sections, remove sections, reserving the juice (approximately ⅓ cup depending on juiciness of grapefruit), and set aside.
4. Put the sugar and wine vinegar in a heavy-bottomed 1-quart saucepan. Cook over medium heat until vinegar is evaporated and sugar is caramelized. Slowly add the stock. Bring to a boil and simmer for 5 minutes. Add the grapefruit rind and juice and simmer 3 minutes longer. Strain into a clean saucepan and simmer until just thick enough to coat a spoon lightly. Adjust seasoning with salt and pepper and keep warm.
5. Serve ½ duckling per person. Garnish each serving with grapefruit sections and some of the sauce. Serve with the blanched vegetables.

VEAL STOCK

ABOUT 2 QUARTS

6 pounds meaty veal bones and knuckles or a combination of veal
and beef
2 tablespoons vegetable oil
2 large onions, washed and quartered
2 carrots, washed, trimmed, and coarsely sliced
2 stalks celery with leaves, washed and coarsely chopped
1 leek (both white and tender green sections), thoroughly washed,
halved lengthwise, and coarsely cut
4 cloves garlic, halved (no reason to peel)
1 small bunch parsley
2 cups water plus more as needed
½ teaspoon dried thyme
2 tomatoes, fresh or canned, coarsely cut,
or 3 tablespoons tomato paste
2 bay leaves
2 whole cloves
½ teaspoon each coarse salt and peppercorns

1. Preheat oven to 450 degrees. Put bones in a roasting pan and sprinkle with the oil. Roast for 35 minutes. Add onions, carrots, celery, leek, garlic, and parsley. Toss to coat all ingredients with fat and continue to roast for 30 minutes longer.
2. Remove pan from the oven and transfer its contents to a clean stockpot. Place roasting pan directly over medium-high heat, add 2 cups cold water, and boil briefly, stirring and scraping all the nice browned bits from bottom and sides. Add resulting liquid to the stockpot. Add enough additional water to just cover contents. Bring slowly to a boil, skimming off any froth or foam that rises to the surface, which would cloud the resulting stock.
3. Lower heat, add remaining ingredients except the peppercorns, and simmer uncovered for 6 to 8 hours, adding more water as needed just to keep ingredients covered. Add peppercorns during last 15 minutes of simmering.
4. Strain stock into a large bowl through a colander lined with a double layer of dampened cheesecloth, gently pressing solids to extract as much of the savory liquid as possible.
5. Cool at room temperature, partially covered, then refrigerate overnight. Carefully lift off and discard all fat that has accumulated on top, pour stock into containers for storage, label, and date. Stock keeps 3 days in the refrigerator and up to 6 months in the freezer.

DUCK STOCK

A variation of the above veal stock recipe. Prepare a veal stock, roasting bones and vegetables until well browned, then simmering about 3 hours. For an especially rich stock, roast duck bones and carcasses in a 450-degree oven for 30 minutes, then transfer them along with all fat in the pan to a pot of simmering veal stock and continue with veal recipe.

☆ ☆ # CHOCOLATE MOUSSE FLOWERPOTS ☆ ☆

SERVES 10

One of Mr. Fitoussi's most exquisite desserts is a chocolate mousse served in a ceramic flowerpot and topped with a single chocolate rose. For serving you will need five 2-cup cachepots or ceramic flowerpots, each to serve two.

> *Crème Anglaise (see below)*
> *Chocolate Mousse (see below)*
> *Chocolate Flowers (see below)*

To assemble the desserts: Divide the custard or crème anglaise into five 2-cup cachepots or other porcelain dishes shaped like flowerpots. Top with chocolate mousse, mounding slightly in the center. Set chocolate flower atop each mousse. Refrigerate for at least 20 minutes before serving. Each flowerpot makes 2 servings.

Note:

To anchor flowers more securely, place on lollipop sticks, then insert in mousse.

CRÈME ANGLAISE

3 cups milk
1 cup heavy cream
10 egg yolks, at room temperature
1 cup sugar

1. Bring milk and cream to a boil in a heavy saucepan.
2. Meanwhile beat egg yolks and sugar in electric mixer on high speed for at least 7 minutes, or until mixture is thick and pale in color and forms a ribbon when beaters are lifted. Slowly beat in 1 cup of the hot liquid. Then stir yolk mixture into remaining milk-cream mixture and cook over medium-low

heat, stirring constantly, until mixture is thick enough to coat the spoon. Do not let it boil. As soon as it begins to bubble around the sides of saucepan, lift pan off heat and whisk rapidly. If custard has not thickened enough, return to heat and continue the cooking and stirring.

3. Strain the custard into a large bowl set into a larger bowl of ice water and cool to room temperature, stirring occasionally. Cover and refrigerate for at least 2 hours.

CHOCOLATE MOUSSE

½ cup sugar
½ cup water
4 egg whites, at room temperature
¼ teaspoon cream of tartar
2 cups heavy cream, whipped to soft peaks
1 cup unsweetened cocoa
3 ounces semisweet chocolate, melted and cooled
3 tablespoons instant espresso powder

1. Heat sugar and water in a small heavy saucepan over medium-low heat until sugar is completely dissolved, stirring occasionally. Increase heat and boil to the soft ball stage (syrup will spin a long thread) or 240 degrees on a candy thermometer.
2. Meanwhile, beat egg whites and cream of tartar until soft peaks form. While beating, slowly pour the hot syrup into the egg whites and continue to beat for about 5 minutes, or until resulting meringue is cool.
3. Carefully fold in the whipped cream, cocoa, melted chocolate, and espresso. Cover and refrigerate for 1 hour.

CHOCOLATE FLOWERS

10 ounces coating chocolate or milk chocolate, coarsely chopped
¼ cup light corn syrup

1. Line a jelly roll pan with wax paper. Melt chocolate with the corn syrup, stirring until smooth. Pour onto prepared pan and spread with a metal spatula to a thickness of ¼ inch. Cool.
2. Transfer paper with chocolate to a clean work surface and place a second sheet of waxed paper over chocolate. Roll chocolate out with rolling pin to ⅛-inch thickness. Cut into 20 1-inch rounds with a cookie cutter. Roll a chocolate round into a tight funnel shape for center of flower. Gather 3 more rounds around center, forming petals. Squeeze together at the base. Place on wax-paper-lined plate. Repeat, forming 5 flowers. Refrigerate until firm.

"21" Club

21 West 52nd Street
New York, N.Y. 10019   582-7200

"21," named for its number on West 52nd Street, is one of the most famous restaurants in the city. It is a must for those visiting New York for the first time. Formerly an ultrachic speakeasy during Prohibition, it still retains the small window in the entrance door, once used to ensure its owners that the signaled knock was made by a customer and not by a cop. The first of its two floors is wood-paneled, crowded, but comfortable, the favorite spot of celebrities and for those who wish to see and be seen. The second floor is airy, with well-spaced tables reserved for clientele with a predilection for serious conversation, good food, and good wine. Rooms are available upstairs for private functions. At lunch, the two most popular dishes are a marvelous hamburger, a chicken hash with spinach sauce, and steak tartare. The restaurant is famous for elegant fish and seafood mousses, roast saddle of baby lamb, and broiled game in season, such as the recipe Mr. Jerry Berns, one of its executive owners, gave us for roast pheasant with the authoritative sauce known as périgourdine. Their "secret" underground cellar is considered the eighth wonder of New York City for both structure and content. After dinner tours are given if requested. Expensive. Reservations recommended.

☆ ☆ "21" 's ROAST BABY PHEASANT, ☆ ☆
SAUCE PÉRIGOURDINE

SERVES 4

If baby pheasant are not available to you, you may substitute Cornish game hens.

4 baby pheasants (1½ pounds each), oven ready and trussed
4 slices salt pork or leaf lard (the solid fat from the chest of a pig)
2 tablespoons vegetable oil
2 stalks celery, diced
2 medium carrots, scraped and diced
1 medium onion, peeled and diced
2 bay leaves
Pinch rosemary
About 1 cup chicken broth
4 teaspoons diced truffle
1 ounce (2 tablespoons) sherry
1 ounce (2 tablespoons) Cognac
1 teaspoon chopped shallots

1. Cover breast of each pheasant with a slice of salt pork or lard.
2. In a large sauté pan, heat oil, add the diced vegetables, bay leaves, and rosemary, and place the pheasants on top. Bake the birds in a 350-degree oven for about 40 minutes, basting occasionally with some of the chicken broth. If the juice runs clear when thigh is pierced with a fork, the birds are done.
3. When birds are cooked to taste, remove them to a serving dish and keep warm, reserving the cooking juices.
4. In a small saucepan combine the truffle, sherry, Cognac, and shallots. Simmer for a few minutes until liquid is reduced to about half. Strain liquids from the roasting pan into the truffle mixture and simmer on low heat for about 15 minutes.
5. When ready to serve, pour the sauce over the pheasant, and serve with cooked wild rice and braised celery or zucchini provençale.

☆ ☆   # ZUCCHINI PROVENÇALE   ☆ ☆

SERVES 4

2 tablespoons olive oil
3 ripe tomatoes, peeled and chopped
1 clove garlic, finely chopped
4 medium zucchini, sliced
2 tablespoons butter
Salt and freshly ground black pepper to taste

1. In a heavy saucepan heat olive oil and add tomatoes and garlic. Sauté over low heat for about 15 minutes.
2. Meanwhile sauté zucchini slices in butter in a separate pan until tender and golden brown.
3. Add the tomato-garlic mixture and simmer for 5 minutes. Season to taste with salt and pepper.

CHOCOLATE POTS DE CRÈME "21"

☆ ☆   ☆ ☆

SERVES 4 TO 6

One of the most popular desserts at this prestigious restaurant is the little ceramic pots filled with a rich chocolate cream.

1 pint light cream
½ cup sugar
4 egg yolks
1 whole egg
2 drops vanilla extract
Pinch salt
2½ ounces bitter chocolate, chopped
Whipped cream for garnish

1. In saucepan heat cream until hot but not boiling, and stir in half the sugar.
2. In a separate saucepan, beat together egg yolks and whole egg. Gradually beat in remaining sugar, vanilla, and salt.
3. Slowly pour the heated cream into the egg mixture, stirring constantly.
4. In a small heavy saucepan melt chocolate over very low heat. Very slowly stir in half the cream-egg mixture. Add remaining mixture, stir to combine, and strain through a fine sieve.
5. Pour into individual ceramic pots or ramekins or glass bowls, place them in a shallow pan containing a little hot water, and bake in a preheated 325-degree oven for 20 minutes.
6. Chill and top with whipped cream before serving.

Vanessa

289 Bleecker Street
New York, N.Y. 10014   243-4225

We don't know who Vanessa is, but she certainly inspired owner Robert Shapiro to create a romantic restaurant with superb eclectic American food. The deep mauve walls, Florentine wallpaper, and lace curtains are a fitting backdrop for the dramatic jumbo flower arrangements created by talented staff members.

But the real drama centers around the food. Twenty-four-year-old chef Ralph Scamardella brings his experience from places such as Le Cygne, the Polo, and Patisserie Lanciani, with results that belie his tender age. The menu changes frequently, but you'll almost always find a homemade pasta dish; fish fillet dipped in a macadamia-nut coating, sautéed and served with a butter sauce; and rack of lamb, roasted to a turn with pine nuts and rosemary. With your meal choose a wine from the well-stocked cellar.

Desserts are not to be missed. The chef tries to have a special cold and hot dessert each night in addition to an impressive choice of homemade ice creams and sorbets, chocolate cake, and mousse. No wonder reservations are a must.

☆ ☆   ## CRAYFISH BISQUE   ☆ ☆
SERVES 4

Chef Shapiro supplied us with such a wealth of recipes that it was almost impossible to choose among them. We are including all but two, beginning with this gorgeous smooth and flavorful crayfish bisque.

3 pounds live crayfish
2 quarts boiling water
Juice of 1 lemon
1 stick (4 ounces) butter
1 large onion, peeled and diced
2 stalks celery, washed and diced
1 clove garlic, peeled and minced
1 cup dry red wine
1 tablespoon tomato paste
2 quarts fish stock or half stock and half water
2 tablespoons dry tarragon
2 tablespoons dry thyme
1 cup heavy cream

1. Drop the live crayfish into the boiling water to which the lemon juice has been added. Return water to a boil and boil the crawfish for 1 minute. Drain the crayfish, let them cool, then remove the meat from the tails. Set tails, heads, and shells aside separately.
2. In a large stockpot melt the butter and in it sauté the diced vegetables and garlic over low heat. When vegetables are golden brown add the heads and shells of the crayfish and continue to sauté gently.
3. Add the red wine and cook until most of it is evaporated. Stir in the tomato paste, fish stock or stock and water, and the herbs. Continue to cook until liquid is reduced by ¼. Stir in the cream.
4. Purée the soup in a blender, 1 quart at a time, and strain through a sieve. Return the sieved soup to the stockpot, bring to a boil, then add the crayfish tails. Serve steaming hot.

☆ ☆ PASTA WITH WILD MUSHROOMS, ☆ ☆ MARSALA, CREAM, AND PARSLEY

SERVES 6

10 ounces fresh wild mushrooms or 1 ounce dry, reconstituted
2 tablespoons sweet butter
1 small shallot, minced
1 clove garlic, minced
¼ cup marsala wine
Pinch nutmeg
1 cup heavy cream (not ultrapasteurized; see page 303)
½ cup minced fresh parsley

1 tablespoon salt
1½ pounds homemade noodles or fettucine (see recipe for
Pasta Dough below)

1. Sauté the mushrooms in the butter with the shallot and garlic until golden brown. Add the marsala and boil until wine is reduced by half.
2. Stir in nutmeg and heavy cream and continue to boil until sauce is slightly thickened. Stir in parsley and set aside.
3. Roll out dough on a floured board or cloth until very thin, and cut into thin strips. If using a pasta machine, set it for the thinnest setting.
4. Meanwhile bring 1 gallon of water to a boil in a large saucepan. Add 1 tablespoon salt and the pasta and boil until pasta is just bite-tender or al dente.
5. Drain pasta, empty into a serving dish, and toss with the sauce.

PASTA DOUGH

1½ POUNDS

4 cups all-purpose flour
4 large eggs
2 tablespoons olive oil
1 teaspoon salt

1. Empty flour onto a pastry board or cloth and make a well in the center. Break eggs into the well and add the oil and salt. Gradually mix flour into the egg mixture and knead resulting dough until it is smooth.

☆ ☆ # SAUTÉED RED SNAPPER WITH PEPPER SAUCE ☆ ☆

SERVES 4

If you've ever found red snapper too mild, try it with this hot pepper sauce. It's delicious but needs a solid-fleshed fish that can hold its own.

2 red bell peppers
2 hot cherry peppers
½ tablespoon chopped shallots
2 tablespoons butter, divided
¼ cup dry vermouth
½ cup fish fumet or clam juice
1 cup heavy cream (not ultrapasteurized; see page 303)
2 pounds skinned red snapper fillet, cut into 8-ounce portions
2 tablespoons flour to coat the fish
Salt and pepper to taste
2 tablespoons olive oil
Watercress or parsley for garnish

1. Roast peppers in a 375-degree oven for about 20 minutes, or until skin is blistered. Remove from oven and put in a paper bag to cool. When cool, carefully remove thin outer skin, then core and discard seeds.
2. Chop the peppers, both the sweet and the hot, and sauté with the shallots in 1 tablespoon of the butter until lightly browned and tender. Add vermouth and boil until wine is reduced by half. Add the fish fumet or clam juice and again reduce liquid by half its original quantity. Add the cream and boil until the sauce is slightly thickened. Pour it into container of an electric blender, cover, and blend until smooth. Return sauce to saucepan, and set aside and keep warm.
3. Coat the fish fillets lightly with flour and sprinkle with salt and pepper. Sauté in the oil heated with the remaining tablespoon of butter for about 2 minutes on each side, or until golden brown.
4. Ladle some of the sauce onto a serving plate, arrange fish on top, and garnish with watercress or parsley.

☆ ☆ # RASPBERRY ICE CREAM ☆ ☆
ABOUT 1½ QUARTS

The ice cream served at Vanessa's is a real treat. It is made at the restaurant with heavy cream and fresh berries. What could be more refreshing and delicious?

3 egg yolks
3 tablespoons sugar
1 cup milk
3 cups heavy cream
1 tablespoon confectioner's sugar
12 ounces fresh raspberries or other seasonal berries (about 2 cups)
4 ounces (½ cup) raspberry liqueur

1. In upper half of a double boiler combine egg yolks, sugar, and milk, stirring until sugar is completely dissolved. Cook over simmering water until custard is thickened, stirring frequently. Set aside to cool.
2. In a mixing bowl combine cream, confectioner's sugar, fruit, and liqueur. Add the cooled custard and combine thoroughly. Empty into freezer container of an ice cream maker and churn until thick, following manufacturer's directions.

☆ ☆ # APPLE TARTS ☆ ☆

SERVES 2

Serve these tarts with whipped cream or crème fraîche (see page 301).

Pâte Brisée (see below)
2 Granny Smith apples, peeled, cored, and thinly sliced
4 tablespoons granulated sugar
2 tablespoons sweet butter

1. On a well-floured board or pastry cloth, roll out pastry to ⅛ inch thickness or less and cut into 2 8-inch rounds. Transfer pastry to baking sheets and arrange half the sliced apples on each round. Sprinkle each with sugar and dot with butter. Bake in a 325-degree oven for 15 minutes. Serve hot.

PÂTE BRISÉE

1 cup all-purpose flour
4 ounces (1 stick) butter, sliced
4 tablespoons confectioner's sugar
4 tablespoons cold water

1. Empty flour onto a pastry board or pastry cloth and cut in the butter. Add the sugar and mix lightly. When flour and butter bind, add the cold water, little by little, until dough forms a ball. Let dough rest for about 1 hour, covered lightly with a bowl, before rolling out.

Vašata

339 East 75th Street
New York, N.Y. 10021   988-7166

Vašata is comfortable, spacious, with an old-world Czechoslovakian country-inn charm, and rich middle-European fare is the rule here. This is the restaurant known for making Long Island duckling famous. Mrs. Vašata searched for many years to find the right source for Long Island duck that she felt was good enough to be served at Vašata. She and her chefs mastered the art of roasting the duck and the result is a tender, crispy dish that satisfies the discriminating taste of the most demanding gourmet.

☆ ☆   # Roast Duck Vašata Style   ☆ ☆
SERVES 2

Here is Mrs. Vašata's recipe.

> *1 Long Island duckling (6 or more pounds)*
> *2 teaspoons salt*
> *1 teaspoon caraway seeds*
> *Pork bones, duck wings, and giblets*
> *Hot water*
> *Cornstarch mixed with cold water*
> *Salt, if needed*

1. Preheat oven to 400 degrees.
2. Wash duckling and rub both inside and out with salt and caraway seeds.
3. Place bird in an open roasting pan on a bed of bones, add a little hot water to pan (more may be added during cooking time so bones do not burn), and roast in the hot oven for about 2½ hours or until tender. While roasting, prick skin all over with tines of a sharp fork so the fat can run off. Baste duck with drippings in the pan. When done the duck should be golden brown and there should not be any fat under the skin.
4. Remove duck from pan and keep warm. Drain most of the excess fat from pan and add hot water to the bones. Cook, scraping sides and bottom of pan, then return to oven for 15 minutes longer.
5. Strain liquid into a saucepan and bring to a boil on top of stove. Stir in about 1 teaspoon cornstarch mixed with a little cold water for each cup liquid in the pan. Simmer for 15 minutes, whisking constantly. Season to taste with salt, if necessary. If too salty, add a little more water.
6. Cut duck in half lengthwise and serve on a bed of the gravy.

☆ ☆ # PALAČINKY ☆ ☆

Makes 12 filled pancakes

Small pancakes filled with apricot jam and rum make a perfect dessert.

4 eggs
¼ cup sugar
1 cup all-purpose flour
Pinch salt
1 cup milk
½ teaspoon vanilla extract
Clarified butter for cooking pancakes
Confectioner's sugar

Filling:
1 12-ounce jar apricot jam
2 tablespoons water
1 tablespoon dark rum

1. In an electric mixer combine eggs and sugar until well blended. Add flour and salt and begin beating. While beating, gradually add milk and vanilla and beat on medium speed until batter is very smooth. Strain into a bowl and let stand at least 15 minutes.
2. While batter is resting, prepare filling. Mix the apricot jam with the water in a heavy saucepan. Bring to a simmer, add the rum, mix well and keep warm.
3. To cook the pancakes: Heat a small heavy 8-inch skillet or crêpe pan and brush bottom and sides generously with clarified butter. Pour in a small amount of batter and swirl pan to coat bottom with a light film of the batter. Cook until light brown on under side, then turn with a spatula and brown the other side. Flip out onto a heated plate and keep warm while making more pancakes.
4. Spread each pancake with apricot filling and roll into a cylinder. Sprinkle with confectioner's sugar and serve at once, while hot, 2 or 3 rolls per serving.

Victor's Cafe

240 Columbus Avenue, New York, N.Y. 10024   595-8599
236 West 52nd Street, New York, N.Y. 10019   586-7714

It's hard to remember Victor's not being crowded, nor the food not being satisfying. Forget that the combination of rice and beans is a perfect protein and just lean back and enjoy the food. There are two Victor's Cafes; we think the one on Columbus Avenue is more fun. This restaurant was a staple of the area long before Columbus Avenue became a haven for New York yuppies. The food is not Spanish, it's Cuban—the difference found in dishes such as suckling pig and ropa vieja, a version of pot roast in which the meat seems to fall into succulent shreds. Victor's will be around long after most of the yuppies have started families and left for the suburbs. It's one establishment that is here to stay.

☆ ☆   # RED SNAPPER VASCA STYLE   ☆ ☆
(Red snapper with green sauce)
SERVES 6

Because of the attractive color of the skin of the red snapper, this fish is usually served with the skin left on the fillets, but it is seldom eaten. The dish is served with cooked rice and garnishes.

6 8-ounce fillets of red snapper, well scaled and washed
12 littleneck clams
12 fresh mussels
12 shrimp, shelled and deveined
2 medium onions, peeled and cut into julienne strips
2 medium green peppers, seeded and cut into julienne strips
3 cups Green Sauce (see below)
1½ tablespoons cornstarch
⅓ cup dry white wine
For garnish: white asparagus, red pimientos, green peas,
and ½ hard-boiled egg

1. In a large skillet put all the seafood, onions, and peppers. Pour the Green Sauce over the seafood, bring to a boil, cover, and simmer for about 15 minutes.
2. Combine cornstarch with white wine and stir into ingredients in the skillet. Cook, stirring gently, for 5 minutes.
3. Serve with the garnish and cooked white rice.

GREEN SAUCE

4 bunches parsley, leaves only
6 cloves garlic, peeled and halved crosswise
½ teaspoon salt
¼ teaspoon freshly ground black pepper
1⅔ cups dry white wine
1 cup white vinegar

1. Pack blender container with parsley and place garlic on top. Add salt and black pepper and slowly pour wine and vinegar into the container, giving it time to run through the leaves to the bottom.
2. Cover container and blend on high speed for 30 seconds.

The Village Green

531 Hudson Street
New York, N.Y. 10014   255-1650

The Village Green is elegant, pretty, and even boasts a piano bar.
The food can best be characterized as continental. The upper floor
of this town house holds the bar and piano, and a few tables. For
dining, opt for the lower level whenever possible. It's quieter and
you can always wander upstairs for a brandy after dinner if you
wish.

The subtle lighting, intimate atmosphere, and easygoing service
make this a romantic place that belies the boisterous village atmosphere outside. The menu offers such tempting appetizers as
oysters topped with beluga caviar and served with ice-cold vodka,
and the main courses include many delicious fish and chicken
dishes plus sirloin steak prosciutto, filet mignon in green peppercorn sauce, and veal sweetbreads with a truffle sauce. The prices
are modest for the quality.

☆ ☆ # CRAB MORNAY AU GRATIN ☆ ☆

SERVES 4

1 pound lump crab meat
1 quart Béchamel Sauce (see below)
½ cup freshly grated Parmesan cheese
¼ cup shredded Gruyère cheese
4 thin slices bread, toasted
4 sprigs parsley

1. Clean the crab meat, discarding any bits of cartilage or shell. Set aside.
2. Combine the béchamel and the cheeses and heat, stirring, until sauce is smooth. Stir in the crab meat.
3. Divide crab meat and sauce into four gratin dishes and place under broiler for about 8 minutes, or until sauce is tinged with brown.
4. Cut each slice of toast into 4 triangles and arrange them around each serving. Garnish each with a sprig of parsley.

BÉCHAMEL SAUCE

1 QUART

½ cup (1 stick) lightly salted butter
1 small onion, finely chopped
½ cup flour
1 quart milk
⅛ teaspoon each nutmeg, salt, white pepper

1. In a saucepan melt butter and in it sauté the chopped onion until onion is transparent.
2. Remove saucepan from the heat, add the flour, and stir until the mixture is smooth. Return to heat and cook, stirring, for 5 minutes.
3. Add milk and continue to cook and stir until sauce is thickened. Strain through a fine sieve and stir in seasonings.

☆ ☆   # CHOCOLATE MOUSSE,   ☆ ☆
VILLAGE GREEN
SERVES 6

Following the light luncheon dish of crab mornay, almost anyone can afford the extra calories of this chocolate mousse.

8 ounces semisweet chocolate
½ cup water
2 cups confectioner's sugar
7 eggs
2 ounces Grand Marnier
1 pint heavy cream, whipped

1. In the top of a double boiler over simmering water put chocolate, water, and sugar. Stir occasionally until chocolate is melted and mixture is smooth.
2. Meanwhile separate eggs.
3. Add Grand Marnier to the yolks and beat thoroughly. Add chocolate mixture and stir until yolks and chocolate are well blended. Fold in the whipped cream.
4. Beat egg whites until they stand in soft peaks. Do not overbeat. Add to chocolate mixture and fold all together until there are no signs of whipped cream or egg whites.
5. Pour into a serving bowl or individual 6-ounce custard cups and refrigerate until needed. If leaving overnight, be sure to cover the surface of the mousse lightly with plastic wrap.

The Water Club

The East River at 30th Street
New York, N.Y. 10016   683-3333

The great cities around the world show off their waterfronts, except New York. To get a great view of Manhattan you have to go to New Jersey or Brooklyn. There is now one restaurant in Manhattan that is not only on the water, its nautical atmosphere makes it seem as if you're actually in the river. The menu is dedicated to American dining—ham, broiled fish, lobster, and wonderful fresh oysters. The service is also typically American—casual. Window tables at any level are choice, but if they're not available you'll probably find you can get a sense of being out to sea wherever you sit.

☆ ☆   # CORN AND CRAB MEAT   ☆ ☆
CHOWDER
SERVES 6 TO 9

One of the most delicious chowders we have ever tasted is served here as a first course. In your own home it can be easily duplicated and would make an exquisite luncheon dish with a salad and a dessert.

½ pound sliced bacon, finely cut
1 medium onion, peeled and finely chopped
2 large cloves garlic, peeled and finely chopped
2 stalks celery, diced
1 large leek, white part only, finely cut
½ teaspoon dry thyme or a small bunch of fresh thyme
1 bay leaf
8 ounces corn kernels, fresh or frozen (1 cup)
1 quart chicken broth
Freshly ground pepper to taste
2 cups (1 pint) heavy cream
2 tablespoons arrowroot or cornstarch
2 tablespoons cold chicken broth or water
½ pound fresh lump crab meat

1. In a 3-quart saucepan or kettle sauté bacon until it is crisp. Drain off all but 1 tablespoon of the drippings, and add the onion, garlic, celery, leek, thyme, and bay leaf, and sauté for 5 minutes, stirring frequently. Add the corn and cook over low heat, stirring frequently, for 10 minutes longer.
2. Add the quart of chicken broth and pepper to taste, and cook for 40 minutes.
3. Add cream and the arrowroot or cornstarch mixed with the 2 tablespoons chicken broth or water, and cook for 5 minutes without letting the mixture boil.
4. Just before serving, add the crab meat.

☆ ☆ SWORDFISH WITH RASPBERRIES ☆ ☆ AND GINGER

SERVES 6

This recipe sounds like one of those pretentious dishes that go out as fast as they come in, but the unusual combination of sweet, hot, and sour turns out to be a rare complement to an otherwise dull fish and makes a dish that is here to stay.

½ cup raspberry or apple cider vinegar or any
fruit-flavored vinegar
1 pint fresh raspberries, divided
¾ cup julienned fresh ginger, divided
2 cups (1 pint) demiglace or homestyle brown gravy
1 tablespoon crushed black peppercorns
Salt to taste
1 or 2 tablespoons honey (optional)
6 swordfish steaks about 1 inch thick, each weighing 8 ounces

1. In a saucepan combine the fruit vinegar, ¾ of the raspberries, and ½ cup sliced fresh ginger. Bring to a boil and cook until raspberries are wilted and the vinegar is reduced to about half its original quantity.
2. Stir in the gravy or demiglace and the black peppercorns and cook for 12 to 15 minutes.
3. Strain to remove raspberry seeds and the peppercorns, pressing through as much of the raspberry pulp as possible, or put through a food mill, and correct the seasoning. If the sauce is too sour, stir in 1 to 2 tablespoons honey. Set aside.
4. Spray a skillet large enough to hold the fish steaks with a vegetable shortening and in it sauté the swordfish for about 5 minutes on each side, or until cooked through.
5. Arrange fish on a warm serving dish. Quickly reheat sauce and pour it over the fish. Sprinkle sauce with remaining ¼ cup ginger. Garnish platter with remaining fresh raspberries.

Wilkinson's Seafood Cafe

1573 York Avenue (near 84th Street)
New York, N.Y. 10028   535-5454

A really good fish house is hard to find. It takes a chef who knows precisely when to take the fish out of the broiler, poacher, and so on, imaginative cooking so that the sauces contain more than butter and lemon and, realistically, a few good meat dishes for that one member of the party who either doesn't like seafood or can't eat it. Wilkinson's does all these things well and does them in a friendly atmosphere that's one step up from the corner bistro. You'll find patrons who savor good fish dishes and know enough about superior food to appreciate it. The luscious desserts are a bonus and somehow seem more justifiable after a lean fish entrée.

☆ ☆ DOVER SOLE WITH ROE SAUCE ☆ ☆
SERVES 2

We begin with a glorious entrée of Dover sole with a sauce as smooth as silk and as rich as Croesus—not a dish that is going to justify a sumptuous dessert.

2 individual Dover sole (see Note) with roe when possible
1 large shallot, minced
½ cup dry white wine
1 cup fresh pasteurized heavy cream, (not ultrapasteurized; see page 303)
Juice of 1 lemon or to taste
Salt and freshly ground white pepper
1 tablespoon minced fresh parsley

1. Have your fish dealer fillet the sole, saving any roe inside. Wash in cold water and dry on paper towels. Set aside.

289

2. Put the minced shallot and white wine into a small saucepan and boil over moderately high heat until almost all of the wine is evaporated.

3. Add the cream and boil hard until it is reduced by half and is thick enough to coat the spoon.

4. Add the roe and simmer over low heat for 2 minutes, or until the roe turns a pale beige. Add lemon juice. Transfer sauce to a blender container and blend on high speed until sauce is almost smooth.

5. Season sauce to taste with salt and pepper.

6. Arrange sole fillets on an oiled rack in a broiling pan and broil 4 inches from the heat for 2 minutes, or until the flesh is white and firm to the touch. Do not attempt to turn the fillets.

7. Place two fillets per serving on warm plates, cover with the creamy sauce, and sprinkle with chopped parsley.

Note:

No true Dover sole swims in American waters. It is imported from seaports on the English channel to our shores. It is, however, difficult for the home chef to procure and its cost usually encourages us to settle for delicate-fleshed, close-grained flat fish that masquerade as sole, such as fluke and flounder, sand dabs, and English, gray, or lemon sole. There will be no roe, of course, so if you wish to be adventuresome, add 2 teaspoons red salmon caviar to the finished sauce. It needs no cooking.

☆ ☆   PRAWNS WITH SHRIMP SAUCE   ☆ ☆

SERVES 4

The next recipe from chef Ron Myers at Wilkinson's is broiled prawns with an extraordinarily flavorful sauce that simmers for 3 hours. Once the sauce is made, the dish is ready to serve in two minutes. Prawns are extra large shrimp, ten or less per pound. If not available settle for the largest you can buy. The original recipe also called for the heads of two lobsters. That's all very simple for a restaurant that serves lobster dishes on its menu, but rather tough on the homemaker who must, to be practical, eat lobster one night in order to save the heads for this sauce. We tried the sauce with and without the lobster heads and found it difficult to distinguish between the two versions. If you want to be truly authentic, next time you eat lobster in your own home, freeze the heads for use in this dish. Discard them when sauce is finished cooking and before it is put in the blender.

20 *large prawns or 2 pounds largest fresh shrimp available*
¹⁄₄ pound (1 stick) sweet butter
5 stalks celery, chopped
2 carrots, trimmed, washed, and chopped
1 large onion, peeled and chopped
¹⁄₂ teaspoon each dry thyme, oregano, and basil
1 pound (2 cups) crushed fresh or canned tomatoes
1 bay leaf
2 teaspoons paprika
1 cup dry white wine
¹⁄₄ cup brandy
4 cups water
2 tablespoons horseradish
Cayenne pepper and salt to taste
Chopped parsley for garnish

1. Shell and devein the shrimp, reserving the shells. Wash the shells well and set aside. Wash and refrigerate the prawns.
2. In a 3- or 4-quart saucepan melt the butter and in it sauté the celery, carrots, onion, thyme, oregano, and basil over low heat for 10 minutes.
3. Add tomatoes and cook for 5 minutes longer, tossing occasionally.
4. Add bay leaf, paprika, white wine, brandy, and water. Add lobster heads (optional and not listed in ingredients) and shrimp shells.
5. Simmer from 2 to 3 hours, or until liquid barely covers the chopped vegetables. Stir occasionally.
6. If lobster heads were used for flavor, discard them at this point. Pour remaining sauce, half at a time, into container of an electric blender and blend until shrimp shells are pulverized and sauce is smooth (see Note).
7. Stir in horseradish and season with cayenne and salt to taste. Return to saucepan and keep warm.
8. Boil prawns for approximately 2 minutes on each side, only long enough for the flesh to turn opaque. Take care not to overcook them.
9. Serve the prawns covered with the shrimp sauce. Garnish with chopped parsley.

Note:
   If you wish, you may put your sauce through the fine screen of a food mill, but we did not find this necessary. The sauce was satiny smooth.

Windows on the World

One World Trade Center
New York, N.Y. 10048   938-1111

Here the food plays second fiddle to the fantastic view—you can see all of Manhattan, New York harbor, and as far as Brooklyn and New Jersey from different windows. If you're lucky enough to get a table at a window (there is no way of reserving one), you can have the deliciously eerie experience of looking down on the clouds from one hundred stories up. Even the weather may be different from what it is on the ground! The menu is standard à la carte fare with one exception, the elegant Cellar in the Sky—but there is no view from there. Many people prefer to go to the Windows on the World bar, which has a limited dinner menu, live music, and a view. Better yet, come for brunch and bring the kids. Well-behaved youngsters are welcome. Boys are required to wear jackets, and no jeans are allowed for anyone.

☆ ☆ ## BEEF MEDALLIONS WITH BRAISED SHALLOTS IN RED WINE SAUCE ☆ ☆
SERVES 4

Medallions are thin slices, about ½ inch thick, from the chateaubriand section of a beef tenderloin. This particular dish is perfect for guests. The sauce may—and actually should—be made at least a day ahead. From then on it requires only minutes to complete the dish for the table. Serve it with cooked vegetables in season. Here it is served with cooked sliced zucchini and broiled tomatoes.

292

½ pound shallots, peeled
2 ounces (½ stick) sweet butter
½ cup red burgundy or Bordeaux wine
¾ cup Sauce Bordelaise (see below)
2 tablespoons olive oil
8 medallions of beef, each 2 to 3 ounces
Chopped parsley for garnish

1. Sauté the shallots in the butter until golden on all sides, shaking pan frequently. Add red wine and simmer for 10 minutes, or until shallots are fork tender. Add bordelaise sauce and simmer until sauce is the desired consistency. Set aside.
2. In a large heavy skillet heat oil until very hot. In it sauté the medallions of beef for 3 minutes on each side for medium rare.
3. Put 2 medallions on each warm serving plate, cover meat with sauced shallots, and sprinkle with chopped parsley. Garnish plates with cooked zucchini and a half a tomato or other colorful vegetable in season.

SAUCE BORDELAISE (Long version)

ABOUT 2 CUPS

The traditional version of this sauce takes several hours to make and in a restaurant is made by the sauce chef. At home we don't have as much time to devote to sauce making, so we've added a short version that even the best chef would be hard put to tell from the real thing.

4 pounds beef and veal bones, chopped by butcher
1 medium onion, peeled and diced
1 large carrot, trimmed, washed, and coarsely cut
2 stalks celery with leaves, washed and coarsely cut
2 tablespoons cooking oil
4 tablespoons tomato paste
1 cup mushroom stems and trimmings or 2 whole mushrooms, chopped
4 tablespoons flour
½ cup red wine
6 cups water
A little salt
15 white peppercorns
2 bay leaves
2 tablespoons beef bone marrow, diced

1. Spread bones in a large roasting pan and roast in a 400-degree oven for 45 to 60 minutes. Add vegetables and cooking oil and roast for 10 minutes longer.
2. Add the tomato paste and mushrooms, and continue to roast for an additional 30 minutes. Sprinkle with flour, stir in half the red wine, and reduce.
3. Add remaining red wine and water. Transfer to top of stove and bring liquid to a boil. Skim off fat and foam from surface and season the liquid lightly with salt. Add peppercorns and bay leaves. Cook slowly for about 2 hours, or until liquid is reduced to about half its original quantity.
4. Strain through a fine sieve into a clean saucepan, bring to a boil, and skim off excess fat. Cook to desired consistency, or until at least 2 cups of the sauce remain. If the sauce is too thin, mix 1 tablespoon cornstarch with a little red wine and stir into the boiling sauce.
5. Remove from heat and add the diced marrow.

BORDELAISE SAUCE (Short version)

ABOUT 1½ CUPS

1 12-ounce jar commercial homestyle brown gravy (see Note)
1 tablespoon dry sherry
1 tablespoon dry red wine
1 teaspoon tomato paste
Freshly ground black pepper
1 tablespoon chopped beef bone marrow (optional)

1. Pour ¾ cup of the gravy into a saucepan. Stir in the sherry, red wine, tomato paste, and pepper to taste. Bring to a boil and cook to the desired consistency.
2. Remove from heat and add, if desired, the beef bone marrow.

Note:
Recipe may be doubled, using the entire contents of the jar and doubling all other ingredients. Save the jar to store any leftover sauce in the refrigerator, where it will keep for a week to ten days. It's good on almost any cooked meat or fowl or makes an interesting addition to spaghetti sauce.

☆ ☆ # HAZELNUT DACQUOISE ☆ ☆

SERVES 12

One of the many tempting desserts served at Windows on the World.

1 cup egg whites (about 8)
1 pound (2 cups) fine granulated sugar
½ pound toasted, skinned, and ground hazelnuts
2½ cups Amaretto Butter Cream (see below)

1. Whip egg whites until foamy; gradually beat in sugar and whip until meringue is stiff. Fold in hazelnuts.
2. Using a pastry bag fitted with a ¾-inch tip, pipe meringue onto greased and floured baking sheets into three 12-inch circles. (Trace the circles in the floured surface of the baking sheets before piping meringue.)
3. Bake in a 200- to 225-degree oven for about 1 hour, or until the meringues are pale brown, firm, and dry. Remove from oven to cool.
4. When cool, trim edges with a serrated knife to make sides straight and put the rounds together with Amaretto Butter Cream, leaving the top bare. Sieve the trimmed crumbs and pat around sides of the dacquoise. Keep cold until ready to serve.

AMARETTO BUTTER CREAM

1 cup sugar
⅓ cup water
¼ teaspoon cream of tartar
4 egg yolks
1 cup (2 sticks) sweet butter, at room temperature
4 tablespoons (2 ounces) Amaretto
2 tablespoons very strong espresso, cooled

1. In a small saucepan combine sugar, water, and cream of tartar. Bring slowly to a boil and boil rapidly until syrup spins a long thread.
2. Put egg yolks into bowl of an electric beater and beat until pale and thickened. Gradually beat in the syrup and continue to beat until mixture is very thick.
3. Gradually beat in the butter, bit by bit and, finally, beat in the Amaretto and coffee. Chill until thick enough to spread.

Woods Gramercy

24 East 21st Street
New York, N.Y. 10010   505-5252

Uptown at 718 Madison Avenue, Woods is a small, sparse restaurant that mixes minimalism in design with nouvelle cuisine. But in the branch near Gramercy Park, Zeus Goldberg has added elegant carpeting, plush cushions, a less formal atmosphere that doesn't lose any luxury in the translation. The restaurant's space is broken into several areas with tables far enough apart to let you eat and talk in privacy.

The food is what the owner likes to call "modern American," with an emphasis on pastas and fish. The prices are not inexpensive but the quality is worth it. For those who want to sample this cuisine, but would like to do so on a small budget, try the brunch, or walk into Out of the Woods next door and walk out with an interesting take-out meal. There is a third Woods at 148 West 37th Street.

☆ ☆ ## WOODS'S GRILLED SWORDFISH ☆ ☆
SERVES 8

The grilled swordfish at Woods is served with a tantalizing oriental sauce flavored with grated orange zest and fresh ginger.

½ cup sherry
½ cup soy sauce
1 tablespoon lemon juice
2 cloves garlic, minced
1 tablespoon minced gingerroot
Grated rind of 2 oranges
8 swordfish steaks, about ½ pound each
Sesame oil

296

1. In a flat-bottomed dish combine sherry, soy sauce, lemon juice, garlic, ginger, and orange zest. Let stand for 1 hour.
2. Arrange swordfish steaks in the dish and brush both sides with the marinade. Marinate in the refrigerator for at least 45 minutes, turning steaks at least once.
3. Brush the steaks with sesame oil and grill or broil them about 4 inches from the heat for 8 to 10 minutes per inch, or until cooked through, turning them once.

☆ ☆ WOODS'S CHOCOLATE ROULADE ☆ ☆
SERVES 10 TO 12

The special Woods touch to this popular dessert containing no flour is the dash of coffee liqueur added to the whipped cream filling. It's feather-light and frequently garnished with strawberries.

> *Oil for pan*
> *Wax paper*
> *12 eggs, separated*
> *2 cups superfine granulated sugar, plus about ½ cup*
> *1 cup Dutch-process cocoa*
> *6 ounces semisweet chocolate*
> *¼ cup very strong coffee*
> *1 pint (2 cups) heavy cream*
> *2 teaspoons instant espresso*
> *2 teaspoons coffee liqueur*
> *2 tablespoons confectioner's sugar*
> *Strawberries for garnish (optional)*

1. Oil a 10½- x 15-inch jelly-roll pan, and line it with wax paper, letting the wax paper form a rim. Oil the paper. Set aside.
2. Prepare the cake batter, in reality a soufflé batter: In an electric mixer beat egg yolks and 2 cups of the sugar until the mixture is thick, pale in color, and forms a ribbon when the beater is withdrawn. This will take at least 5 to 10 minutes on high speed.
3. Gently fold in the cocoa, sifting a little at a time over the surface of the beaten eggs, and folding it in until it is incorporated and the batter is smooth.
4. Beat egg whites until they stand in soft peaks (do not overbeat) and fold thoroughly into the egg-cocoa mixture.
5. Pour batter onto prepared pan, spread it well into the corners, and bake in a preheated 375-degree oven for 18 to 20 minutes, or until cake tests done.

6. Remove from oven, cover surface of the cake with wax paper, then with a kitchen towel, and place on a cake rack to cool.

7. While the cake is cooling, prepare the filling: Melt chocolate with the strong coffee over very low heat. It should be the consistency of mayonnaise. Set aside. Remove towel and wax paper from top of cake and run a knife around edge of cake to loosen it from the pan.

8. Lay two overlapping strips of wax paper lengthwise on work-table. They should be wider than the width of the cake. Sift the remaining ½ cup superfine sugar over the surface of the cake to coat it generously, then flip baking pan and cake up-side down onto center of the paper strips. The long side of the baking pan should be parallel to counter edge.

9. Carefully remove baking sheet: Grasp the edge of the wax paper lining the sheet and gently raise baking sheet from right to left. Peel wax paper from the bottom of the cake.

10. Spread surface of cake with the melted chocolate.

11. Whip the cream in an electric blender (page 303) until it is thick enough to spread. Add and blend in instant espresso and the coffee liqueur. Spread the chocolate cream over surface of the cake.

12. Now the fun part: Grasp the wide side of the wax paper clos-est to you with both hands, raise the edge of the cake, and roll about 1 inch over filling. Continue to lift the wax paper, and roll cake and filling with it, making a long roll about 4 inches in diameter. Don't be upset if it cracks a little, especially on the first try. It often does, but that does not spoil the taste. The last roll of the cake should deposit it near the edge of the wax paper.

13. Place a long serving board on far side of the roll, parallel to it, and lift wax paper and roll onto the board. Carefully cut around wax paper with a sharp knife, then pull it gently out from under the roll.

14. Refrigerate for about 2 hours before serving. Sift confec-tioner's sugar over top of the cake and garnish with strawber-ries, if desired.

Note:
If you moisten your work surface with a damp sponge, it will keep wax paper from slipping.

Notes and Techniques

☆ ☆ ☆ ☆

Although the specific suggesstions that follow will be old hat to sophisticated home chefs, they do bear repeating, and may help the less experienced, aspiring cooks who read this book achieve success more readily.

Garlic:

To peel and chop garlic, place an unpeeled clove on the chopping block or board and give it a whack with the flat side of a heavy knife or cleaver, just hard enough to crush it. The papery outer skin can then be lifted away and discarded. Give the clove another hard whack. Scoop the smashed garlic onto the side of the knife and transfer it to the skillet or casserole. In some dishes (salads, for example), garlic should be neatly minced after the first whack. Garlic odor can be removed from fingers by rubbing your hands with salt before washing.

Gingerroot:

Fresh ginger is now widely available, but usually comes in a piece too large to use at one time. Buy young, pinkish roots. They can be stored, unpeeled, in a paper bag in the refrigerator or on a cupboard shelf, or peeled, cut into pieces, and refrigerated in a jar, covered with sherry or vodka; or they can be minced, double-bagged in freezer bags, and frozen—very young roots can be frozen unpeeled.

HERBS:

If you wish to grow your own fresh herbs, Nicols Garden Nursery, 1190 North Pacific Hwy., Albany, OR 97321, specializes in herb plants and seeds, herbal teas, elephant garlic, gourmet vegetable seeds from around the world, and ecological low-maintenance flowering herbal turf. They guarantee that their plants will arrive in perfect condition.

MUSHROOMS:

New varieties of mushrooms seem to appear in the stores daily. If you cannot find a variety you want, one of the best sources of wet-packed and dried mushrooms imported from Europe is the S. E. Rykoff Company, P.O. Box 21467, Los Angeles, CA 90021. Maison Glass, 52 East 58th Street, New York, NY 10022, also carries both wet-packed and dried mushrooms of various types.

PEPPERCORNS:

The most widely used spice in the world, pepper is probably the most important spice in the kitchen. Once pepper is ground, it quickly loses fragrant oils and piquancy, so it should always be ground fresh. Although black peppercorns abound, it is more difficult (but well worth it) to find unground white peppercorns. Once a novelty item used only by restaurants, green peppercorns, preserved either in salt or vinegar, will last indefinitely in the refrigerator after they are opened. It's a good idea to use several different grinders, one for each type of pepper. Szechwan peppercorns are best ground with a mortar and pestle.

SWEET AND HOT PEPPERS:

Sweet bell peppers, both green and red, have been around for years. Recently, yellow and purple sweet peppers have appeared on the market. While the yellow are fruity and juicy, the purple are disappointing—only the skin is purple, and the green flesh is less flavorful than the traditional sweet green bell pepper.

The "heat" in fresh, green, hot chile peppers can be reduced by removing stems, seeds, and veins, and soaking the flesh in cold water for thirty minutes to an hour. Hot pepper juice can burn skin, so care must be taken to wear rubber gloves and wash hands thoroughly in soap and water after working with hot peppers. Be very careful not to get any juice in your eyes, as it can be very painful.

SHALLOTS:

Once rarely found in supermarkets, shallots are now quite common. A pint of shallots will go a long way and will keep a long time without drying or sprouting if you store them in a cool, dark place. They should not be kept in the refrigerator. One medium shallot weighs about ½ ounce and makes one tablespoon when peeled and minced.

CLARIFIED BUTTER:

Put a pound (or less) of unsalted (sweet) butter in a small saucepan and melt over low heat. Pour the clear liquid into a container, discarding the milky substance at the bottom of the pan. The process can be repeated and the resulting oil strained through a muslin cloth—it will be pure and crystal clear. Clarified butter needs no refrigeration and is an excellent medium for sautéing as it does not burn.

CONCASSE OF TOMATOES:

Peel 2 ripe tomatoes, quarter them, and squeeze out seeds and excess liquid. Chop into small pieces and stew in 1 tablespoon hot butter until most of the moisture is cooked away and the tomato pulp is soft. For variation, flavor with chopped dill and/or tarragon. Freeze in small amounts in double freezer bags and reheat to use as garnish.

CRÈME FRAÎCHE:

Stir 1 tablespoon plain yogurt into one container or 1 cup (8 ounces) of heavy sweet pasteurized cream and let stand at room temperature for 24 hours, or overnight. Refrigerate, and use as needed.

PESTO FOR WINTER USE

Half fill a blender container with very fresh, rinsed and dried sweet basil. Add 6 cloves garlic, peeled and halved crosswise, ½ cup pine nuts or walnuts (optional), and ½ cup olive oil. Blend, and purée at high speed, adding a bit more oil if needed. Continue to add basil leaves and oil, while blending, until container is almost full.

Place mixture in dry jars, filling to within one inch of the top. Fill with salad oil, cover tightly, and store in the refrigerator or cupboard. One 8-ounce jar is sufficient pesto for one pound of spaghetti, to serve four.

SWEET BASIL PRESERVED IN OIL:

(Makes about 1 cup preserved basil)

4 cups fresh green basil leaves, rinsed if necessary, and thoroughly dried
½ cup olive oil, plus additional oil as needed, and to cover surface

Put one cup of the basil leaves and ½ cup oil in blender container. Blend at high speed until leaves are finely chopped. Continue to add leaves by the handful, while blending, adding a little more oil from time to time as needed. Scrape the mixture into a small glass container and add enough oil to cover the surface of the basil by ½ inch. Cover tightly and store at room temperature.

To use, dip out the amount of basil needed and strain the oil back into the container. Add more oil if needed to cover surface again by ½ inch.

RED CHILE PEPPER OIL FOR ORIENTAL RECIPES:

In Oriental cooking, a dozen red chile peppers are often fried whole in a little hot cooking oil until they become black. They are then discarded and the rest of the dish cooked in the nut-flavored peppery oil that remains. See the recipe given by Shun Lee Palace for Orange Beef.

TARRAGON-FLAVORED VINEGAR:

Save the last of the wine in the bottles, and collect in a half-gallon bottle until it is half full. Pack it full of tarragon leaves with their stems, fill bottle full of cider vinegar, and allow to mature for at least a month. As used, fill the bottle alternately with wine and vinegar.

WHIPPED CREAM ROSETTES FOR GARNISHING:

Whipped cream that is to be used for decorating should be whipped in an electric blender. It will not have the volume that it would have if beaten with a rotary beater or wire whisk, but will not "weep" as readily. Whip only 1 cup at a time for best results. As soon as the cream begins to thicken, turn off the blender, and stir with a rubber spatula. Leave the top off the container, and continue alternately blending and stirring several times until the cream is very thick. Transfer to a pastry bag fitted with a large, fluted tube, and pipe out rosettes onto a baking sheet lined with wax paper. Freeze until solid, remove rosettes with a spatula, and drop them into a double freezer bag. They will remain fresh and ready to use, as needed, for a couple of months.

WHAT YOU MUST KNOW ABOUT CREAM

Most of the cream and milk products available to the homemaker today are "ultra" pasteurized, meaning they have been subjected to ultra-high temperatures that render them literally sterile, with no viability. This gives them a shelf life of 35 to 40 days as compared with the shelf life of 10 days for the fresh pasteurized products. As a result they are welcomed by supermarket managers. Ultrapasteurization gives the cream a burnt flavor, destroys all the original bacteria, both good and bad, its enzymes and all its thickening properties. The cream doesn't even have the grace to turn into edible sour cream. There must be at least one dairy in your area, supplying the good restaurants, that has a few conscientious retail outlets that you can track down to supply you with the pure pasteurized products, especially pure pasteurized cream, which gets thicker as it stands in the refrigerator, can be made into crème fraîche by the addition of a little yogurt, and can be reduced by boiling over direct heat to saucelike thickness without the need for flour or starch thickeners, properties essential to the good cook or master chef.

It's a sad commentary on the times when shelf life comes ahead of quality and flavor. Types of cream in both regular pasteurized and the ultrapasteurized impostors are:

Heavy (whipping) cream is rich and thick with 35 to 45% butterfat content.

Light (coffee) cream is an all-purpose cream with 18 to 20% butterfat content. Good for tea or coffee.

Half-and-half is a mixture of milk and light cream with 12 to 14% butterfat content. It will not whip but may be substituted for light cream in puddings.

SOURCES OF SPECIAL COOKING EQUIPMENT AND SPECIALTY FOODS

☆ ☆ ☆ ☆

Bazaar Française, 666 Sixth Avenue, New York, N.Y. 10010—Fine cooking utensils; catalog

Bridge Kitchenware, 214 East 52nd Street, New York, N.Y. 10022 —Fine cooking utensils

Byrd Mill, RFD 5, Louisa, Va. 23093—Whole grains, stone-ground flours and meals

Casa Moneo, 210 West 14th Street, New York, N.Y. 10011—Spanish and Mexican foods; catalog

Charles & Company, 340 Madison Avenue, New York, N.Y. 10017 —Assorted delicacies and cheeses; catalog

H. Roth & Sons, 1577 First Avenue, New York, N.Y. 10028—Hungarian and middle European foods, herbs, spices; catalog

Kam Man Food Products, 200 Canal Street, New York, N.Y. 10013 —Vietnamese and Chinese foods

Kassos Brothers, 570 Ninth Avenue, New York, N.Y. 10036—Greek foods

Katagari, 224 East 59th Street, New York, N.Y. 10022—Japanese foods and supplies

Kendall Brown, P.O. Box 3365, San Rafael, Calif. 94912—Raspberry vinegar

Maison Glass, 52 East 59th Street, New York, N.Y. 10022—Various
delicacies, special oils and vinegars, caviar, foie gras, St. André
triple cream cheese; catalog

Manganaro's, 488 Ninth Avenue, New York, N.Y. 10018—Italian
specialties; catalog

Maryland Gourmet Mart, 1072 First Avenue, New York, N.Y. 10022
—Game, assorted delicacies; catalog

Nichols Garden Nursery, 1190 North Pacific Hwy., Albany, Oreg.
97321—Live herb plants, annuals and perennials, guaranteed to
arrive in good condition; catalog

Poseidon Confectionery Co., 629 Ninth Avenue, New York, N.Y.
10010—Greek pastries and fresh phyllo sheets

Paprika Weiss Importer, 1546 Second Avenue, New York, N.Y.
10029—Paprika and other Hungarian and Middle Eastern food,
spices, herbs, utensils; catalog

Trinacria Importing Co., 415 Third Avenue, New York, N.Y. 10016
—Near and Middle Eastern foods and utensils

INDEX